"This interdisciplinary book is bound to become a classic in studies of family media and learning. Educators and parents will appreciate the compelling stories and rich information that illuminates how families are navigating media and learning in an increasingly global society."

—**Lynn Schofield Clark**, *author of* The Parent App: Understanding Families in a Digital Age

"*Children and Families in the Digital Age* offers valuable insights into the many experiences children have with media. With an all-star cast of contributors, Gee, Takeuchi, and Wartella bring cutting edge research to bear on critical issues of our day, including: how children learn from media, what role parents play in shaping children's mediated experiences (and what role children play in shaping parents' mediated experiences!), and how we can provide better support for families as they navigate the digital era."

—**Amy Jordan**, *Associate Dean for Undergraduate Studies, Annenberg School for Communication, University of Pennsylvania, USA*

CHILDREN AND FAMILIES IN THE DIGITAL AGE

Children and Families in the Digital Age offers a fresh, nuanced, and empirically based perspective on how families are using digital media to enhance learning, routines, and relationships. This powerful edited collection contributes to a growing body of work suggesting the importance of understanding how the consequences of digital media use are shaped by family culture, values, practices, and the larger social and economic contexts of families' lives. Chapters offer case studies, real-life examples, and analyses of large-scale national survey data, and provide insights into previously unexplored topics such as the role of siblings in shaping the home media ecology.

Elisabeth Gee is Delbert & Jewell Lewis Chair in Reading & Literacy and Professor at Mary Lou Fulton Teachers College, Arizona State University, USA.

Lori M. Takeuchi is Senior Director and Research Scientist at the Joan Ganz Cooney Center at Sesame Workshop, USA.

Ellen Wartella is Sheikh Hamad bin Khalifa Al-Thani Professor of Communication and Director, Center on Media and Human Development at Northwestern University, USA.

CHILDREN AND FAMILIES IN THE DIGITAL AGE

Learning Together in a Media Saturated Culture

Edited by
Elisabeth Gee, Lori M. Takeuchi, and Ellen Wartella

NEW YORK AND LONDON

First published 2018
by Routledge
711 Third Avenue, New York, NY 10017

and by Routledge
2 Park Square, Milton Park, Abingdon, Oxon, OX14 4RN

Routledge is an imprint of the Taylor & Francis Group, an informa business

Library of Congress Cataloging-in-Publication Data
A catalog record for this book has been requested

ISBN: 978-1-138-23860-2 (hbk)
ISBN: 978-1-138-23861-9 (pbk)
ISBN: 978-1-315-29717-0 (ebk)

Typeset in Bembo and Stone Sans
by Florence Production Ltd, Stoodleigh, Devon, UK

CONTENTS

FOREWORD

Sonia Livingstone

Where shall we start, and where shall we focus our gaze, when making sense of the influx of digital devices that fill our homes and workplace, absorbing the attention of both children and parents, promising so much yet often proving frustrating, disappointing, worrying. It is tempting to start with the technologies themselves, for they highlight clear differences between how things used to be, including in our own childhoods, and how they are now. But as social scientists and historians know well, recent decades have seen many changes, among which digital media are among the most salient but are not, in any simple terms, the most influential. Indeed, as the contributors to this book carefully demonstrate through painstaking empirical work, to understand modern families we must start by situating them at the intersection of the global movements of people and cultures, growing insecurity and risk in financial and employment futures, internal contestation over gender, authority and social norms and, yes, also, transformed means of communication, information, entertainment, and relationships within and beyond the home. Then, as this book also convincingly demonstrates, rather than focusing our analytic gaze on either the technology or the child, we should examine their mutual dynamics, along with the emerging interactions among parents, teachers, siblings, and friends with and around digital media. For all of these are changing in complex ways. But do they bring new opportunities to learn? And do the less well-off, including the growing segment of Hispanic-Latino families in the United States, benefit in practice?

These are important questions, given the huge investment—national, community and individual—in all kinds of digital devices, networks and contents, and, even more expensive, the training, expertise and reshaping of societal infrastructures to accommodate and harness them supposedly for public good. While other books explore the associated transformations in the public, private and third sectors, this one undertakes perhaps the most difficult task: working in depth with over 200 families to understand how they are finding ways to engage with the media in their domestic lives. Building on prior insights that stress the value and potential of social and digital connections (youth-led, interest-driven, peer-supported), the authors variously demonstrate ways in which digital media afford new sites for learning individually and together, at home and, especially, between home and school. They thereby qualify and contest the multiplicity of myths that abound in academic, policy, and public discourses about digital media—that children know it all already (as so-called "digital natives"), that parents know nothing about it (as so-called "digital immigrants"), that time with media is time wasted, that families are being broken apart by the multiplicity of personal screens, and that the risks of digital media vastly outweigh the opportunities, and more.

But this does not mean all is plain sailing in the lives of modern families in the digital age. The fieldwork presented here, among many other findings, tells tales of school-provided laptops increasing the home-school disconnect for some low-income parents, of teachers underestimating how parents may use digital technologies to both support and complement learning in school, and of parents hampered by the belief that media may support entertainment or learning but not both. Yet, in the best instances, problems such as these have become familiar to the expert community of scholar, policy makers, and practitioners that shape families' future prospects. And while this does not, in and of itself, mean that the problems are being swept away, it does provide the basis for learning within that community. For while we rightly love to share best practice in digital media learning, it is often from past mistakes that we can learn the most.

Here we find some of the most creative suggestions emerging from the experiences of today's families. To recognize how children develop expertise in searching, evaluating, and communicating knowledge as they act as online information brokers for their families. To relish the playful engagement of a father mixing media sources to support his little son's fascination with space exploration. To notice that it is around co-viewing of the supposedly trashy telenovela that mother and teenage daughter get to have those sensitive conversations that it is otherwise hard to begin. My hope is that this book can help bring such instances to wider public attention, countering talk of harmful media, passive kids, and clueless parents. Also important, of course, would be a digital media industry that worked with parents, teachers, and kids to scaffold such positive experiences for greater benefit. Families need a media that represents the diversity of their audiences, that encourages imaginative play and shared learning among family members and that minimizes oppressive, stereotyped, and overcommercialized contents. So let us hope the industry reads this book too.

CONTRIBUTORS

Brigid Barron is Professor of Education and the Learning Sciences at Stanford's Graduate School of Education. Her research investigates how digital technologies can serve as catalysts for collaborative learning across home, school, and community settings with the goal of creating more equitable opportunities for the development of expertise and interest-driven learning.

Briana Ellerbe is a doctoral student at the Annenberg School for Communication and Journalism at the University of Southern California. Her research interests include the ecological contexts of communities of color, the educational and developmental experiences of children, and media's potential to serve as tools for equity, education, and more diverse and complex representations.

Elisabeth Gee is the Delbert & Jewell Chair in Reading & Literacy at Arizona State University. Her current research interests focus on understanding the nature of literacies and learning associated with new digital technologies, particularly video games, in out-of-school contexts such as the home and family.

Carmen Gonzalez is an Assistant Professor in the University of Washington's Department of Communication. Previously she was a postdoctoral research associate at Rutgers University, working with Vikki Katz on a digital equity study funded by the Bill & Melinda Gates Foundation.

Vikki Katz is an Associate Professor of Communication, and Affiliate Graduate Faculty of Sociology, at Rutgers University. She is also a Senior Research Fellow at the Joan Ganz Cooney Center at Sesame Workshop. Her research focuses on low-income and immigrant children and their families, and on the influence that technology has on their learning activities, daily routines, and access to a range of social opportunities.

Alexis R. Lauricella is the Associate Director of the Center on Media and Human Development at Northwestern University and a Lecturer in the department of Communication Studies. Her research focuses on children's learning from media and parents' and teachers' attitudes about young children's media use.

June Lee is the Director for Measurement and Evaluation at the ELMA Philanthropies. She was previously Vice President for International Research at Sesame Workshop.

Amber Maria Levinson is a Research Associate at Stanford Graduate School of Education as part of the TELOS Initiative (Technology for Equity in Learning Opportunities), and recently spent 2 years as a postdoctoral scholar with the Joan Ganz Cooney Center at Sesame Workshop.

Sonia Livingstone is Professor of Social Psychology in the Department of Media and Communications at the London School of Economics and Political Science. She leads the project Preparing for a Digital Future, which follows the recently completed project The Class, both part of the MacArthur Foundation-funded Connected Learning Research Network. Among other prior work, she directed the 33-country network, EU Kids Online, funded by the EC's Better Internet for Kids programme, with impacts in the UK and Europe. She is author or editor of 19 books and many academic articles and chapters.

Alexia Raynal is Research Manager at the Joan Ganz Cooney Center at Sesame Workshop where she designs research projects and research-based communication products to promote access to deeper learning for all children in the digital age.

Deborah Silvis is a doctoral student in Learning Sciences and Human Development at the University of Washington. Her research interests include understanding what constitutes media ecologies, studying families' everyday learning in home settings, and Science and Technology Studies.

Sinem Siyahhan is an Assistant Professor of Learning Sciences and Educational Technology at California State University San Marcos. Her research focuses on understanding the affordances of video games for family learning, communication, and connection.

Reed Stevens is Professor of Learning Sciences, in the School of Education and Social Policy at Northwestern University. His research examines and compares cognitive activity in a range of settings including classrooms, workplaces, and science museums.

Lori M. Takeuchi is Senior Director and Research Scientist at the Joan Ganz Cooney Center at Sesame Workshop. She conducts research on how children use digital media across the various settings of their lives, and the implications these tools hold for their learning and development.

Katie Headrick Taylor is Assistant Professor of Learning Sciences and Human Development at the University of Washington. She studies children's digital literacy practices, spatial literacy as it pertains to youth mobility and mapping, new ways of teaching spatial literacies, and how to leverage new technologies to engage young people in civic processes that drive community change.

Ellen Wartella is the Al-Thani Professor of Communication, Professor of Psychology, and Professor of Human Development and Social Policy at Northwestern University. She also is the Director of the Center on Media and Human Development at Northwestern.

Heather Weiss is Co-Director of the Global Family Research Project, a non-profit organization that fosters collaboration among child- and family-serving organizations to create equitable learning pathways for children across time and place. She and her colleagues created and maintain the Family Involvement Network of Educators (FINE), providing the latest research, policy examples, professional development tools, evaluations, and other resources to support family and community engagement practice and policy (see Globalfrp.org).

Jason C. Yip is an Assistant Professor at The Information School and Adjunct Assistant Professor at Human Centered Design & Engineering at the University of Washington. He is also a Senior Research Fellow at the Joan Ganz Cooney Center at Sesame Workshop. His research examines how technologies can support parents and children learning collaboratively together.

1

INTRODUCTION

Elisabeth Gee, Lori M. Takeuchi, and Ellen Wartella

Media, as defined by Merriam-Webster, is "a channel or system of communication, information, or entertainment." Media have been a part of the human experience since ancient times, and over the millennia taken the form of cave paintings, maps for navigation, and the development of writing systems. In the past few decades, however, the Digital Revolution has yielded and continues to yield new systems and channels at what seems to be an ever-increasing rate. Common use of the term media includes the technological devices—also referred to as "tools" or "platforms"—as well as the content they deliver. Today, media include cell phones, tablets, laptop and desktop personal computers, DVD and Blu-ray players, streaming video services, game systems, websites, and social media, in addition to print newspapers and books, cinema, television, and radio.

Media play a prominent role in families with children. Parents use media to teach, entertain, preoccupy, bribe, and soothe their children, and some even use media to learn how to be better parents. Children use media to play, learn, explore, express themselves, and stave off boredom. Together, family members use media to communicate, coordinate, bond, and even disengage from one another. Given how much time adults and children alike spend with media, debates abound over the effects that the rapidly proliferating digital forms in particular are having on family life. But these sentiments are hardly new, as evidenced by one developmental psychologist's observation more than 40 years ago:

> Like the sorcerer of old, the television set casts its magic spell, freezing speech and action and turning the living into silent statues so long as enchantment lasts. The primary danger of the television screen lies not so much in the behavior it produces as the behavior it prevents—the talks, the games, the

> family festivities and arguments through which much of the child's learning takes place and his character is formed.
>
> (Bronfenbrenner, 1979, p. 170)

Indeed, Urie Bronfenbrenner's remark rings as true today as ever, with television being just one of many sorcerers on the scene, albeit a stubborn one. While TV still dominates children's screen time—2- to 10-year-olds watch, on average, 1:21 hours of video content in the form of television and DVDs per day—digital devices are occupying increasing proportions of children's time. Children spend 17 minutes with video games, 14 minutes with computers, and 14 minutes with mobile devices, which, along with TV, contribute to an average daily screen time of 2:07 hours (Rideout, 2014). Adult media habits are shifting as well. E-mail, "productivity software," and smartphones have revised the ethos of the American workplace such that employees are expected to accomplish far more in a day than ever before, and continue working even after they've physically left the office. Although location once demarcated one's roles as employee versus parent, today parents can tote their work to a school play and even to the dinner table. When parents do finally break from work, they may be drained and, consequently, satisfied to hand their child a tablet while they catch up on Facebook or Netflix. For the single parent or the unemployed, these patterns are likely to reflect even greater strains on family together time.

As parents and children alike engage with a greater variety of media on a daily basis, how are family routines, rules, and norms evolving? To evoke Bronfenbrenner's concerns, what can we expect in the way of the behavior digital media produce as well as the behavior they prevent? The portability and connectivity of new devices have spawned the type of family whose members are too often, according to MIT sociologist-psychologist Sherry Turkle, "alone together, each in their own rooms, each on a networked computer or mobile device" (2011, p. 280). Reports in the popular press alternate, rather predictably, between dramatizing how digital tools might damage family relationships, and extolling their potential to help families stay in touch, exchange information, and support learning. These stories, which sometimes are and sometimes are not grounded in rigorous empirical research, leave readers fearful or hopeful, and oftentimes just plain confused. In effect, these stories leave parents and educators, as well as policymakers and media developers, unprepared to help families navigate an increasingly complicated technological landscape.

Background

This volume aims to offer valuable guidance to these audiences, and contribute to the national debate on media's potential to foster family engagement and learning. Drawing from the work of an interdisciplinary group of researchers who have been collaborating on studies of media-related practices and beliefs among families with children ages 2–12, we present new findings about media use in families, with an emphasis on how media shape learning at home. The Families and Media Project, which commenced its work in 2013, drew its inspiration from a growing body of research that began to delineate the ways in which family culture, values, practices, and social and economic circumstances shape young people's learning and participation in a rapidly evolving, increasingly global society.

The Digital Youth Project was a significant source of this inspiration. The multi-year, multi-institution study led by Mizuko Ito and funded by the MacArthur Foundation's Digital Media and Learning Initiative is still the largest study of youth media practices to date. Between 2005 and 2008, the Digital Youth Project (DYP) employed a mix of qualitative and quantitative methods across 20 distinct studies to document adolescents' through young adults' understanding and use of new media. By focusing on youth-centered practices of play, communication, and creative production, the DYP located "learning in contexts that are meaningful and formative for youth, including friendships and families, as well as young people's own aspirations, interests, and passions" (Ito et al., 2009, p. 6). DYP investigator Heather Horst (2009) identified family as one of these meaningful and formative contexts. She examined the many ways in which home- and family-specific circumstances—such as parent work schedules and income, family routines and rhythms, and the physical layout of the home—structure how youth engage with and around media. Living in cramped versus spacious quarters, for instance, may determine whether family members watch TV together or separately and, consequently, opportunities for conversation.

Other prior work in this space has focused on parental involvement in children's media use. Barron, Kennedy, Takeuchi, and Fithian's (2009) research with adolescents, their parents, and other learning partners articulated eight basic roles that parents play in nurturing their children's interest in technological endeavors. With roles like learning broker, resource provider, nontechnical consultant, employer, and learner, the taxonomy highlights the fact that parents do not need to be technologically fluent to foster such fluency in their children. Similarly, Plowman, McPake, and Stephen (2008) found in their survey of 346 families and 24 case studies that parents are often unaware of the extent to which they model technological practices to their preschool age children. By assuming that their children independently learn how to operate the DVD player or log on to their favorite websites, the authors argue, parents underestimate their influence in transmitting technological know-how and values around media to their children.

Recent large-scale quantitative work provides further context for the qualitative research described above. In 2012, Wartella, Rideout, Lauricella, and Connell (2014) surveyed 2,326 parents of children ages 0–8 on their attitudes and practices surrounding their children's digital media use. They found that home media environments varied greatly from family to family, with parents' own media practices strongly influencing their children's media use. About a quarter of the parents were deemed "media-centric," averaging 11 hours of media use a day. Their children were heavy media users as well and reported spending about 4.5 hours with media per day. By contrast, "media light" parents, also about a quarter of those queried, spent less than 2 hours a day with media; their children spent just more than 1.5 hours with media on a daily basis.

These are just four of many studies published in the 2000s that have emphasized the importance of family as an important context for learning. They underscore the functions that family members and family circumstances play in shaping how youth use and learn with media and, in doing so, have helped debunk the myth of the "digital native" (Prensky, 2001), that generation of individuals naturally inclined toward and gifted with all things hardware and software. The Families and Media Project takes root in the scholarship described above, but extends its inquiry to understand how *all* family members—not just children—learn with media across the developmental lifespan, and how they are doing so *together*.

Given our interest in the shared experience of media use, our work also builds upon the co-viewing research that emerged in the 1970s around television viewing. These studies demonstrated that children who watch educational television with actively engaged adults learn more from shows than children who watch alone. Today, co-viewing has taken on a moniker that better describes what happens around more interactive forms of media (Takeuchi & Stevens, 2011). *Joint media engagement*, according to Stevens and Penuel (2010), refers to "spontaneous and designed experiences of people using media together . . . [including] viewing, playing, searching, reading, contributing, and creating, with either digital or traditional media." Unlike the studies reviewed above, a focus on JME requires us as researchers to examine the interactions between learning partners as they engage with and around media. What is going on inside the room? What are family members saying to one another as they watch TV, play video games, or surf the web together? These in-the-moment interactions reveal quite a lot about how learning takes shape among family members, as do the interactions that play out asynchronously and sometimes even away from the medium that initially sparked the connection between family members. How do media provide anchors that sustain continued engagement between family members over longer stretches of time?

In a rare study for its day, Stevens, Satwicz, and McCarthy (2008) applied a JME lens to understand how young people play video games in the naturalistic environments of living rooms and dens. They describe the "learning arrangements" that 9- to 13-year-old siblings and their friends set up around the games and gaming systems they ordinarily play. Unlike most studies of games and learning, this one focused less on what youth were learning from the games and more on the spontaneous and oftentimes tacit forms of teaching and learning that transpired between players (and observers) to improve gameplay. The authors also extended their inquiry beyond home to understand how the "in-room" learning connected to the youths' lives and identities in the world outside. Like Stevens et al., the Families and Media Project set out to understand how media—as well as the human interactions around media—drive children's learning across the boundaries of home, school, and the other settings where they spend significant portions of their days.

Focus on Hispanic-Latino Families

Rather than surrender to our fate as an "alone together" society, the Families and Media Project aims to highlight the positive interactions that take place between adults and children around the growing number of devices at home and, in doing so, create a more hopeful future for the American family. *American* is a key descriptor here. Our research acknowledges the cultural and socioeconomic diversity that defines our nation by oversampling typically underserved and understudied populations, including low income, African-American, and Hispanic-Latino families. In fact, the Families and Media Project prioritized the study of Hispanic-Latino[1] families, as they comprise a significant and growing proportion of families with school-age children in the United States. Recent survey research on Hispanic-Latino families suggests that newer media are being widely adopted by Latino families and that, in fact, the digital divide between Latinos and Whites has significantly narrowed over the past decade (Livingston, 2011; Zickuhr & Smith, 2012). Seventy-six percent of Latino adults own cell phones—compared to 79 percent of Blacks and 85 percent of Whites—and are also more likely to use their phones to access the Internet in lieu of home broadband (6 percent of Hispanics, 6 percent for Blacks, 1 percent for Whites). Notably, Latino adults are acquiring smartphones and tablet computers at an equal or higher rate than White and Black non-Latino adults (Rainie, 2012; Wartella et al., 2014; Zickuhr & Smith, 2012). With increased access to these platforms and services at home, libraries, and other community settings, out-of-school time and locales present untapped opportunities to use digital media to fulfill Hispanic-Latino children's education needs.

While the surveys cited above were useful in describing access, they told us little about the *content* and *contexts* of Hispanic-Latino families' media use and learning. And in place of the vanishing access gap between Hispanic/Black and White youth, there is evidence of an emerging "participation gap" demarcating more or less empowering uses of digital media (Watkins, 2011). To design educational programs, services, and tools that Latino families can both benefit from and willingly embrace, the Families and Media Project set out to understand how media fit into their existing household routines, and how they hold up to parent beliefs and family value systems. At the outset of the project, we were cognizant that the racial identifiers "Hispanic" and "Latino" obscure a diverse reality that includes multiple countries of origin (Mexico, Puerto Rico, Cuba, El Salvador, etc.), ethnic origins (European, indigenous, Asian, African, etc.), generations (first, second, third), and settlement regions (urban, suburban; Northeast, Southwest, West). Reasons for and experiences immigrating to the United States vary not only by a family or individual's country of origin, but by the community they settle into upon arrival. Immigrants from rural towns in Puebla, Mexico who settle in the Coney Island neighborhood of Brooklyn, for instance, live vastly different lives from Salvadoran immigrants who move to the Mission District of San Francisco. The education and life opportunities made available to their children (born abroad or in the States) consequently differ.

Because the routines, beliefs, and values we sought to understand could widely vary between these subcultures, the Families and Media Project ran field studies of Hispanic-Latino families in six different sites across the United States: New York City, Phoenix, Tucson, Denver, Chula Vista (near San Diego, CA), and San Francisco. Although we can only begin to document differences in media use across our collective field sample of 227 families, it is a good starting point for generating new questions and theories to test in subsequent research.

About the Families and Media Project

The Families and Media Project (FAM) is a multi-institution consortium composed of researchers from the Joan Ganz Cooney Center, Arizona State University, California State University at San Marcos, Northwestern University, Rutgers University, Stanford University, Sesame Workshop, and the University of Washington at Seattle. A distinct strength of the FAM consortium is its interdisciplinary composition, with scholars representing the learning sciences, communications, child development, and media studies. We came together with a common goal of producing research that could guide practitioners—including educators, policymakers, and media producers—in developing programs, policies, and products that:

- positively impact the learning, communication, and lifestyle needs of families with children;
- support family engagement with media—in real time and asynchronously—by taking advantage of technological affordances that may overcome the various challenges of using media together;
- better address the needs of today's families, including single-parent households, nonnative speakers, and parents with demanding work schedules;
- help families be smarter media consumers and wiser in their content selections; and
- improve education, promote healthy lifestyles, and positively influence family development outcomes.

With funding from the Heising-Simons Foundation, the Bezos Family Foundation, AARP (American Association of Retired Persons), and the Bill and

Melinda Gates Foundation, the Families and Media Project commenced its work in 2013 with the launch of two national surveys and seven qualitative field studies located in eight study sites around the nation, all focusing on families with children ranging in age from 2 through 12. Investigators from seven institutions designed and oversaw these separate studies, which held the common aims listed above but were otherwise customized to investigators' own research agendas, questions, methodological preferences, and local site considerations. As such, methods varied across the studies, but investigators shared a few data collection protocols that allowed them to make cross-study comparisons. Data collection took place in 2013 and 2014 and analysis and write-up continued through 2016.

The following descriptions of the nine studies that make up the Families and Media Project are intended to provide an overview of the topical, geographic, and methodological scope of FAM. The Appendix offers longer accounts of each study, including their research questions, methods, and participant sampling and demographics.

1. *National survey of educational media use*: Vicky Rideout of VJR Consulting and GfK, in collaboration with the Joan Ganz Cooney Center, surveyed 1,577 parents online on how their 2- to 10-year-old children use educational media, with whom, and to what effect. It also queried parents on their beliefs about the educational potential of media. The survey oversampled Black and Hispanic-Latino parents to ensure adequate representation of these populations. (See Study 1 in the Appendix.)
2. *Parents and children learning together study*: Brigid Barron and Amber Levinson of the Stanford Graduate School of Education recruited eight families with children ages 4–6 to participate in ethnographic interviews and joint play sessions to better understand joint media engagement. The study explored parents' beliefs about the nature of screen media (television, video, electronic games, apps, etc.) in their children's lives, how such media were used to support learning, and the role of both child and parent interests in family media practices. (See Study 2 in the Appendix.)
3. *Siblings and video games study*: Elisabeth Gee of the Mary Lou Fulton Teachers College at Arizona State University and Sinem Siyahhan of California State University at San Marcos recruited Mexican-American families in the Phoenix area with one older (ages 7+) and one younger (ages 4–6) sibling to investigate how digital gaming might promote language and literacy development as well as collaborative problem solving in the context of family routines and activities. (See Study 3 in the Appendix.)
4. *Children's mobility study*: Katie Headrick Taylor and Reed Stevens of the Northwestern School of Educational and Social Policy took a spatiotemporal approach to tracing the distribution and flow of digital media practices of 12 focal children (ages 9–13) from nine families living in the Chicago area. Data are based on ethnographic observations of children using technology

in the home and across various settings of activity over the course of 6 weeks. (See Study 4 in the Appendix.)

5. *Parent social networking survey*: Ellen Wartella and Alexis Lauricella of the Northwestern School of Communication conducted an online survey of 163 low-income parents to understand how they use social networks—both real and virtual—to help them make critical parenting decisions around their children's education, health, and well-being. (See Study 5 in the Appendix.)
6. *Three-community study of reduced cost broadband programs*: Vikki Katz of the Rutgers School of Communication and Information visited three primarily Latino school districts in Chula Vista, CA, Tucson, AZ, and Denver, CO, studies to interview parents and children (50–60 families per site) on how they made use of free/reduced cost broadband programs (i.e., local EveryoneOn initiatives), and how their participation shaped family access to information resources and bridged home and school learning. (See Study 6 in the Appendix.)
7. *Information search brokering study*: Jason Yip of the University of Washington's Information School studied the learning processes, challenges, and strategies of 10 Latino youth (ages 11–14) as they brokered online information searches for their ELL parents. (See Study 7 in the Appendix.)
8. *Modern families study*: Lori Takeuchi of the Joan Ganz Cooney Center adapted Headrick Taylor and Stevens' mobility study methods to understand how media are being used for learning in "modern families" in which children live physically apart from at least one parent as a result of divorce, military deployment, staggered immigration, or any other reason. The Cooney Center observed and interviewed 15 Latino children (ages 6–9) and their families living in the New York metro area over the course of 6 weeks. (See Study 8 in the Appendix.)
9. *Language and literacy ethnography*: Amber Levinson of the Stanford Graduate School of Education used ethnographic methods to document how seven San Francisco Latino immigrant families with 5- to 7-year-old children used screen media to engage in language and literacy experiences. The study also included an "intervention" in which families received a tablet device loaded with language and literacy apps to see what these families might do with new tools. (See Study 9 in the Appendix.)

Crosscutting Themes

Each chapter in this volume addresses a topic or issue that emerged as significant in one or more of the FAM studies. While we have organized the chapters according to their relative emphasis on the media-related practices and learning of children, parents, or families, all chapters reflect several common themes and assumptions about how we might best understand the nature of learning and the role of media in the context of home and family life.

First, our work foregrounds the dynamics of family interactions and routines, and how the meaning and use of media are caught up in these dynamics. Other scholarship on families' and children's use of media often places the devices at the center of inquiry, reinforcing a sense of technological determinism; that is, that technology drives human behavior. This view is implied, for example, in popular reports that social media is responsible for a breakdown in family communication. In contrast, we emphasize the importance of understanding people and their relationships, values, and beliefs as key influences in how media are taken up by families. While the properties of a particular technology play a role in how it is utilized, how people actually make use of the technology can be unpredictable, shaped by many factors, including people's own ingenuity. This viewpoint is reflected in Brigid Barron and Amber Levinson's (Chapter 2) discussion of the creative ways that parents and children recruited a variety of digital and nondigital resources to support their learning, including curation of media, interest-driven searches, conversational anchoring, content creation, and co-play. For example, one father in their study explained how he and his 4-year-old son went on a "multimedia space binge," using books from the library, online videos, and drawing pictures to explore an interest they shared in space exploration. As another example, in Chapter 10, Levinson describes how Latino parents took advantage of translation apps to engage in the familiar practice of helping children with their homework, as well as to improve their own English language skills.

While in general, chapter authors have stressed the more positive ways that families have incorporated media into their lives, we have also noted instances where families have struggled with making the best use of these technologies, or when these technologies have exacerbated already problematic situations and relationships. Barron and Levinson, for instance, note that some parents did not feel confident or well-informed enough to take full advantage of digital media's affordances for learning at home. In Chapter 6, Vikki Katz, Carmen Gonzalez, and Alexia Raynal reveal how, for some low-income parents, school-provided laptops increased their sense of a disconnect between home and school learning and their parenting approaches. For example, some parents felt marginalized since they did not have the skills to monitor what their children were doing on the laptops at home, or they restricted the home use of laptops due to concerns about financial liability.

Second, and tied to this decentering of technology, is our broad, inclusive view of learning in families. Recognizing that learning is both "lifelong and lifewide" (Stevens, Bransford, & Stevens, 2005), the authors in this book discover learning in at times unexpected situations and activities. All too frequently, families and the home are viewed by educators primarily as environments to support or supplement children's school achievement. Even efforts to recognize and affirm family cultural knowledge often seek to recruit this knowledge to facilitate academic learning, thus viewing this home-based knowledge through the lens of school subjects and priorities. This limiting view can affect families' perceptions of media's potential to support learning. In Chapter 7, Sinem Siyahhan and June Lee describe how parents' as well as children's perceptions of the educational value of television shows and video games were related, with few exceptions, to whether the media might help children develop school-related skills or content knowledge. They also felt that, for the most part, media could not be both educational and entertaining, a rather sad commentary on both educational media and school learning.

Instead, we explore learning as it takes place in connection with families' goals, routines, and practices associated with digital media. Looking at learning in this way brings new issues into focus. For example, in Chapter 8, Jason Yip, Carmen Gonzalez, and Vikki Katz describe the challenges facing youth who serve as online information brokers for their families, who not only had to develop information searching skills, but also had to find ways to summarize and communicate complex material, at times beyond their own understanding. These findings offer a compelling illustration of how, for these youth, being effective information brokers was dependent on a diverse set of abilities, such as using nondigital resources, negotiating their parents' demands and expectations, recruiting help from social networks, and coping with the pressure of helping their families navigate situations that were at times stressful and emotionally charged. These abilities go far beyond what we commonly associate with digital literacies or other conceptions of technological skills.

As another example, in Chapter 4, Katie Headrick Taylor, Deborah Silvis, and Reed Stevens offer insights into the forms of problem-based learning that result from young people's efforts to assemble and organize technological tools, relevant people, and information in order to pursue their goals, often recruiting the help of other family members and affecting household routines more broadly. While in one sense, the challenges and frustrations that these young people experienced when coping with dead batteries, unpredictable Internet connections, missing passwords, and other issues could be viewed as barriers to learning, the authors demonstrate how such experiences contributed to participants' ability to troubleshoot technical breakdowns, engage in joint problem-solving, and other instrumental forms of learning. As the chapter authors point out, these efforts typically are invisible to adults, but are central to learning with technology.

Along these same lines, Lori Takeuchi and Briana Ellerbe, in Chapter 9, describe learning as it occurs in families with and around TV shows with ethno-cultural themes. While few would consider the *telenovela* a source of cultural enrichment and moral development, the authors examine how one mother used a popular Mexican soap to anchor sensitive conversations about religion, ethnic identity, and social pressures with her adolescent daughter. They also describe how one father trusted *Dora the Explorer* to foster in his second-generation Latino children pride in their ethnic heritage and a little Spanish language practice beyond what they get at home. In both cases, though the adults and children were drawn to the same programs for different purposes and experienced the content in different ways, their co-viewing experiences solidified family members' identities in relation to one another, as well as the family's ethnic identity more generally. In Chapter 7, Sinem Siyahhan and June Lee also note how parents valued media that strengthened children's fluency in Spanish and their ties to Mexico, even if the media was not overtly "educational."

A third common thread across chapters is explicit attention to the wide variety of ways that family members of all ages support each other's learning with and through media. While prior work has shown how children as well as parents can serve as information brokers and teachers in the home media ecology (e.g., Katz, 2014), much of this scholarship has focused on direct teaching-learning interactions around media. Barron et al.'s (2009) research, cited above, offers perhaps the broadest characterization of the different roles that parents can take in supporting their children's skills and interest in digital technologies, but their focus was on parents only. Also cited above, Plowman et al.'s (2008) discovery that parents are often unaware of their influence on their preschool age children's technological practices is telling, and perhaps true of family influences more generally. In this volume, our authors begin to uncover some of these previously unexplored dynamics. Elisabeth Gee, Lori Takeuchi, Sinem Siyahhan, and Briana Ellerbe, in Chapter 3, explore the typically overlooked forms of direct and indirect influence that siblings can have on children's digital media use and the broader home media ecology. The more obvious, direct forms of influence that siblings can have include overt or implicit teaching roles, or introducing new forms of technology into the home. Indirect forms of influence, however, can be just as powerful, and include how siblings affect parents' beliefs about children's media preferences or abilities, or how siblings serve as points of comparison in children's self-perceptions of their own technology skills.

In Chapter 5, Alexis Lauricella, Briana Ellerbe, and Ellen Wartella describe how parents obtain parenting information and support in diverse ways through social media channels like Facebook. Particularly intriguing is how parents acquire such information serendipitously through their online social networks, perhaps while browsing friends' posts or links shared by others. While parents most commonly used Facebook to share updates with extended family about children's development and family events, many reported that they gained instrumental and even emotional support as an indirect benefit of their Facebook activities.

Lastly, a shared goal across chapters is to offer implications for the many professionals concerned with enhancing the value of digital media in families' lives, and in particular for supporting learning of all family members. Some implications have been explicitly spelled out, such as the value of involving parents as partners in planning technology initiatives (see Chapter 6) or the need for more social opportunities for parents to gain awareness of how to harness the potential of media for learning (see Chapter 2). Other implications can be gleaned more indirectly from study findings and the new perspectives they offer on media and learning in family life, such as the role of media as "boundary objects" (Chapter 9) that support intergenerational learning, or the significance of "collecting," trouble-shooting, and problem-based learning in young people's use of digital media at home (Chapter 4).

While specific implications are too numerous to list comprehensively, here we draw attention to a few broad areas of concern and potential impact. First, our studies offer new insights for educators interested in supporting the kind of connected, interest-driven learning experiences that Ito et al. (2009) describe as particularly important for engaging less privileged young people. In particular, this research suggests the critical role of parents, siblings, and other family members in helping children identify and explore these interests, make connections across potentially disparate learning experiences, and resolve issues and barriers to using media to pursue these interests. Indeed, while discussions of interest-driven learning often focus on *individual* interests, a number of our chapters indicate how *shared* interests among family members can be focal points for collaborative, social learning activities.

Second, the chapters offer implications for enhancing connections between home and school media use and learning. These implications stress the importance of understanding parents' perceptions of new media as well as the kinds of media-related practices that are actually taking place in the home. For example, children are taking on roles as teachers, information brokers, and gatekeepers for their siblings and parents, yet the skills they develop and the demands they face frequently go unrecognized by teachers, as resources and opportunities for learning. In particular, understanding families' out-of-school use of media and digital technologies may help educators develop more expansive notions of digital literacies and learning activities that go beyond typical school- or workplace-oriented tasks.

Third, earlier in this chapter, we identified *joint media engagement* as a central concept that informed the FAM group's inquiries, and across this volume, the authors describe forms of joint media engagement that go far beyond how we have typically conceptualized such engagement. Joint media engagement occurs, for example, in the process of troubleshooting media-related problems and can extend to asynchronous interactions over time and space (Chapter 4). Recognizing and designing for these more diverse forms of joint media engagement, as well as supporting parents in taking full advantage of such opportunities for learning, are valuable tasks for designers as well as educators.

Lastly, many of the chapters offer implications for supporting parents' learning through and about media and digital technologies. Our findings indicate how actively parents are involved in navigating the rapidly evolving media landscape, seeking information, resources, and support, while trying to align new media practices with their values, parenting approaches, and perceived needs of their children and families. All parents need assistance in sorting through the wide range of often conflicting opinions and evidence about digital media's potential for learning and other positive outcomes, and many parents do not feel confident about their ability to make informed decisions about their family's media access and practices. Clearly there is much work to be done in making such assistance more available to parents, and providing it in a way that respects diversity in families' values, lifestyles, and backgrounds.

Organization of the Book

We have organized this book into three major sections, focusing on children's media engagement, parent engagement with media, and family media engagement. While there is not a standard chapter format, each chapter focuses on one or two key topics and findings, and is intended to be accessible to a nonspecialist audience. Many chapters draw on findings from more than one of the nine FAM studies, and a number of authors contributed to more than one chapter. This approach, we feel, strengthened the overall contribution of each chapter, and reinforced our goal of bringing interdisciplinary perspectives to bear on the complex, messy, and fascinating nature of family learning and engagement with media in today's world.

Note

1. We use the terms "Hispanic-Latino," "Hispanic," and "Latino" almost interchangeably throughout the book to describe individuals who trace their roots to Spanish-speaking countries. While half (51 percent) of this population holds no preference for one term over the other (Taylor, Lopez, Martinez, & Velasco, 2012), in the communities we studied, "Latino" was the term of choice.

References

Barron, B., Martin, C. K., Takeuchi, L., & Fithian, R. (2009). Parents as learning partners in the development of technological fluency. *The International Journal of Learning and Media, 1*, 55–77.

Bronfenbrenner, U. (1979). The ecology of human development: Experiments by nature and design. *American Psychologist, 32*, 513–531.

Horst, H. (2009). Families. In M. Ito, S. Baumer, M. Bittanti, D. Boyd, R. Cody, B. Herr-Stephenson, et al. (Eds.), *Hanging out, messing around, geeking out: Living and learning with new media* (pp. 149–194). Cambridge, MA: MIT Press.

Ito, M., Baumer, S., Bittanti, M., Boyd, D., Cody, R., Herr-Stephenson, R., et al. (2009). *Hanging out, messing around, geeking out: Living and learning with new media.* Cambridge, MA: MIT Press.

Katz, V.S. (2014). *Kids in the middle: How children of immigrants negotiate community interactions for their families.* New Brunswick, NJ: Rutgers University Press.

Livingston, G. (2011). Latinos and digital technology, 2010. Washington, DC: Pew Hispanic Center. Retrieved from www.pewhispanic.org/2011/02/09/latinos-and-digital-technology-2010

Plowman, L., McPake, J., & Stephen, C. (2008). Just picking it up? Young children learning with technology at home. *Cambridge Journal of Education, 38*(3), 303–319.

Prensky, M. (2001). Digital natives, digital immigrants part 1. *On the Horizon, 9*(5), 1–6.

Rainie, L. (2012, January). Tablet and e-book reader ownership nearly double over the holiday gift-giving period. Washington, DC: Pew Internet & American Life Project.

Rideout, V. J. (2014). *Learning at home: Families' educational media use in America.* A report of the Families and Media Project. New York: The Joan Ganz Cooney Center at Sesame Workshop.

Stevens, R. Bransford, J., & Stevens, A. (2005). The LIFE center's lifelong and lifewide diagram. Seattle, WA: LIFE Center. Retrieved from http://life-slc.org/about/citationdetails.html

Stevens, R., & Penuel, W. R. (2010). *Studying and fostering learning through joint media engagement.* Paper presented at the Principal Investigators Meeting of the National Science Foundation's Science of Learning Centers, Arlington, VA.

Stevens, R., Satwicz, T., & McCarthy, L. (2008). In-game, in-room, in-world: Reconnecting video game play to the rest of kids' lives. In K. Salen, *The ecology of games: Connecting youth, games, and learning* (pp. 41–66). Cambridge, MA: MIT Press.

Takeuchi, L., & Stevens, R. (2011). *The new coviewing: Designing for learning through joint media engagement.* New York: The Joan Ganz Cooney Center at Sesame Workshop.

Taylor, P., Lopez, M. H., Martínez, J. H., & Velasco, G. (2012). When labels don't fit: Hispanics and their views of identity. Washington, DC: Pew Hispanic Center. Retrieved from www.pewhispanic.org/2012/04/04/when-labels-dont-fit-hispanics-and-their-views-of-identity

Turkle, S. (2011). *Alone together: Why we expect more from technology and less from each other.* New York: Basic Books.

Wartella, E., Rideout, V., Lauricella, A., & Connell, S. (2014). *Parenting in the age of digital technology*. Evanston, IL: Center on Media and Human Development, School of Communication, Northwestern University.

Watkins, S. C. (2011). Digital divide: Navigating the digital edge. *International Journal of Learning and Media, 3*(2), 1–12.

Zickhur, K., & Smith, A. (2012, April). *Digital differences.* Washington, DC: Pew Internet & American Life Project.

SECTION 1

Child Engagement

Section Editor: Katie Headrick Taylor

2

MEDIA AS A CATALYST FOR CHILDREN'S ENGAGEMENT IN LEARNING AT HOME AND ACROSS SETTINGS

Brigid Barron and Amber Maria Levinson

> My kind of outlook is like hypocritical, incoherent, and confused. That has a lot to do with the fact that I'm in that generation that was very much like plopped in front of the TV. Most of my peers were plopped in front of the TV. I wasn't. Then technology has changed so dramatically that a lot of people in my age bracket are just like we don't know what to do.
>
> Barbara, mother of 6-year-old Cati

> Well [my son] likes devices and everything, and I want to guide him so that he is applying what he likes toward learning [. . .]. I don't know much about programs that might be able to help him, for example to read, to translate, to support him with English.
>
> José Rubén, father of 6-year-old Brandon

Six-year-old Cati's mother, Barbara, is a humanities teacher and in the quote above she expresses how many parents are feeling about the rapidly developing digital landscape. She, like her mother before her, attends to expert guidelines for media use. For example, she restricted television viewing until Cati was two, as recommended by the American Academy of Pediatrics (AAP) in 2013 and she frequently discusses the shows they do watch, particularly focusing in on character representation and stereotypes. Following AAP recommendations available at the time, she tries to limit screen time, whether that is television or access to the families' iPad or smart phones. When they do purchase interactive media, it tends to follow the recommendations of Cati's peers or the parents of her friends. Despite Barbara's deep ambivalence about screen time, Cati is enthusiastic about playing a variety of interactive games. On long car trips or when Barbara is too tired to engage, Cati is allowed to play *Angry Birds*, *Fruit Ninja*, *Math Bug*, or *Little Wings*—all popular games with free versions in the App store. When Cati is spending time with her peers at their homes all bets are off, as Barbara has a "do what the Romans do" parenting philosophy. She is not about to impose restrictions on the routines of the technologically sophisticated and immersed parents of Cati's school friends and besides, she trusts the other parents to do no harm. And, she does not want media to become "forbidden fruit" and thinks it is important for Cati to be part of her peers' "culture"—a culture that increasingly incorporates the latest devices and digital resources.

Barbara's uncertainty and caution mirror some of the feelings of the other 14 families we recently recruited to participate in studies of family media use. However, she is on the low end of *a continuum of enthusiasm* for media as learning resources and consequently how actively she sought out high-quality interactive media that might advance her child's learning or interests. In fact she was one of the two parents in our study who believed that there was nothing much to be gained for cognitive or social development from the advances in tablets and apps so eagerly taken up by children today. The remaining 13 families ranged from minimally to extremely enthusiastic and all 15 families had developed their own unique combinations of practices for capitalizing on digital and traditional media for valued outcomes ranging from language learning to conceptual interests to social development. We are intrigued by families' resourcefulness and ingenuity in working around challenges and leveraging modern tools to accommodate tight economic and time constraints. At the same time, many families felt they needed more information and support to understand how to use technology to best support their children's development, as expressed in the second quote, from father José Rubén, above.

Barbara and José Rubén are not alone in their desire for more information and clarity about how to best leverage and manage digital media use (Lee & Barron, 2015; Rideout, 2014). Expert recommendations send the message that good parenting requires limiting screen time to avoid displacing human interaction, reducing physical activity, and exposing children to negative content (American Academy of Pediatrics, 2013). Policy-oriented reports also recommend active mediation by parents (Blum-Ross & Livingstone, 2016) or what we call joint media engagement (Takeuchi & Stevens, 2011). However, few examples are provided about what powerful social interactions might look like or how to realistically enable quality screen time under the daily constraints parents face with respect to time or knowledge of how to find quality content.

Our goal in this chapter is to help fill this gap. We examine a range of examples of how digital and traditional media have been used by children and their families to support learning and emphasize the role of both children and parent interests as contributors to the media practices that emerge. At the same time, we surface differences in how parents conceptualize the presence of media in their children's lives and speculate about the role that parents' theories of the value of media has on the degree to which they leverage it as a learning resources. We also draw attention to the equity issues at stake and note the importance of a family's access to the tools, infrastructure, and knowledge that make these informal learning interactions possible. We draw on data collected from two samples of families who represent different socioeconomic and language groups, exploring emergent practices of media use for learning and parent-child interactions around media.

Background: Digital Technologies and Learning Ecologies

Young children learn long before school starts through everyday routines, imaginative and constructive play, and conversations with caregivers and peers. Play themes and topics of interest are often generated from books, movies and television, and increasingly the vast store of digital interactive media that can often be accessed from smart phones or other mobile devices such as tablets. Touch screen tablets that do not require typing or even the need to be able to read have dramatically expanded very young children's access to powerful content, generated new communicative possibilities and made possible novel modes of expression and creativity. Having access to a smart phone or tablet can be likened to having an encyclopedia, a creative production tool, a television, and a gaming device all in one's pocket. In fact there is so much variety that as we think about particular children and their access to learning resources it is helpful to think about how their unique learning ecologies are constituted across digital and physical spaces. From this perspective, the main driver of development is not the technological tool at hand but the unique configurations of activities, material resources, relationships, culturally grounded practices, and the interactions that emerge from them within and across settings (Barron, 2006).

This view also highlights the active role of both children and adults in creating learning opportunities, often based on their interests and cultural histories. When preschoolers get interested in topics or characters or relational themes they often incorporate them into their play scenarios, ask their caregivers questions, and request related toys or books. When caregivers notice and encourage these interests they can lead to what Crowley and Jacobs (2002) called "islands of expertise," reflected in considerable knowledge about topics of interest. Crowley and Jacobs give the example of a child whose interest in the topic of trains was sparked by a book. Book reading was followed by trips to museums and viewing videos related to trains. Over time he and his parents built up a great deal of shared knowledge including vocabulary, schemas for train scenarios, and knowledge of mechanisms that allow for train travel. This shared knowledge in turn can support rich conversations that include explanations, elaborations, and analogies to related domains that prepare the child for future conversations. Developing islands of expertise can also set in motion other social processes such as parents providing topically related books or media, connecting their children to other people or places to build interests, or instigating inquiry questions or projects that drive further learning (Barron, Martin, Takeuchi, & Fithian, 2009).

New technologies provide opportunities to extend this type of interest-driven learning by making information and activities so easily accessible. Nationally representative survey data support this conjecture, showing that parents report that educational media regularly inspired a number of related non-media learning rich activities. The survey was given to parents with children 2 to 8 years old. Of this group they found that 87 percent of children who were weekly users of educational media often or sometimes talked about something they saw in educational media. A majority also often or sometimes engaged in imaginative play based on something they saw in such media, asked questions based on content in educational media, asked to do an activity or project inspired by that media, and teach their parents something they did not know before based on learnings from the media content (Rideout, 2014). Additional analyses showed that for Hispanic families, the frequency of these interactions was linked to parents' use of media for their own learning (Lee & Barron, 2015).

Although survey data is important for identifying general trends, naturalistic studies of learning interactions are also essential, particularly to help parents and educators imagine new possibilities for their own practices. This chapter is intended to help surface some of the innovative learning practices families develop when they have access to media and digital technologies, and describe how they manifested for particular families. Our analysis was organized by two questions: (a) How were families using digital media as a resource for learning, and (b) how did their use relate to family values, needs, expertise, or beliefs about the benefits of digital media for learning and development?

Participating Families

To better represent the diversity of families who use media and their needs and perspectives, we include families with very different profiles of education, income, language, and work. This sampling is important as much of the existing research on family media use has focused predominantly on mainstream culture and middle-class families. There has been less attention to the question of how we might create opportunities for more equitable access to digital learning resources for families who may have fewer financial resources and/or are from language-minority groups.

To address this need, we recruited families living in Northern California that varied in their educational, language, and occupational backgrounds. Seven of the families were low-income, primarily Spanish-speaking and the parents were immigrants to the United States. These families were the focus of a longitudinal dissertation study (Levinson, 2014; also see Study 9 in the Appendix) on families' use of media and technology for language and literacy learning, from which a small subset of findings are discussed here. The remaining eight families were predominantly English-speaking, longtime US residents with moderate to high incomes; they were the focus of a study that collected the primary data within a 2-week window (Barron, Levinson, Matthews, & Vea, in preparation). All families had focal children between the ages of 4 to 8 years old. Both studies used mixed methods, including ethnographic interviews, the video recordings of technology use, and surveys. Both studies also included documentation of families' use of provided tablets. Our approach in combining these two studies is not to contrast the groups but to take advantage of the range of backgrounds and experiences from both. Most families owned a variety of devices including televisions, smartphones, and/or computers. All but two families had high-speed Internet access (although one of these did not own a computer), and the remaining two had mobile-only access.

Findings

The notion of "joint media engagement" (Takeuchi & Stevens, 2011) focuses our attention on family practices that include media as a resource for sense-making and creativity. To address our two research questions, we highlight four interrelated ways that media came to be a learning resource among families and make links to how these were connected with family needs and forms of expertise. These included (a) curation of media, (b) interest-driven searches and linked activities, (c) content creation and co-play, and (d) "conversational anchoring," when technology was used intentionally to help ground referents in conversations, often resulting in unplanned teaching–learning interactions. In the examples that we surfaced these were not independent practices, rather they were frequently interdependent and related in unique and interesting ways. Our goal in naming and describing them as unique categories is to further develop our field's analytic language and capacity to see what is powerful about media for learning interactions.

Curation of Media

> I found the Mega Builders and things like that after I started looking to record different *How It's Made* for him. We don't record every one of them. I look for specific ones. His favorite one is where they actually showed how a Ferrari was made. Things like that.
>
> Marie, mother of 6-year-old Joshua

We typically think of curation as a practice limited to experts who are charge of collections of culturally significant objects owned by museums or art galleries. With the rapid proliferation of digital assets, digital curation is becoming more widespread. Playlists, recommendation sites, rating and review organizations, and yearly top 10 lists might all be considered forms of curation. The theme of parents "curating" or intentionally selecting media content for their children was prevalent in interviews, although parents' approaches, feelings about screen media and curation styles varied widely, even among families of similar income or education levels. Most parents believed that media could be used for learning, however parents varied in their tendency to actively curate—research, select, organize, present—their children's choices to maximize learning. This variability was related to a number of factors including their own expertise with media, their beliefs about its value, and their concerns about possible negative effects of screen time on development.

Curation of media around children's interests was sometimes born of the need to have quality down time for busy parents. For example, Marie was a single working mom and her son Joshua was 6 years old and in first grade at the time of interview. They were a busy pair. Joshua's weekdays consisted largely of school and after-school program activities, with only a few hours spent at home. Weekends were spent in large part running errands, visiting family, riding his bike outside, and, on Sundays, watching football. Joshua also enjoyed media and his mom spent time supporting his strong interest in building and engineering by finding, recording, and organizing particular shows. This curation focused on segments factual TV programs that his mother selected for him based on topics that she knew he found of interest, such as *How It's Made* or *Mega Builders*. Marie prerecorded the shows for Joshua to watch when they had time to sit down and relax after a busy day. This allowed her to filter commercials and have confidence that he was seeing content that is connected to his interests and information rich. She explained:

> I picked those because, besides that I can DDR them and get rid of all the commercials, we can sit there for 20 minutes. **He can get like three or four different stories on how things are made and then we can move on. He gets some information**. He gets time to sit down.

In Marie's view, much of the value of these programs for Joshua lay in the questions and discussions they inspired. For example, one of the factual shows Marie recorded for Joshua was about how knives are made. Marie described how after watching the show, Joshua was helping to make dinner and, recognizing in his own kitchen the Henkel brand of knife he had seen portrayed, told his mother about what he had seen—how the steel was melted and then hardened to make the knives. Joshua also asked many questions about how cars or other machines featured on the shows are made, which he discussed with his grandfather. According to Marie, "He'll ask a lot of questions about [the programs], if it's something he's been really interested in," sometimes the same day or sometimes weeks later.

Among the seven dual-language families, parents actively curated media in Spanish to reinforce children's heritage language, and several used English-language media to expose their children to English, which was not often spoken in the home. These parents were all committed to having their children develop a strong foundation in both languages, and saw media as helpful resources. Some parents, such as Karina (stay-at-home mother of a 6-year-old daughter, Bryanna) reported that their children also taught them English based on media content.

Interviewer: What do you see as the value of these programs for [your daughter]? What does she get out of these programs?

Karina: Ah, so she can speak more English, because in the beginning she didn't speak much English.

Interviewer: Yes?

Karina: Now it's like, little by little she has progressed and now I put on both [languages] for her. And she tells me, she asks about things that, sometimes she teaches me things. Because I don't know English and there are things she teaches me.

Another mother, Rebeca, a waitress and janitorial worker, used media as a way to reinforce Spanish with her younger daughter. Although Rebeca's older daughter was fluent in both English and Spanish, her younger daughter Yelitza, age 3, had preferred English, even though Rebeca spoke Spanish exclusively with the girls at home. Rebeca credited children's media with helping Yelitza expand her Spanish:

> Yes, yes, yes for example more . . . I think it's more with *Dora*, with the *Dora* program, or *Super Why* where they teach the colors, and she says "Look, it's pink," so she already knows more or less how to distinguish the colors. [. . .] Because before she would say "pink, blue," [in English] and I'd tell her "no, it's rosado or azul."

Another father, Geoff, from the English-speaking sample, also curated Spanish-language content for his 4-year-old son Zach, though in this case Spanish was a language Zach had been introduced to in preschool rather than as a primary home language. Geoff hoped that watching *Dora* exclusively in Spanish might motivate Zach to speak the language more and he went to considerable effort to purchase these episodes as they were not readily available in the US market.

Latino immigrant parents also curated media from their countries of origin in order to expose children to aspects of their heritage culture. For example, Mexican families enjoyed the classic sitcom *El Chavo del Ocho* together, and parents from El Salvador and Perú used YouTube or subscribed to cable packages in order to show children programs that they themselves had grown up with (also see Chapter 9, this volume). Besides co-engaging with media alongside their children, Spanish-speaking parents also used technology in a variety of ways to improve their own English.

Among the Spanish-speaking families who were learning English, unique opportunities arose for both parents *and* children to learn together, since in many cases both parents and children were in the process of learning English. Érica Martínez, a stay-at-home mom who had recently arrived from Mexico with her two children and aspired to find a local job, was not a confident English speaker and used technology frequently to try to improve. She used the English language learning app Wlingua on her smartphone as a way of improving her language skills, and used the app collaboratively with her son David, aged 6.

Some parents curated media to be able to hand off a tablet without concern that the content was a waste of time or worse, a negative influence. For example, Geoff, a former CEO of a small technology startup and primary caregiver to 4-year-old Zach, spent a significant amount of energy finding and collecting both apps and shows that would help his son learn more about topics of interest. He saw the iPad as an essential parenting tool but he wanted apps that would allow for playful and interest-driven exploration rather than drill and practice. For example, his son's persistent interest in firefighting was fed by digital episodes of *Fireman Sam*. Zach would in turn share what he learned about fire safety with his parents. It also led to project ideas. He became interested in experimenting with how a magnifying glass could start a fire, a purchased inspired by a segment of this very same show.

Finding media that helped with early academic skills was common. The Latino immigrant families engaged in a rich set of practices using technology to connect home and school, which are explored in more depth in Chapter 10. These included finding specific educational resources to support children's academic learning. As an example of the latter, when 8-year-old Naomi was encountering difficulty with timed math quizzes in school, her mother downloaded an app that challenges players to complete the maximum number of operations in a limited time, so that Naomi could practice under time pressure. Érica guided her son Saul to use the online library, MyOn, which his school subscribed to, in order to support his English and reading skills. While families did curate resources to bolster academics, some families also expressed that they did not know where to find digital resources that would best support their children's learning (see José Rubén's quote at the start of this chapter).

Parents of preschoolers also curated media to encourage early learning. Kirsten relied on trusted channels such as Sprout to provide games and shows with age-sorted content for her 5-year-old son, Liam. She particularly selected games that would help him learn shapes, colors, letters, and spelling. Parents' professional background also influenced their approach. Amy, a computer scientist, and her husband Perry gave their now 4-year-old daughter Melanie access to a tablet when she was two and a half. In addition to screening for high-quality content focused on counting and learning letters, they also brought to bear their technical expertise as programmers and screened every purchase for the quality of the interaction. They had found that many apps had programming bugs and were unwilling to let Melanie suffer through the frustration of buttons that did not work or had inconsistent interfaces.

Not all parents were eager to explore interactive media. Miguel, father of 5-year-old Estela, was wary of digital technologies, but placed more trust in traditional media such as television and video. Estela watched television shows as well as occasional YouTube videos of the same programs (such as *Caillou* and *Curious George*), but her parents did not download other apps for her to use. Like other children, Estela gained access to digital apps on other people's devices, primarily when she was at her cousins' house. Estela's parents, using the "do as the Romans do" approach mentioned by Barbara (the mother in our opening example), trusted Estela's aunt and uncle to regulate her digital use appropriately when she was with them. At home, however, apps were not part of Estela's routine.

Interest-Driven Searches

> We had a space binge recently. It was a multimedia space binge. There was an Apollo 11 book from the library; I have this really beautiful Apollo 11 art book, lots of YouTube videos, and drawing. A rocket, planets, and stuff that kids can draw. So it was cool. We'd learn about something in one format and we'd take it into the other. Then we'd learn something else and we'd go back to the first one and have a new insight.
>
> Geoff, father of 4-year-old Zach

Searching the Internet for information related to topics of interest and to connect to video-based learning resources is a daily practice for many adults and teens. Some families in our study described using the Internet to more deeply explore topics of children's interest, whether sparked at school or elsewhere. In these examples, media use contributed to children's developing "islands of expertise" (Crowley & Jacobs, 2002) and in our study the topics inspiring the search ranged widely from spiders, to trains, to fires and firefighting. For example, Diana used resources on the *National Geographic* website to explore her 4-year-old daughter's interest in jellyfish and fires. In some cases these explorations were also linked to offline projects. For example, father Geoff described his and his son Zach's "multimedia space binge," where they gathered information from various types of media. Beginning with a library book about Apollo 11, the two moved across media platforms and practices, extending their interest through drawing and viewing online videos together. Their shared enthusiasm and interests supported extended exploration and activity. In addition to their common interest in space, this father and son pair shared an interest in cooking and would search together for recipes.

Some families described explicit bridging of interests between home and school, a theme developed in Chapter 10 of this volume. In that chapter Levinson describes how 6-year-old Brandon Orozco and his father José Rubén engaged in parent–child exploration of history and historical figures, a topic that caught the child's interest at school. Brandon had a keen interest in people in history, and developed a practice with his father where the two searched for videos on YouTube about Martin Luther King, Jr., George Washington and other famous leaders Brandon had heard of in school and wanted to know more about in the moment. A curious and inquisitive child, Brandon often asked questions about these famous people, who may have come up because of a particular holiday such as Martin Luther King, Jr. Day or other thematic units his first grade class was studying at the time. Chapter 10 details how Brandon's father José Rubén turned to online video with Brandon as a way of learning more together and deepening Brandon's understanding.

In addition to more in-depth searches for content related to interests, parents used media as a conversational prop to illustrate concepts, anchor discussions, and make meaning, sometimes leveraging the "anytime, anywhere" quality of mobile media to help children understand or learn more. We found that parents used the Internet, on computers or especially via mobile devices that can connect on the go, as a tool to seek visual and/or textual information "in the moment," as a just-in-time teaching tool in ways not possible without this technology. We call this form of activity *conversational anchoring* and describe several examples below.

Conversational Anchoring

> Because [with a video] it's easier for him, for him to visualize it and understand it better, and everything, [. . .] [In the videos] they represent it or . . . like he understands the representations better that way.
>
> José Rubén, father of 6-year-old Brandon

Kari, a stay-at-home mom of two with an advanced science degree, described how her husband enjoys hiking, and how the family had gone on a nighttime hike to do some stargazing. Elise, aged 5, was having trouble recognizing the Orion constellation as her parents were pointing it out in the sky, so they used one of their smartphones to look up an image of the constellation and help Elise identify it. On a separate excursion, Kari and her daughters were outdoors and saw a space shuttle flown by on top of an airplane as it was being transported, but it passed quickly and the girls could not get a good look. Kari used her smartphone to look up images of the shuttle transport that had been published online so they could look at the shuttle in more detail, and from there went on to explore images of animals that had traveled into space. Both examples—looking up the constellations on a hike and the images of space shuttles—began with an outdoor activity, and Kari saw these situations stemming at least in part from her own background as a scientist. In a similar example, Diana, mother of 4-year-old Mimi, did a search on their iPad to bring up an image of a painting referenced in a poem they were reading. It turned out it was one that they had also seen previously in a museum.

José Rubén and his son Brandon, who began exploring YouTube videos in order to learn about history-related topics, also used online video as a way to illustrate his answers to Brandon's questions. In one case, Brandon's questions were actually sparked by watching media: one of the Disney *Ice Age* movies. As José Rubén described, "[Brandon] said 'Dad, at that time what was it like? There weren't any buses? There weren't . . .?,' so we watched documentaries where it's shown and everything." In this way, media and particularly Internet video became a go-to resource for Brandon and José Rubén to learn about topics Brandon was interested in, taking advantage of both the information available as well as the visual nature of the material and in the case of historical figures, even seeing and hearing people from the past. For Geoff and Zach, experiences out in the world would inspire searching YouTube videos to get multiple view points on a situation. As he explained,

> So, we could be saying, 'Oh, when there's a fire, they have to spray from the top, and then they jump on the roof and cut a hole in it.' Then he can go see it on YouTube. He can see the helmet cam view. And he can see the helicopter view. He can see a stop-motion view and all this kind of stuff. It's really cool.

Media-inspired conversations could also bring up deeper lessons. Manuel, a construction worker and father of two girls, used movies as an opportunity to discuss behavior, values, and ethics with his 5-year-old daughter, Alicia. He described how he initiated discussion with his daughter around *Charlie and the Chocolate Factory* in this way:

> I start asking her questions. What did she understand? What did she like? What did she learn? And the man who sends out the tickets for the children to win, he wants to see their intelligence, their manners and the way that we adults raise our children, no? Greed, envy, how to treat others and how they respond. [. . .] [Alicia] says, 'Oh, that girl is difficult, she is this or that, she won't win. [. . .] and I asked her, 'What do you think the other kids did who had to leave?' And she answered right away, that it was because they were badly behaved.

Similarly, for Barbara's daughter Cati, the movie *The Princess and the Frog* became a springboard for discussing issues of race and racism, stereotypes in media, and how they do not reflect the reality of their own experience. Barbara's partner Jo also used media as a resource to talk with Cati about their shared interest in photography. Jo was a former photographer and she encouraged Cati to take her own photographs and videos on the iPhone and they would discuss these as well as photos found from other sources. Jo was also a baseball fan and this too became a source of learning and conversation that Cati actively took up, learning and sharing her knowledge of the positions and state of play.

Content Creation and Co-Play

> I try to tell them that, because I've always loved music, photography, film, videos, making videos. So I have told them too, for example, "you can start making your video with the phone," and that's why Naomi is starting to want to report and record.
>
> Eduardo, father of Naomi, aged 8

Some families also engaged in *producing* video and/or watching themselves onscreen as recorded by others. This topic was explored in more depth with the study of Latino families, which included numerous home visits and interviews. Parents enjoyed taking photos of their children and sharing these with friends and family by e-mail or using social media. The children in the study were aware that their parents' mobile phones could create images, as well as display them. Children themselves enjoyed taking photos or videos of outings and gatherings, but also sometimes around the house. For example, 6-year-old Bryanna Parra enjoyed using the video camera or the audio recording app on her mother's iPhone to record herself singing or making sounds, and took videos of her parents or friends when they visited. Melanie, aged 4, also took digital photos and her programmer father Perry created a screen saver to showcase their favorites. Cati, aged 6, took photos and videos with the family iPhone, an interest she shared with one of her parents who was a professional photographer.

In other families, media production took the form of home movies shot by parents. For example, 5-year-old Alicia and her 2-year-old sister regularly asked to watch a home video their parents recorded of Alicia's preschool graduation. When they watched, the girls waited eagerly for Alicia's appearance on the stage and enjoyed singing along with the songs the class had performed.

Naomi, aged 8, was particularly interested in media production, and used her iPod Touch to create her own "talk shows" along with her 6-year-old brother Eduardo, Jr. Naomi's father was a media production aficionado himself, and encouraged the children to create. In the quote at the start of the section, Naomi's father describes how he inspired the children's activities based on his own interest. More generally, shooting video during outings and taking photos was a popular family activity, and the family also enjoyed reviewing what they had recorded, connecting their photo or video camera to their large television set and looking through family photos and videos together. The children's own talk shows, influenced in part by the Nickelodeon show *iCarly* about a teenage girl with her own webcast program, featured Naomi in the role of presenter discussing topics (in Spanish) that ranged from describing the local surroundings, to fears, to wildlife and environmental conservation, which was a focus at her elementary school. Although no clear audience was mentioned in the children's recordings, Eduardo, Jr. tells their audience that "if you are in Mexico it doesn't matter, we will send it to you on Facebook," indicating that some of their viewers were relatives in his parents' native country.

The video transcript excerpt that follows was drawn from a video that Naomi and her brother recorded using Naomi's iPod touch. The inspiration from television shows shines through in several features of the video. Naomi in particular used a tone and manner that mimicked TV presenters, even including "commercial breaks." At the opening of the segment, Eduardo is recording Naomi as she introduces the show and the themes of the day, beginning with *el miedo* (fear) and, after the "commercial break," the theme of *la naturaleza* (nature). Throughout the video, the children alternate roles talking to the camera. As Naomi and Eduardo narrate their video, they naturally interweave the local and the global in their subject matter; bringing together a topic of widespread concern (the environment) as well as details of their local surroundings. In a later segment of the same show, Naomi and Eduardo turn their attention to "electronic things," before tying back to the theme of nature. We first present their dialogue in Spanish and then provide the English translation.

Naomi: Bienvenidos otra vez, miremos, ahora tendremos que hablar de la naturaleza. Aquí hay muchos ejemplos de la naturaleza. Como puedes cuidar al mar, que no haga basura, o . . . y que todas las plantas están a salvo. Veremos, este árbol esta tan bonito de mi calle, [camera shows tree outside bedroom window] que hasta había un colibri, aquí hay uno.

Eduardo: Ya ven? Si esta en México no importa, le vamos a mandar en el Facebook. [Referring to the street scene below] allí están todos los carros, que . . . están en [name of city]. Hay un biciclero, las hojas, y más para allá abajo hay nuestra escuela. Y también podemos ver la gente cruzando, los árboles, la escuela que antes yo iba allí, y por allá . . . [speaking inaudibly to Naomi] allá mas allá pasando por el freeway, allá vive mi tía y mi primo.

Naomi: Welcome back, now we will be talking about nature. Here there are many examples of nature. The way you can take care of the ocean, not litter, or . . . keeping all plants safe. As we can see, this tree is so pretty on my street [camera shows tree outside bedroom window] that there's even a hummingbird, there's one right here.

Eduardo: You see? If you are in Mexico it doesn't matter, we will send it to you on Facebook. There are [referring to street scene below] all the cars that . . . are in [city]. There is a biker, the leaves, and farther down there is our school. And we can also see people crossing the

> street, the trees, the school where I used to go, and that way [speaks inaudibly to Naomi]. Farther that way past the freeway is where my aunt and cousin live.

On the less enthusiastic end of the spectrum, Olga, parent to 8-year-old Wayne, was one of the most skeptical about the value of media as a learning resource. She heavily restricted Wayne's access to devices and digital content, though she made exceptions under certain conditions. For example, when a favorite babysitter brought over an *Angry Birds* game she allowed them to play together. However, Olga also recognized the value of technology for building and creating, but primarily for older children like Wayne's 12-year-old brother, Alex. Wayne was allowed to participate from the sidelines; for example, Alex built worlds in *Minecraft* or designed games in *Scratch* and allowed Alex to play the games that he had designed.

In addition to content creation, some parents actively played games with their children. For example, on weekends 5-year-old Elise played an iPad *Lego* game with her father, an activity linked to her tangible toy experience with physical *Lego*. Brandon played computer-based card games with his mother, Carmen, and some families also used game consoles at home together. Marie and Joshua played the math game *Top It!* together, and this was one of the games that they chose to share with the research team during our play session. Top It is a two player game during which players take turns dealing two pairs of numbers, entering the sums of the numbers on a keypad, and then judging which of the two numbers is bigger. Throughout the 6.5-minute session, Joshua's enthusiasm and excitement was palatable. During that time they play nine rounds and, as illustrated in Figure 2.1, Joshua counted on his fingers, used gesture to make number shapes with his hands, and Marie frequently pointed to the symbols on the screen as she verified magnitude judgments between the numbers. This 1-minute of interaction provides an example of sustained joint attention (Tomasello, 1999) focused on the iPad as well the multimodal and embodied nature of what is often thought of as "screen time." Throughout the session, Joshua was highly focused on the challenging computational problems presented and visibly excited by the game. He responded enthusiastically to the feedback from both the app and his mother, clenching hands, bouncing and leaning forward, expressing both positive affect and physical affection.

Marie learned about the game through Joshua's older cousin, whose teacher had recommended it. Joshua had been playing the game with his mother and cousins for more than a year when his teacher introduced the analog version in school. According to Joshua's mom, the iPad experience was useful for him as he often struggles when presented with a new game to learn. In this case, he knew right away what game they were playing and so he could jump right in. This kind of transfer of skills from digital to analog is a positive indicator of learning, though we need more research to understand the interactions and game features that facilitate it.

1. Joshua deals the four cards yielding a 7/3 combination on the left and a 3/6 combination on the right.
2. Marie: Your turn.
3. Joshua silently counts on his fingers to add seven and three, counting on from seven.
4. Joshua enters a ten on the iPad keypad to indicate the sum of the 7/3 pair and a nine for the sum of the 3/6 pair.
5. Joshua makes the shape of a "nine" with his fingers. Marie turns her head to look at his hands.
6. Marie: What is it?
7. Joshua: Nine! [louder, remaking the shape to show her]
8. Marie: Nine [laughs].

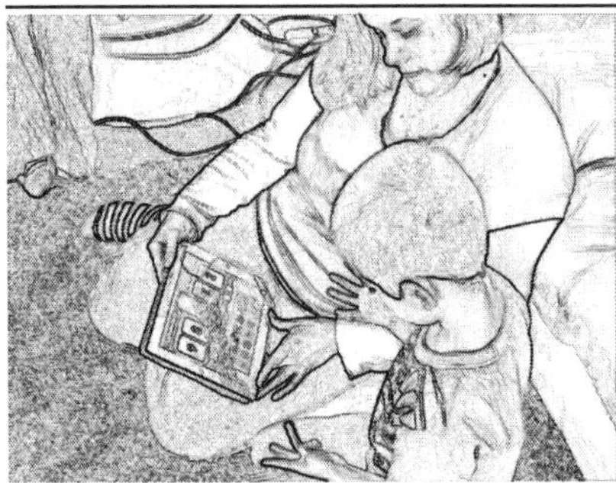

10. Marie: Ten is greater than nine [pointing to the numbers as she says them].
11. Maries deals the next set of four cards yielding a 9/8 pair on the left and a 7/2 pair on the right. She enters a 9 as the sum for the 7/2 pair and looks to Joshua.
12. Marie: Can you do it? [referring to the 9/8 pair].
13. Joshua counts on from nine with his fingers using both hands with five on his right hand and three on his left, whispering as he counts and then enters 17 on the number pad.
14. Marie: Good job.

15. Marie: Good job. Is that the last one?
16. Josh: Yep.
17. iPad voice: Great game. Way to play!
18. Joshua: Tied.
19. Marie: Hey, we're tied!
20. Joshua: Yeah. [gets up on his knees]
21. Maries raises hand palm up for a high five and Joshua enthusiastically slaps her hand.

FIGURE 2.1 Marie and Josh enjoying a game of "Top It"

Conclusions and Implications

In bringing together data from two studies of family media use, we sought to identify rich examples of learning with media that are emerging among families as well begin to conceptualize as how these relate to parents' own histories, values, interests, beliefs, and social networks. We close with conclusions and recommendations for parents, educators, designers, and researchers that can guide future work based on our findings.

For Educators and Parents

Parents vary in their approaches to media for their children, and struggle to find resources. We found variability in parents' enthusiasm for using media for their children's learning that was tied to parents' perception of whether it could advance learning as opposed to being just a source of entertainment. This continuum ranged from a stance we might call resistant or hesitant, to extreme enthusiasm. On one end of the continuum were families who either felt media were not a productive use of children's time, or who felt uninformed about how media could support learning. Two parents, both among the high socioeconomic status group, said that they did not conceptualize media as a meaningful or desirable learning tool for their children and they consequently were not proactive about finding high quality content. In one of these cases children's media use was heavily restricted. In the other, little attention was paid to the content of media used by children and reflected the parents' own histories with media (e.g., Barbara's memory of her peers being "plopped" in front of the TV led her to feel ambivalent about her daughter's media use but wanted her to be able to participate in media with her peers). Among other families there was more openness and enthusiasm, yet many parents had a sense that information on the topic was not readily available. Even parents who *did* engage in technology practices that supported children's learning sensed that there was much they did not know, including how to locate the best content. Many parents, including most in the Latino immigrant sample, were not aware that mobile devices could be used for reading e-books, creating original stories, and other rich learning activities, and thus they had not sought this type of content for their children. Some parents in this group stated that they wanted to use technology to support their children's learning, but did not feel confident about doing so.

Parents who were enthusiastic leveraged resources in multiple ways. The active curation of media was more prevalent for parents who saw the potential benefits of digital content for particular learning goals including language, early literacy, art, or science. Beyond simply choosing and regulating media use, parents also engaged *with* their children in using media (particularly via the Internet) to conduct *interest-driven searches* and deepen knowledge jointly across settings. Questions sparked at school, in the neighborhood, or with friends could be explored in more depth later at home. For example, Brandon and his father expanded on Brandon's school-sparked interest using online video, bringing topics from the school setting into the home. Among the Latino immigrant sample, families harnessed media to expose their children to English, which many parents did not feel confident speaking. They also reinforced children's heritage language and culture with media resources.

In other examples, media was used for *conversational anchoring*, as a means to illustrate and expand on ideas rather than researching topics based on mutual curiosity. With young children, media seemed particularly effective in that it provided access to a variety of representations, such as photographs, videos, and poems as opposed to text-only options. In this way media could be used as a means for *collaborative* learning, rather than solely as a way to teach or illustrate. These findings suggest that there is a significant opportunity for educators, parents, and librarians to productively share examples of interactions and media resources that will help them expand their ideas about how to use media in novel ways that extends to conceptual and creative activity.

For Designers

The options for learning with media are not transparent to families. Our results show the ways in which families' own experiences and values shape practices with media, and surface innovative practices that families have developed from their own ingenuity. However, there are few resources available to systematically guide parents who want to know more about how to productively harness media for their children. These findings suggest the need for design work that can help families explore resources and approaches to using media. This work needs to go beyond technical designs to include social learning opportunities in the places where families spend time including schools, libraries, museums, and workplaces. This is an ideal context for research-to-practice partnerships (e.g., Coburn & Penuel, 2016).

Opportunities to produce, rather than simply consume, is one area that can be developed further in technology design and has the potential to contribute positively to learning and development. We know from studies of adolescents that media creation is correlated with creative confidence and technical expertise (Barron, Gomez, Pinkard, & Martin, 2014; Barron & Martin, 2016). Our examples show that some children were beginning to explore the power of technology to record and experiment with their own ideas. In their "talk show," Naomi and Eduardo used their experience watching media programs, particularly Naomi's with iCarly, as a template for creating their own show that shares themes from their lives as well as topics that they may have been introduced to in school. In this way Naomi and Eduardo, who consumed a variety of different media programs, also leveraged this experience to express their own voices and share—

to a palpable audience—topics of concern and interest to them. This example also illustrates Dugan, Stevens, and Mehus' (2010) point that media programs that are not necessarily designed as "educational" can give rise to learning interactions and activities. In addition, as Naomi's father expressed, media production was a practice that was not only encouraged and supported in their household, but was also modeled as he pursued his own production practice and drew the children into it. There is room for additional content creation games and tools, designed specifically for families with young children.

For Researchers

We need to understand more about how media can help connect learning experiences and best practices for families. In many examples shared here, media provided opportunities for families to connect experiences across time and setting and in some cases facilitated playful or interest-driven learning (Barron, 2006) that connected to school topics. This is an important finding that needs to be followed up by more research. Future studies that include analyses of collaborative discourse and links to learning measures would be productive for further conceptualizing the potential for digital media to be a rich resource for joint attention and conceptual development. We also found variability among families in how they conceptualize and leverage media. Parents' own media history and confidence played a role in the extent of their curation and all parents expressed interest in knowing more about how to find good content. Future research can do more to articulate how parent's perceptions influence choices as well as define how parents might be helped to better find and leverage digital resources that are productive for learning. Research on parents as learners and learning partners can advance both our theories of human development and yield frameworks and tools that might help parents become stronger brokers of opportunities. Design-focused research that can help articulate the needs of families with fewer economic resources is particularly important. Although divides in access are decreasing, along with achievement gaps at kindergarten (Bassok, Finch, Lee, Reardon, & Waldfogel, 2016), there are significant equity issues at stake with respect to access to the quality of devices, software, connections to the Internet and most importantly the social resources that can help parents leverage digital media resources to support learning.

In closing, the increasing prevalence of digital technology in homes of diverse backgrounds and income levels make it vital to understand family media practices and how these can support learning and development. This chapter highlights practices that provide direction for working with parents to conceptualize their and their children's media engagement. These accounts can inform educators' notions of students' home activities, which educators can draw upon when aiming to connect learning across settings. There is significant work to do to ensure that schools, libraries, and other institutions that serve children provide digital and human resources to those families who may currently have the least access to high-quality tools and who may benefit the most.

Acknowledgments

This research was supported by grants from the National Science Foundation (REC-238524, REC-354453) through the LIFE center (http://life-slc.org/) and by grants to the Joan Ganz Cooney Center from the Heising-Simons Foundation. Any opinions, findings, and conclusions expressed are those of the authors and do not necessarily reflect the views of the sponsoring agencies. We are grateful for the participation of the families involved.

References

American Academy of Pediatrics. (2013). Children, adolescents, and the media. *Pediatrics, 132*(5), 958–961.

Barron, B. (2006). Interest and self-sustained learning as catalysts of development: A learning ecologies perspective. *Human Development, 49*, 193–224.

Barron, B., Gomez, K., Pinkard, N., & Martin, C.K. (Eds.). (2014). *The Digital Youth Network: Cultivating new media citizenship in urban communities*. Cambridge, MA: MIT Press.

Barron, B., Levinson, A., Matthews, J., & Vea, T. (in preparation). Digital media as a catalyst for learning: Contributions of parent & child learning biographies, expertise and interests.

Barron, B., Martin, C. K., Takeuchi, L., & Fithian, R. (2009). Parents as learning partners in the development of technological fluency. *International Journal of Learning and Media, 1*, 55–77.

Barron, B., & Martin, C. K. (2016). Making matters: A framework for assessing digital media citizenship. In K. Peppler, E. R. Halverson, & Y. B. Kafai (Eds.), *Makeology: Makers as learners*, Vol. 2 (pp. 45–72). New York: Routledge.

Bassok, D., Finch, J. E., Lee, R., Reardon, S. F., & Waldfogel, J. (2016). Socioeconomic gaps in early childhood experiences: 1998 to 2010. *AERA Open, 2*(3), 1–22.

Blum-Ross, A., & Livingstone, S. (2016). *Families and screen time: Current advice and emerging research. Media Policy Brief 17*. London: Media Policy Project, London School of Economics and Political Science.

Coburn, C.E., & Penuel, W.R. (2016). Research-practice partnerships: Outcomes, dynamics, and open questions. *Educational Researcher, 45*(1), 48–54.

Crowley, K., & Jacobs, M. (2002). Islands of expertise and the development of family scientific literacy. In G. Leinhardt, K. Crowley, & K. Knutson (Eds.), *Learning conversations in museums* (pp. 333–356). Mahwah, NJ: Lawrence Erlbaum Associates.

Dugan, T.E., Stevens, R., & Mehus, S. (2010). From show, to room, to world: A cross-context investigation of how children learn from media programming. *International Conference on the Learning Sciences, 1*, 992–999.

Lee, J. & Barron, B. (2015). *Aprendiendo en casa: Media as a resource for learning among Hispanic-Latino families*. New York: Joan Ganz Cooney Center at Sesame Workshop.

Levinson, A.M. (2014). *Tapping in: Understanding how Hispanic-Latino immigrant families engage and learn with broadcast and digital media* (PhD dissertation). Stanford University.

Rideout, V. (2014). *Learning at home: Families, educational media use in America. A report of the Families and Media Project.* New York: The Joan Ganz Cooney Center at Sesame Workshop. Retrieved from www.joanganzcooneycenter.org/publication/learning-at-home/

Takeuchi, L., & Stevens, R. (Eds.). (2011). *The New Coviewing: Designing for learning through joint media engagement.* New York: Joan Ganz Cooney Center.

Tomasello, M. (1999). *The cultural origins of human cognition.* Cambridge, MA: Harvard University Press.

3

THE INFLUENCE OF SIBLINGS ON THE DIGITAL MEDIA ECOLOGY OF LATINO CHILDREN

Elisabeth Gee, Lori M. Takeuchi, Sinem Siyahhan, and Briana Ellerbe

Siblings have always played a significant role in the lives and learning of young children. While parents are often described as children's "first teachers," for many children, older siblings are a close second, serving as playmates, role models, and guides. Younger siblings as well as older siblings provide children with opportunities to develop social skills, such as empathy, the ability to negotiate conflicts, and collaboration (Howe, Ross, & Recchia, 2011).

In the United States, a significant majority of young people aged 18 and under live with at least one sibling (McHale, Updegraff, & Whiteman, 2012). In 2010, almost 40 percent of this age group was living with one sibling, about 25 percent were living with two siblings, and over 15 percent were living with three or more siblings. Children from Hispanic and African-American backgrounds have higher numbers of siblings than white or Asian-American children (ibid). A widely cited study from two decades ago reported that children spend more time with siblings than with parents during the ages of preschool to middle childhood (McHale & Crouter, 1996), yet the role of siblings in children's development and learning has received very little attention from researchers or educators. This lack of attention to siblings is reflected in the literature on digital media's role in the lives of young children, which tends to focus on parent or other adult caregivers' roles and interactions with children around media (e.g., Nikken & Schols, 2015).

In this chapter, we explore some of the many potential ways that siblings might influence the home media ecology and the opportunities that children have to learn with and about digital media. These influences can be both positive and negative; for example, older children might teach younger siblings how to use new digital tools, while in other cases siblings might restrict access to these tools. Developing an understanding of sibling influence is complicated by the considerable diversity in sibling relationships across families. These relationships vary by sibling age, gender, birth order, personality traits, and number of siblings, as well as by parents' expectations for siblings' roles and interactions with each other. We draw on data from two studies, *Joint Media Engagement, Play, Literacy, and Learning among Mexican-American Families* (AZ) and *Learning with Media in Modern Families* (JGCC) (see Appendix, Studies 3 and 8), and use family cases to illustrate different ways that siblings affect children's access to and use of digital media in the home. We follow these cases with a more general discussion of several key themes that crosscut different forms of sibling influence and further illuminate how and why siblings can be such powerful sources of digital media-related learning.

Siblings and Learning in the Home Media Ecology

Considerable attention has been given to the role of parents in structuring and regulating the use of digital media in the home and in family life (e.g., Horst, 2009; Plowman, McPake, & Stephen, 2008). Of course, children are not just passive recipients of digital media provided by parents, and they do not simply acquiesce to parental rules or guidance. In general, children of all ages play an active role in shaping family culture and practices (McHale et al., 2012) and the use of digital media is no exception. Children negotiate rules, subvert them, and establish their own rules and norms for behavior. Influenced by popular media and peers, children persuade parents to purchase toys, games, software, and hardware such as tablets, game consoles, and computers. They learn to use digital technologies independently and surpass their parents' skills through their own experimentation as well as through peers, school, and online resources.

Not surprisingly, the presence of siblings is an important aspect of the home learning environment in general, and of the digital media environment in particular. Siblings have both direct and indirect influences on children's learning and development. As McHale et al. (2012, p. 913) observe, "Sibling influences emerge not only in the context of siblings' frequent and often emotionally intense interactions but also by virtue of siblings' roles in larger family system dynamics." In other words, siblings have a *direct* influence on each other because they tend to spend a lot of time together (often more than they spend with parents), particularly when they are young, which gives them greater opportunities to shape each other's thinking and behavior. This time spent together, in the most intimate context of the home, also means that siblings have opportunities to develop deep knowledge of each other's perspectives and feelings (Howe & Recchia, 2014). In addition, time spent with siblings, and what is learned in this time together, often carries a heightened emotional valence due to factors like competition for parents' attention or the desire for a sibling's approval. The social and cultural significance often given to the relationship among siblings can make these direct interactions particularly impactful. For example, an older sibling may be positioned as a caregiver or protector of a younger child, or siblings may be expected to share toys and play together. Age differences among siblings can intensify power dynamics, with older siblings attempting to exert control over younger brothers or sisters. At the same time, age differences offer opportunities for teaching and mentoring.

Siblings also have an *indirect* influence on each other's learning and development as they shape how the family functions as a whole. There are at least three main forms of indirect sibling influence (McHale et al., 2012). First, siblings influence parents' parenting knowledge, beliefs, and behavior. As parents gain experience with first-born children, they develop parenting strategies that they apply to younger siblings. They also form beliefs about children's learning and development that can affect how they respond to and interpret younger siblings' behavior. Second, siblings can create "resource dilution"; that is, tangible and intangible resources such as money, space (i.e., having your own bedroom), parent time and attention, need to be spread across more children. A reduction in resources available to any one child does not necessarily have negative consequences; as we will describe later, for example, the need to share digital tools can lead to increased opportunities for co-learning and collaboration. Third, siblings serve as points of social comparison, starting as early as infanthood, when parents assess babies' personalities and development in relation to older siblings (i.e., "she is so easy-going compared to her brother," or "he is the smart one").

In addition, families with siblings are subject to more varied and potentially conflicting social and cultural norms for parenting and children's behavior (Davies & Gentile, 2012). For instance, determining what video games are appropriate may be complicated enough for parents when they have only one child, but such decisions become even more complex when they must take into account the needs and desires of siblings of different ages. In addition, parents must accommodate changes over time, both in general norms for parenting and in specific expectations for children's media use, which can affect sibling dynamics. They may, for example, provide younger siblings with tools such as cell phones or tablets at earlier ages, creating tension over how resources are distributed or placing more demands on older siblings to model appropriate media use (ibid).

While it's apparent that siblings play an important role in children's home experience and development, how siblings affect children's digital media use and learning more specifically is less clear. Making generalizations about sibling influences has been particularly difficult. Researchers adopting quantitative survey methods have attempted to identify relationships among variables such as the presence of siblings, age differences between siblings, or the quality of sibling relationships and factors such as amount of media use. Taken as a whole, such studies have yielded mixed results; for example, some research has found that the presence of siblings was associated with increased media use, while other studies found the opposite (Bagley, Salmon, & Crawford, 2006; Davies & Gentile, 2012). Empirical studies in more controlled, laboratory settings have focused on the nature of sibling interactions and their effects in situations such as co-viewing television shows. Such research also has yielded mixed results, with some studies indicating positive effects of sibling co-viewing, such as increased enjoyment and understanding of characters, while other studies found negative effects, including lack of comprehension of programs (Haefner & Wartella, 1987; Wilson & Weiss, 1993).

Given the complexity of sibling relationships, it is perhaps not surprising that efforts to determine the effects of isolated variables have been inconclusive. Furthermore, such research tells us little about the role of siblings in children's digital media use and learning in the dynamic and multifaceted context of family life. A small number of naturalistic studies provide more insight into the dynamics of sibling teaching and learning around digital media and in general. Takeuchi (2012) used case studies of two 8-year-old girls to provide an in-depth portrait of how children's technology access, use, and learning are shaped by a multiplicity of forces, and in particular how home and family are central to young children's engagement with digital media. While siblings were not a primary focus of the analyses, the case studies suggested a variety of ways in which siblings play a role in children's media engagement, for example, by acting as gatekeepers, playmates, and role models of technology-related behaviors and attitudes. Takeuchi (2012) concluded that "the involvement of siblings and other relatives in a child's technological upbringing should be studied with the same attention and rigor with which parents have been studied" (p. 55).

Other studies have focused more narrowly on siblings' interactions around specific kinds of digital media, particularly video games (e.g., Coyne, Jensen, Smith, & Erickson, 2016; Go, Ballagas, & Spasojevic, 2012). These and other studies of sibling interaction around different media, such as books and board games, offer a glimpse into distinctive and powerful features of sibling teaching and learning. For example, while older siblings are more likely to be teachers or managers in relation to the use of media, younger siblings play an active role in soliciting explanations and assistance. The comfort that younger children feel in seeking support from siblings seems to be important in shaping the teaching and learning situation (Azmitia & Hesser, 1993; Gregory, 2001). Older siblings can become very adept at scaffolding younger children's media use and learning, through coaching, "bending the rules" in game play, offering hints, and otherwise actively supporting their engagement. Even very young children engage in teaching less experienced siblings; teaching appears to be a natural and universal cognitive ability (Strauss and Ziv, 2012), though specific teaching practices are shaped by culture and exposure to formal schooling (Maynard, 2004). Just as importantly, children can improve their own skills and knowledge through teaching their siblings; for example, children who helped their younger siblings with reading books showed more improvement in their own reading scores than children who did not have these teaching opportunities (Smith, 1990).

Teaching and learning interactions around digital media, similar to sibling interactions in general, are shaped by the nature and quality of sibling relationships more broadly. And as Howe and Recchia (2014) point out, a characteristic of sibling relationships is that they vary considerably on attributes such as closeness and warmth, and can be fraught with emotions such as jealousy and rivalry as well as caring and affection. This variability exists even in sibling relationships within the same family; for example, two brothers close in age might have a contentious and competitive relationship while at the same time adopt a protective and nurturing stance toward their younger sister. Some variability can be attributed to sibling personality and temperament, that is, a child who is generally easy-going or tolerant may have a more relaxed relationship with siblings than a child who is anxious or competitive.

In this chapter, we describe the dynamics of sibling influence through case studies of four families. Case studies allow us to illustrate the multiple forms of sibling influence within each family while at the same time identifying common themes. We drew on an earlier analysis of sibling influence (Gee, Siyahhan, & Cirell, 2016) that identified five broad categories of direct and indirect sibling influence: direct interactions, access to social networks, access to technology and tools, mediation of parental beliefs, and mediation of family routines. We reviewed family data from the JGCC and AZ studies, and selected four families that represent diverse configurations of sibling age, gender, and family socio-economic status. Each family exemplifies a form of sibling influence that was particularly prominent in the family. We make no claims about the representativeness of the families and their dynamics, but rather use the cases to illustrate the significance of siblings in the media learning ecology of young children in general, and point to the need to reconceptualize how we understand the dynamics of media-related learning in the home. Following the discussion of cases, we discuss several themes that we identified as particularly important, drawing on data from our studies as well as the existing literature on sibling relationships and learning.

Sibling Influences in Four Families

The families in these studies are quite different, but they share some similarities as well. All of the families are of Hispanic-Latino origin: the families in the AZ study were all Mexican American, and the families in the JGCC study were from varied Hispanic backgrounds. While culture obviously plays a big role in the families' identities and experiences, here we do not emphasize cultural background as a prominent factor in the dynamics of sibling influence. Our case studies focus primarily on how siblings directly affect each other's digital media learning opportunities, since such direct influences were easier to document, though we also identify indirect influences if they became apparent.

Tacit and Explicit Teaching and Learning between Brothers: The (Little) Professor and His Student

Sofia (Garcia) Edwards (age 44) and sons Liam (age 9) and Dylan (age 12) live in a two-bedroom apartment in Brooklyn Heights. Sofia was born and raised in Mexico City, and came to New York City as a young adult to attend art school. She married a Canadian citizen, whom she divorced when Liam was very young and who now plays no role in the boys' lives other than making meager child support payments. Both Liam and Dylan have Asperger's Syndrome (a mild form of autism) and, according to Sofia, neither are very social or interested in sports, which has resulted in her indulging them with iPads, Wii Us, Nintendos DS, robotics materials, Flip Cams, and pretty much any technology they ask for. Sofia also admits to doing so because she sees the potential that these tools hold for the boys becoming the next Bill Gates and Steve Jobs, two tech geniuses among the many who share the Asperger's Syndrome diagnosis.

Sofia enjoyed a comfortably middle-class upbringing in Mexico City as part of *la izquierda intellectual* (the "intellectual left"), and so prioritizes the education and cultural enrichment of her sons, despite her very limited budget as a single parent and full-time student working on her bachelor's degree. She sends the boys to separate private schools in Manhattan (both on scholarship), music, and the necessary doctors' appointments, and holds a part-time job that pays $9 per hour to make this all possible. Sofia relies heavily on technology to facilitate this: Her cellphone (a regular one; she cannot afford a smartphone) is essential in coordinating her sons' school transportation with bus drivers and babysitters. She does her coursework readings on an iPad or Kindle, usually on her 35-minute subway commutes to and from campus, and scours the Internet to obtain information on everything from health to parenting to entertainment. In doing so, Sofia models confidence and competence with technological tools in front of her sons.

Whether or not Dylan inherited this savvy from his mother, he long ago surpassed her as the tech whiz of the family. As a toddler, he would regularly take household items apart and put them back together again. As Dylan grew older, he sought opportunities to build in both physical and digital realms—assembling LEGO kits, programming mods to his favorite video games, and starting his own YouTube channel to show off his game cheats—all on his own initiative but with the material and social support of his encouraging mother. The YouTube channel is an example of what his mom calls the "little professor" syndrome (Klin, Volkmar, & Sparrow, 2000), one well documented among children with Asperger's: Dylan loves explaining how things work to other people, whether they are interested in hearing about it or not. Liam, on the other hand, is more like the student sitting in the back of the classroom compared to his brother, the professor. He is content to communicate through shrugs and nods if that is all that is required to get his point across. Also in contrast to Dylan, Liam is "the artist" (vs. the technologist), a designation that everyone in the family recognizes and celebrates, and his realm has until only recently been the nondigital: music, drawing, crafts, etc.

But all this changed when Liam started playing video games. Although Dylan has been gaming since early in his childhood, according to Sofia:

> They didn't play at all together for a long time, and then Dylan . . . Liam started being interested in Dylan's stuff just to be with him. Just to interact with him. So Dylan likes to be the teacher, so then he started teaching him.

Before this shift, the brothers rarely interacted in sustained activities. Parallel play was the norm, as is common among children with Asperger's syndrome (Klin et al., 2000), though Dylan and Liam's separate interests (digital vs. unplugged) also likely played a role. Now the brothers play games like *Super Mario 3D World* together, sometimes taking on separate characters in multiplayer mode, and sometimes switching off playing the same character. On one visit, we observed Liam playing Princess Peach while Dylan stood behind him, watching for the most part but occasionally chiming in with a suggestion or single word of encouragement or instruction. At one point, Liam handed the controller to Dylan, who took it without comment, scaled Princess Peach to the top of the 3D World's golden pole, then handed the controller back to Liam, whose Princess Peach could now progress to the next world. The entire transaction took place without a word exchanged between them. The teaching and learning arrangements around gameplay that the boys set up are, as illustrated in this example, as often tacit as they are didactic, due to the brothers' close relationship.

The boys still engage in parallel play, though of a different nature. A common scenario we observed involved one brother playing a game on the TV console while the other played a separate game on a handheld console or tablet and within touching distance, allowing the two to keep tabs on each other's maneuverings. One would often peer up from his own screen to watch his brother navigate a particularly sticky situation, sometimes offering words of advice or cheer, sometimes saying nothing at all, and then resuming his own gameplay. What makes these interactions particularly endearing is that Dylan and Liam have separate, designated gaming spots in the house, each equipped with its own flat-screen TV and gaming console: Liam's is on a big armchair in the living room and Dylan's spot is in their shared bedroom. Rather than playing in their separate spots, they end up playing on separate devices but in one another's physical company. This setup makes those tacit teaching and learning arrangements possible.

Sofia is pleased that her 9- and 12-year-old sons have finally established a routine that they find mutually enjoyable: Liam gets to spend more time with his brother, and Dylan has a protégé to shower with his technological knowledge. Since Dylan has other followers that number in the hundreds—if not thousands—on his game cheats YouTube channel, Sofia admits to rewarding Dylan for helping Liam by creating a system of "credits" that he can use to purchase materials he needs for this other digital hobbies.

The Left Out Leader: Finding Her Voice in a Room Full of Boys

Jolena, aged 8, lives in a two-story row home in Philadelphia with her mother, Renelle, her soon-to-be step father, Mario, and her four brothers, Dominic (11), Nadair (9), Jaelon (6), and Isaiah (2). In this male-dominated household, Jolena's daily activities often revolve around the media use of her brothers, and illustrate the role of gender in siblings' interactions with each other and with digital media.

In one instance of gameplay, Jolena looks on as her brothers play an intense game of *Grand Theft Auto: Liberty City* in their bedroom. Dominic, the oldest of the four brothers, takes control of the game as Nadair and Jaelon look on, shouting suggestions for moves to take in the game. Jolena attempts to chime in, then asks for a turn with the controller. However, her brothers tell her that she cannot have a turn, because she "doesn't know how to play" and "always loses her weapons." The brothers chuckle in agreement at the statement while Jolena timidly tries to defend her gameplay skills. Renelle reassures Jolena with a hug and kiss then tells her that she can do anything that she wants to with practice.

This scene is not uncommon in the Vasquez household, as the boys spend a majority of their free time in their bedroom in front of their Xbox 360. They are so enthusiastic about their games that Renelle struggles to get them to even eat a meal between arriving home from school and running upstairs to play. However, technology is an extremely useful tool in household management for Renelle and it helps her to keep her children entertained inside of the home, as she does not feel they are safe playing in their neighborhood. She also believes in the educational potential of media and technology use, so does not hinder gameplay, but rather monitors it by making sure that none of her children fight and that they each get a fair share of time on all of their shared household devices including the living room TV, tablet, and laptop. Because the boys spend so much time on the Xbox 360 and she is aware that Jolena is not as interested, she bought Jolena her own tablet for movies, placed a used PS2 in Jolena's personal bedroom for her to play fishing games, and gives Jolena first priority over the laptop. In this way, the boys' interests and activities, in addition to her mother's worries about technology and the safety of her neighborhood, have shaped Jolena's experience with her own media access and routines.

While Jolena is happy to have these additional devices all to herself in her own bedroom, to her, it does not compare to the presence and friendship of her brothers. At only 8 years old, she believes that her family is the most important thing in her life, and sometimes feels that video games separate her from her brothers. She joyfully talks about technology-free time that her family spends at the beach, when they play in the water and build sandcastles together. But at home, she often feels left out, as if she's "not even there" when they play games, and has even gone so far as to say that she wishes her brothers were girls. Then, she could at least spend time with them painting their nails, watching *Good Luck Charlie*, and playing board games like *Chutes and Ladders*.

In media activities that involve all of her brothers, Jolena often feels invisible; she is timid and follows rather than leads. However, in situations where she can help or teach a younger sibling, she takes on a demeanor of confidence and agency. When Jolena's 6-year-old brother Jaelon wants to play a game, for instance, but is too short to switch the games in the console, Jolena gladly inserts a Batman game into the Xbox 360. She continues to assist him throughout gameplay by reading the video captions to him as he plays, instructing him through his tasks.

She also loves teaching her 2-year-old brother Isaiah through computer games on the laptop. She is proud of her knowledge and enthusiastic in her methods of teaching. Jolena pulls up a *Starfall* game and helps her brother with letter recognition: "B is for Boy. You are a boy. Now you try!" She takes his index finger, guiding it along the laptop's mousepad, as he does not have the dexterity to maneuver the mouse himself. In her process of instruction, she also code switches to more of a "baby" voice, so that her brother can better understand her instructions. For example, instead of saying "Do you want to make a pumpkin?", she asks, "You wan' make punkin?" In addition to letter recognition and teaching him to maneuver the device, she also tries to teach him to navigate the screen and to read and speak. Every once in awhile, she lets go of his index finger and instead instructs him verbally: "Go here, Bubbi." She pulls up a reading game and guides Isaiah: "Say 'green pepp-er.' Wanna listen to it?" Jolena selects the audio option of the reading game. Finally, Jolena chooses some number and math games to show Isaiah. She speaks along with the voiceover, as if to show that she has mastered the topics and is familiar with the games. Each time that Jolena picks the correct number, she exclaims, "Yay! We did it Bubbi!" even if all he did was let his hand be guided by Jolena's to pick the right number. In some cases, she lets Isaiah attempt to pick the number on his own without her verbal or physical guidance. In these cases, she prompts him by saying, "Which number Bubbi? You pick!"

Big Sister, Second Mom: Brokering Technology and Beliefs

In this case example, we look more closely at how siblings can serve as *brokers* for each other's access to, use of, and learning about digital media. We chose the term "broker" to reflect the active role that siblings sometimes take in obtaining digital tools, negotiating rules and routines, and establishing norms for the use of digital media. Siblings also broker the beliefs and assumptions that parents and other adults may hold about children's use of digital media and its effects. That is, while parents' beliefs are influenced by their direct experiences with children around, for example, video game play, these beliefs can also be shaped by the opinions and assertions of children about their own and their siblings' experiences.

The family in this case, the Quinteros, included Laura (age 38), Alfredo (age 46), and three children: Paulina (age 17), Karen (age 12), and Jesus (age 6). Laura and Alfredo met in the United States, but they both were born and raised in rural communities in Mexico. Jesus and his older sibling Karen were born in United States. Paulina is Laura's daughter from a previous relationship; Laura came to the United States when Paulina was just a few years old. Laura has little knowledge of English and all members of the Quintero family speak mostly Spanish at home. Laura works as a housekeeper and Alfredo works as a landscaper, yet their household income hovers near the poverty line for a family of five. The family lives in a small, two bedroom, one bath apartment in Phoenix.

Not surprisingly, given their limited income, the Quintero family's technology devices tend to be older, sometimes given for free or purchased used from family or acquaintances. For example, the family lived for a while with Laura's sister and her family, and when they moved, the aunt left an old TV that is currently in the living room. Alfredo got the family's first cell phone when Paulina was in first grade. At the time of our interviews, the family had the TV in the living room and a small, very old TV in each bedroom. They had two laptop computers, one in the living room and one in the girls' bedroom that belongs to Paulina. There was a Wii in the living room that was used by the whole family and a DVD player in the parents' bedroom that Jesus used to watch videos.

Paulina played a key role in acquiring some of the family's first technological devices. When she was younger, she did chores for relatives to earn money to buy her own devices. She bought her own MP3 player when she was in elementary school, and upgraded to an iPod in high school. She bought her own cell phones, recently passing down her old phone to her younger sister. Paulina also bought the Wii from her godfather, though it is kept in the living room and the whole family uses it now. Paulina's needs and interests also prompted her parents to buy digital devices that in turn became available to her younger siblings. For example, her parents bought a VHS player when Paulina was 4 years old so she could watch movies; in parallel today, one of Jesus's favorite pastimes is watching movies on a somewhat newer DVD/VHS player. Paulina was also the reason that the parents purchased the family's first computer, though it was old and, as Paulina described, "We didn't know how to use it, because it was a PC and at school they only had Macs." Thus, both directly and indirectly, Paulina has had a significant effect on the technology available to her younger siblings in the home.

Paulina was mature and articulate for a 17-year-old. Her experiences as a young child, first in Mexico and then with her economically struggling family in the United States, contrasted significantly with the experiences of her siblings, particularly Jesus. She sounded much older than her years in describing the differences:

> I remember when I was young I didn't have toys, I only had one doll and that was it. You can notice a difference, Anthony had his first laptop when he was three years old, and my first laptop was this year.

Perhaps because of this experience, Paulina was much less attached to her technological devices than one might expect of a teenager, and this affected her interactions with Jesus. As she explains,

> I'm not addicted to my computer, I only use it when I have to look up an address or for homework, I'm not on it all the time, days can go by without me turning it on. Sometimes I have to babysit him (Jesus), and I'll take him off the computer after 30 minutes, I tell him to use his toys and color or read a book. . . . but he just wants to be on his electronic devices.

This belief in moderation did not prevent Paulina from regularly interacting with Jesus around digital media. Both sisters played games on their cell phones with Jesus, and the whole family played games like *Wii Sports* and *Just Dance* on the game console. In addition to playing games with him, Paulina frequently watched Jesus play, coached him, and had conversations with him about gaming, including about why he should not play particular games.

It's not unusual for older sisters to take on the role of "second mother" for younger siblings, particularly with an age difference as large as that between Paulina and Jesus. Paulina's childhood experiences were quite different from Jesus's, contributing to a sibling "generation gap" in their experiences with digital media. Paulina was responsible, directly or indirectly, for the family's initial acquisition of many digital devices, which in turn shaped family interactions, routines, and norms around digital media. Her parents' lack of familiarity with digital media increased the importance of Paulina's role in bringing technology into the home and creating opportunities for all family members to be exposed to various forms of digital media.

Experiences with their first-born children can have significant effects on parents' subsequent parenting behavior and expectations for their younger children (McHale et al., 2012). In the Quintero family, this was apparent in the parents' expectation that Jesus would enjoy watching movies on his own, including placing the DVD player to be in the bedroom he shared with his parents. However, since Paulina, and even the middle child, Karen, had much more limited access to digital media when they were Jesus's age, there was no precedent for his desire to "be on his electronic devices" as much as possible. Paulina aligned herself with her mother in viewing Jesus as much more enmeshed with digital media than she is or was. When Laura was asked what Jesus's use of digital media would be like when he was Paulina's age, she responded that "I think there is already a big difference." Paulina chimed in, jokingly, "I can see him with three phones, the computer, everything, antennas." Together Paulina and Laura construct a generational "digital divide" that may well have consequences for Jesus's identity as a digital media user now and later on.

Big Brother as Gatekeeper to Technology, Tools, and Learning

Leon, aged 6, lives with his parents Victoria and Julian, older brother Santiago (age 11), and 5-month-old sister in a midsize three-bedroom house in Phoenix, Arizona. Television watching is the primary family activity around media and is enmeshed with almost all family routines. Playing video games is the second common media activity in the family, and it is also the most contentious media activity between the boys.

Leon and Santiago often get into conflicts and argue over usage of the devices in the home. This happens more frequently around video gaming than television watching. Each family member has access to a television, but there is only one television and one handheld device available for gaming. The gaming devices were initially purchased for Santiago as birthday or Christmas gifts, so he claims ownership over them, and the living room where the Xbox is located is considered Santiago's gaming room in the family. Santiago has been playing video games since he was 6 years old, and according to his mother, he always keeps up to date with the newest games and gaming devices. For instance, when the Xbox One came out, Santiago insisted that his parents buy the device, and they did so despite their limited budget.

In the previous case, we used the term *brokering* to refer to the more general involvement of siblings in shaping the media learning ecology of the home. Here, we describe the narrower role of siblings as *gatekeepers*; that is, actively controlling, and often limiting, access to digital media and related learning opportunities. In this family, Santiago takes on the role of a gatekeeper by choosing the games Leon plays and when he can play them. Santiago downloads games for his younger brother to play into a special folder on his iPad. Leon does not mind the dedicated space on the iPad and his brother's choice of games for him, which are quite different than the ones Santiago himself plays. Leon enjoys adventure–action–simulation games such as *Flappy Birds*, *Sonic Dash*, and *Ice Village*. Santiago, on the other hand, is "obsessed" with playing *Call of Duty*, and finds the games Leon plays "simplistic" but continues to provide them on the iPad.

Santiago's position as the older brother, the owner of the devices, and the expert gamer (both in the sense that he has been playing video games longer than any other family member and the content of the games he plays is different, perhaps more "hard core," than others in the family) allows him to set rules for Leon around accessing technology. For instance, Leon can only play games and use apps in the folder Santiago created on the iPad for him. Leon cannot play Santiago's iPad games. In addition, Leon has to ask for Santiago's permission every time he wants to use the iPad, and usually can use the device only when Santiago is playing Xbox games in the living room. Leon uses the iPad for educational purposes as well as entertainment. Both boys are restricted to downloading free apps, but even with this constraint, Leon found and downloaded an app to learn Japanese to be able to communicate with a schoolmate who does not speak English, and he downloaded an app about numbers and colors for his little sister Alma.

Arguments tend to erupt between the siblings when Santiago wants his iPad back. He usually does not provide advance warning to Leon, and instead takes the device from him no matter what his younger brother is doing with it. Leon usually protests, and Victoria has to intervene to resolve the conflict. Because these conflicts became frequent, Victoria created a rule that if she sees the siblings fighting over the device, she takes it away immediately. The siblings break this rule quite frequently, and it has had little effect on Santiago's control over the iPad.

Thus, Leon's opportunities to use the iPad for any purpose are unpredictable and constrained both by his brother and by his mother's efforts to reduce conflicts between the siblings. However, the effects of Santiago's gatekeeping on Leon's digital media-related learning are not entirely negative. While Leon's access to the iPad is sporadic, his brother does support his iPad use by finding and downloading apps that he thinks will appeal to Leon. Still, by restricting what apps Leon can use, Santiago may be preventing him from expanding his skills or pursuing his own interests. Notably, Leon was able to circumvent his brother's restrictions by downloading educational apps for his sister and himself, but those were unusual instances that might have been much more common if Leon had more control over the iPad.

Discussion

These cases illustrate some of the many ways in which siblings can influence the home media learning ecology. These influences frequently were interconnected and reinforcing, though at other times could seem contradictory. For example, children who introduced digital media into the home, like Paulina and Santiago, increased the digital learning opportunities for their siblings. These same children, however, might impose rules and restrictions on the media use of their siblings. Parents can amplify or moderate the influence of siblings through the decisions they make about, for example, buying a digital tool for a particular child, and setting rules about sharing or joint media use. Also important are less tangible aspects of family dynamics and relationships, including how siblings are positioned in relation to digital media (as "experts" or "addicted") and the quality of their relationships in general.

In this section, we will discuss several broad factors that we identified as important aspects of siblings' influence on children's learning in the home media ecology. Rather than attempting to generalize about the role of sibling age or number of siblings in the home, we have identified several key elements of how siblings relate to each other and to digital media in the home. These factors are drawn from our larger study of families and digital media, and informed by more general concepts from the literature on the role of siblings in family culture and relationships. They include *sibling identity*, in particular as users of digital media; perceived *ownership* for digital tools, practices, and spaces in which media are used; and *sibling attachment and bonding* as they affect siblings' desire to engage in joint media use or to teach and learn from each other. We illustrate each theme with examples from our family cases.

Sibling Identity

Siblings can play an important role in children's identity development, even through early adulthood. There can often be a sense of "push and pull" in siblings' desire to differentiate themselves from each other yet also share interests and model themselves after a sibling whom they admire or want to be close to. The process of differentiation can take place consciously and unconsciously, driven by the child as well as other family members. A child may construct a particular identity as a means of getting attention or to fill a niche in the family ecosystem. Parents' and other family members' differential treatment of siblings also can contribute to the construction of children's identities (Edwards, Hadfield, Lucey, & Mauthner, 2006).

Our case studies illustrate how children's identities were caught up with their use of digital media and the learning opportunities available to them. One common way that families constructed identities for each other was in relation to a child's (or parent's) perceived competence in relation to a media tool or practice. In other research, Go et al. (2012) found that siblings exhibited distinctive identities around their expertise in video game play. Among our families, we saw, for example, how Liam was characterized as the "artist" in contrast to Dylan, the technology expert, or how Jolena was excluded from her brothers' game play because she was labeled as incompetent. In the Quinteros family, Paulina cultivated the identity of the tech-savvy older sister who was not "addicted to computers," in contrast to her younger brother. Santiago, taking on the identity of an older and more expert gamer, assumed responsibility for selecting Leon's games, reinforcing Leon's position as the less knowledgeable child.

Broader social norms and stereotypes also played a role in the identities that were co-constructed by children, siblings, and parents. The dichotomy of the technologist versus the artist, how Liam and Dylan were characterized, reflects a common social stereotype. The child who is "addicted" to digital media and the girl who "doesn't know how to play" are other examples. These "social selves" serve as resources for the construction and enactment of individual identities that can be both empowering and limiting (Burkitt, 2008, p. 3). These identities are not static, however: people take on different identities or are "positioned" differently in various situations by themselves and others. This is illustrated perhaps most clearly in Jolena's case. In the context of her brothers' gaming, she is positioned as inept and incompetent. Her mother attempts to reinforce a more positive identity for Jolene as a technology user through reassurance and providing her with unobstructed access to her own media devices. Perhaps most meaningful, however, are the opportunities that Jolena has to teach her younger brother how to use digital media for various purposes. In these situations, she can take on the identity of a skillful tech user as well as a supportive teacher—the latter role being one that her older brothers were unwilling to assume with her.

In summary, the identities, or senses of self that children fashion as technology users may strongly affect their ongoing engagement with learning through and about digital media, at home, in school and even later in their career choices. Siblings, as well as parents and teachers, play a significant yet currently under-appreciated role in this construction of identities. Parents and educators can take active roles in helping children construct positive identities for themselves and others, as Jolena's mother did, by challenging negative attributions and creating situations in which children can see themselves as skilled and competent. Our examples also suggest how *ownership* of digital tools, and by extension ownership of practices and spaces associated with digital media, can be caught up with identity and children's learning.

Ownership for a Digital Tool, a Space, or a Practice

People can feel ownership (a sense that "this belongs to me") for many things: objects, places, ideas, and practices. In addition to the more practical consequences of ownership, for example, in access to digital tools, ownership also becomes part of our sense of self. People who line up to buy the most recent iPhone are enacting a particular kind of identity, and so are people who choose to have a dedicated TV room or gaming night. Ownership of digital media in the home most commonly refers to the digital device itself; that is, "mom's phone" or "Santiago's tablet." In the case of devices that are not mobile, ownership can be ascribed based on where the device is located; that is, the game console belongs to the boys since it is in their bedroom, or the TV is common property since it is in the living room. Somewhat less concretely, but still significantly, ownership can be applied to media *practices*; who has the right to choose software apps, video game play as "belonging to" boys, or digital media use in general as the realm of children, not parents, and so forth.

Families vary considerably in the extent that ownership of media tools, spaces, and practices is individual or shared, how ownership is negotiated, and the consequences of ownership. Parents with greater economic resources typically had more freedom to provide children with their own digital devices, though they did not always choose to do so. Parents also shaped perceptions of ownership by where they located digital devices. In the Vasquez family, locating the Xbox 360 in the boys' room reinforced their ownership not only of the game console, but also of their gaming practices (and made it easier to exclude Jolena). In the Quinteros family, even though Paulina "owned" the Wii, its placement in the living room contributed to the whole family's participation in gaming.

The concept of media ownership in families, and in particular among siblings, is important for several reasons. First, media ownership offers learning opportunities of different sorts, and siblings can play an important role in shaping such learning opportunities. For example, the need to share one device can require learning to cooperate and negotiate shared rules, but it also can lead to conflict, aggression, and exclusion. Sharing devices can also expose children to a wider range of software and media practices, as they see what siblings do, what siblings choose to download, what videos siblings tend to watch, and when they deliberately choose software for each other. Second, media ownership is caught up with a sense of responsibility and control. Parents' decisions about what technology to buy for whom, and where to locate it, are often influenced by whether they think a child is able to appropriately manage her or his own media use. Siblings often step in voluntarily, or are expected by parents, to serve as "surrogate parents" and monitor younger children's time spent with media, the apps they use, and whether they are engaging in risky behaviors. The presence of older siblings may mean that younger children have more exposure to media and practices that might otherwise be considered too risky or mature for them, but at the same time may place a greater burden on siblings to oversee their media use. And lastly, as we noted above, media ownership is caught up with individual and family's sense of identity and belonging. In the Edwards family, Dylan and Liam each had their own well-equipped gaming spots but they chose to play in the same space, to literally "keep in touch" with each other. Jolena's mom put the PS2 in Jolena's bedroom, but overlooked the importance that Jolena placed on playing with her brothers.

Attachment and Bonding

Siblings have been described as the "third rail" in family systems (Feinberg, Solmeyer, & McHale, 2012); that is, like the rail that carries electrical current in subway systems, sibling relationships can be significant, emotionally charged forces in children's development and the overall dynamics of families. In the families we studied, it was evident that sibling attachment and bonding can be driving factors in children's digital media-related learning. For older siblings, the desire to be with and to care for young siblings motivated some of their interactions around digital media. For younger children, the desire to spend time with and be closer to their older siblings was a factor in their efforts to master a video game, for example. In turn, a shared interest in digital media was also a means of sibling bonding and family bonding in general.

Parents have been involved in managing sibling relationships, and in particular, negotiating conflicts among siblings, long before the rise of digital media.

A common parental concern is how to enhance the positive and minimize the potentially negative role that digital media might play in sibling and family relationships, and thus in children's learning. Unfortunately, in the literature on parenting, there has been more emphasis on avoiding the negative, for example, by restricting media use, or conversely, giving children their own devices to avoid conflicts over sharing. More structured interventions tend to focus on training parents to teach their children conflict resolution or emotional regulation skills.

Alternatively, evidence suggests that spending time in structured, constructive activities, and in activities with parents is related to positive child development (Larson & Verma, 1999). From this perspective, using digital media as part of efforts to build on many siblings' desire to spend time with and bond with each other might be a productive approach. Sofia Edwards' attempt to scaffold Liam and Dylan's time together around digital media is one example of this.

Concluding Thoughts, Future Directions

We started this chapter by acknowledging that siblings have always played important roles in children's learning and development. The introduction of digital media into the home and children's lives has not diminished siblings' roles, and has perhaps heightened their significance. We have identified the direct as well as indirect forms of influence that siblings can have on children's engagement with digital media as teachers and learners, through gendered interactions around digital media, and as technology brokers and gatekeepers. As our examples suggest, siblings may take on roles associated with digital media-related learning that parents do not, or cannot, due to siblings' potentially greater familiarity with digital media as well as their distinctive relationships with each other. Overall, we can conclude that parents, educators, researchers, and media designers ought to be more cognizant of sibling roles in digital media-related learning, looking for ways to understand and enhance their more positive influences and to intervene when siblings create barriers to learning.

Our discussion of *sibling identity*, *ownership of digital tools, spaces, and practices*, and *attachment and bonding* points to the importance of sibling influence on forms of digital media-related learning beyond a more instrumental mastery of digital skills or a particular tool. At a more fundamental level, sibling interactions and relationships can shape how children view themselves and whom they aspire to be as digital media users and creators. Parents' decisions about ownership—what technology to buy, who has control over how the technology is used, where it is located in the home, and kinds of media practices are encouraged—affect the kinds of instrumental learning experiences available to children, but just as importantly, the kinds of roles and relationships they develop with siblings around digital media. As our examples illustrate, siblings can engage with each other in many ways with and around digital media. They may seek out opportunities to teach and learn from each other as a means of strengthening their relationships and spending time with each other. Indeed, among the families we studied, the eagerness of many children to share their knowledge of digital media and otherwise mentor their siblings was a finding that surprised us. As other chapters in this volume demonstrate, the role of digital media in family relationships is much more rich and complex than common stereotypes of the "disconnected family" suggest.

References

Azmitia, M., & Hesser, J. (1993). Why siblings are important agents of cognitive development: A comparison of siblings and peers. *Child Development, 64*(2), 430–444.

Bagley, S., Salmon, J. O., & Crawford, D. (2006). Family structure and children's television viewing and physical activity. *Medicine and Science in Sports and Exercise, 38*(5), 910–918.

Burkitt, I. (2008). *Social selves: Theories of self and society*. London: Sage.

Coyne, S. M., Jensen, A. C., Smith, N. J., & Erickson, D. H. (2016). Super Mario brothers and sisters: Associations between coplaying video games and sibling conflict and affection. *Journal of Adolescence, 47*, 48–59. doi:10.1016/j.adolescence.2015.12.001

Davies, J. J., & Gentile, D. A. (2012). Responses to children's media use in families with and without siblings: A family development perspective. *Family Relations, 61*(3), 410–425.

Edwards, R., Hadfield, L., Lucey, H., & Mauthner, M. (2006). *Sibling identity and relationships: Sisters and brothers*. New York: Routledge.

Feinberg, M. E., Solmeyer, A. R., & McHale, S. M. (2012). The third rail of family systems: Sibling relationships, mental and behavioral health, and preventive intervention in childhood and adolescence. *Clinical Child and Family Psychology Review, 15*(1), 43–57.

Gee, E., Siyahhan, S., & Cirell, A. (2016). *The influence of siblings on the digital media ecology of young children*. Paper presented at the American Educational Research Association Conference, Washington, DC, April 2016.

Go, J., Ballagas, R., & Spasojevic, M. (2012). Brothers and sisters at play: exploring game play with siblings. In *Proceedings of the ACM 2012 conference on Computer Supported Cooperative Work* (pp. 739–748). ACM.

Gregory, E. (2001). Sisters and brothers as language and literacy teachers: Synergy between siblings playing and working together. *Journal of Early Childhood Literacy, 1*(3), 301–322.

Haefner, M. J., & Wartella, E. A. (1987). Effects of sibling coviewing on children's interpretations of television programs. *Journal of Broadcasting & Electronic Media, 31*(2), 153–168.

Horst, H. (2009). Families. In Ito, M., Baumer, S., Bittanti, M., Cody, R., Stephenson, B. H., Horst, H. A., . . . & Perkel, D. (Eds.), *Hanging out, messing around, and geeking out: Kids living and learning with new media*. Cambridge, MA: MIT Press.

Howe, N., & Recchia, H. (2014). Sibling relations and their impact on children's development. In R.E. Tremblay, M. Boivin, & R. DeV. Peters (Eds.). *Encyclopedia on Early Childhood Development*. Available at: www.child-encyclopedia.com/peer-relations/according-experts/sibling-relations-and-their-impact-childrens-development

Howe, N., Ross, H., & Recchia, H. (2011). Sibling relations in early childhood. In C. Hart, & P. K. Smith (Eds.), *Wiley-Blackwell handbook of childhood social development* (pp. 356–372). New York: Wiley-Blackwell.

Klin, A., Volkmar, F. R., & Sparrow, S. S. (Eds.). (2000). *Asperger syndrome*. New York: Guilford Press.

Larson, R. W., & Verma, S. (1999). How children and adolescents spend time across the world: Work, play, and developmental opportunities. *Psychological Bulletin*, *125*(6), 701–736.

Maynard, A. E. (2004). Cultures of teaching in childhood: Formal schooling and Maya sibling teaching at home. *Cognitive Development*, *19*(4), 517–535.

McHale, S. M., & Crouter, A. C. (1996). *The family contexts of children's sibling relationships*. New York: Ablex.

McHale, S. M., Updegraff, K. A., & Whiteman, S. D. (2012). Sibling relationships and influences in childhood and adolescence. *Journal of Marriage and Family*, *74*(5), 913–930.

Nikken, P., & Schols, M. (2015). How and why parents guide the media use of young children. *Journal of Child and Family Studies*, *24*(11), 3423–3435.

Plowman, L., McPake, J., & Stephen, C. (2008). Just picking it up? Young children learning with technology at home. *Cambridge Journal of Education*, *38*(3), 303–319.

Smith, T. E. (1990). Academic achievement and teaching younger siblings. *Social Psychology Quarterly*, *53*(4), 352–363.

Strauss, S., & Ziv, M. (2012). Teaching is a natural cognitive ability for humans. *Mind, Brain and Education*, *6*(4), 186–196. doi:10.1111/j.1751-228X.2012.01156.x

Takeuchi, L. (2012). Kids closer up: Playing, learning, and growing with digital media. *International Journal of Learning and Media*, *3*(2), 37–59.

Wilson, B. J., & Weiss, A. J. (1993). The effects of sibling coviewing on preschoolers' reactions to a suspenseful movie scene. *Communication Research*, *20*(2), 214–248.

4

COLLECTING AND CONNECTING

Intergenerational Learning with Digital Media

Katie Headrick Taylor, Deborah Silvis, and Reed Stevens

Technology is transforming how and what young people and their families learn together. While families are demographically diverse and idiosyncratic, using technology together (and apart) is a quality of household life that unites us (Rideout & Hammel, 2006). Together, parents and children continue to push the possibilities of intergenerational learning with technology. For instance, parents read books and articles with their children across multiple devices and applications, teach their children how to cook using YouTube and digital recipe boxes, and help with homework remotely using online collaborative tools like Google Docs and Skype. However, tracking families' ways of innovating is difficult, as technologies, and the ways in which they are taken-up in practice by parents and children, are increasingly "on-the-move" (Taylor, 2013; Taylor, Stevens, & Takeuchi, in press), spanning locations, days, and sometimes weeks.

In this chapter, we examine this complexity of learning with digital media in the home to highlight young people's adeptness at negotiating with, trouble-shooting, and making technology work when it resists their efforts. To do this work we ask *how do technologies and digital media reorganize family activities, and create new ones, in and around the household?* We draw from a sociocultural perspective to develop an understanding of digitally mediated learning based on daily routines that children and families have around educational uses of technology. We conducted an observational study of children and families' engagement with technology in and around their homes, and our analysis and findings are based on video records of these observations. Our analysis compared cases of digitally mediated, collaborative activities *that were organized by, or produced, teaching and learning opportunities in the home*. We found that young people's digital media use was often *active* and followed a pattern of "collecting and connecting." This finding highlights the often difficult and intensive effort children and their parents expend on the *opportunity* to engage with digital media well before the desired activity even takes places. We argue this research provides a counternarrative to the popularized view that children are passive consumers of digital media.

We use *collecting* to refer to young people assembling and organizing the necessary materials and resources (including people) into one place before being able to engage in a desired activity with digital media. We use *connecting* to refer to young people engaging in the digital media activity they were planning—or some version of it—before and during collecting. Collecting made connecting possible though there were important aspects of collecting that stood alone for learning how to negotiate tool use and organize or stabilize activities so that interest-driven learning could take place (relatively) easily.

We argue that adequate analyses and theories of how young people learn with digital media cannot exist without careful attention to the collecting phase, a pervasive activity in families' daily routines. The (often immense) effort children spend collecting has been left out of extant accounts of how young people and their families engage with digital media, treated as mundane "noise" or messiness *outside* of the learning process (Star, 1999). Making this work invisible hides young people's adeptness at negotiating with trouble-shooting, and making technology work when it resists their efforts; they learn to organize necessary resources to make good on their planned activities and are free to then focus on interest-driven tasks rather than on the tools functioning correctly.

In what follows, we briefly describe background literature that informed our study. In that overview, we provide a possible framework for thinking about home-based, intergenerational learning with technology as a "mangle," based on Pickering's (1995) "mangle of scientific practice." From there, we touch on our research study design and how we analyzed the data we gathered before focusing on our findings. Each findings section connects a pattern we saw across the families we observed to the over-arching themes of connecting and collecting. We define these patterns and then provide in-depth descriptions of representative cases. The example cases come from a corpus of instances in which children tried to Skype a family member in another state, learned to play Led Zeppelin's *Kashmir*, FaceTime-d a friend on an iPod Touch, played Minecraft with a sibling on separate tablet computers, and learned to seed a pomegranate with *YouTube* (for a complete list of analyzed moments, see the Appendix). These are the kinds of technology and media-based activities we observed across all participating families, and they are rich with learning opportunities. We conclude with what we see as some insights of this research that point to possibilities for connecting families' digitally mediated practices to other learning and teaching contexts.

From Mediation to *Re*-Mediation

People's actions are "mediated" by tools (Wertsch, 1998). We act in the world with the help of tools; these tools shape how we perceive the world as we act with/in it. The nature of mediation has changed with the ubiquity of *mobile* technologies in daily life. Acting in concert with a family member no longer requires *physical* and *synchronous* copresence, as our devices distribute activities across space and time (e.g., Hjorth & Hendry, 2015; Taylor, Takeuchi, & Stevens, in press). In the same way that classrooms can no longer be viewed as "containers" for learning and engagement (Leander, Phillips, & Taylor, 2010), the walls of homes are permeable by distant people, media, and activities that are initiated from afar (Pink, 2012).

Taking a sociocultural perspective, we understand young people's learning and engagement with digital media as a technologically "re-mediated" (Cole & Griffin, 1983) social practice. Many home-based activities, such as doing homework (Goodwin & Goodwin, 2013), learning to cook a new recipe, and practicing a musical instrument, are recognizable as the "unplugged" versions of a decade or two ago. But mobile devices and digital media in homes have reorganized these activities while creating new ones (e.g., Ito et al., 2010). Therefore, to "have a theory of the world that we live in" (Pink et al., 2016, p. 3), we need to account for the ways in which new technologies influence daily life and learning. In what follows, we consider the different variations of learning configurations, or ways that people and materials get arranged together, and how technology has created different possibilities for how these configurations might look.

Learning Configurations

Paradise and Rogoff (2009) describe children learning from adults as a "side by side" configuration; young people learn daily tasks "at the elbow" of an adult in the home. In home-based ethnographies of learning with technology, this configuration persists in many instances, with media being a focal point of the activity. This learning configuration has been described as a version of joint media engagement (JME). JME is an organizing framework for looking at participation with media, not as an individual pastime, but as supporting configurations in which "young [and older] people organize themselves to teach and learn together" (Stevens, Satwicz, & McCarthy, 2008, p. 48). The first studies that developed JME looked at families watching television together (Takeuchi & Stevens, 2011). But we know now that "co-viewing" media occurs around a variety of mobile technologies as well (e.g., Taylor, Takeuchi, & Stevens, in press). Depending on the technologies being used, JME or co-viewing is initiated, carried out, and terminated in different ways. For example, the ways two siblings simultaneously watch YouTube videos on separate tablet computers organizes materials and arranges their bodies differently than when they watch the same video together on a desktop computer. When these activities involve parents or caregivers, as opposed to siblings or peers, the learning configurations can look different because of power dynamics, developmental nuances, and so forth.

But how do mobile, network-based technologies change the configuration of JME when people no longer have to be in the same country, let alone the same room, to engage with media content together? Two of the authors with a colleague have described this phenomenon as "distributed co-participation," joint engagement in an activity occurring across several locations and over different times of the day because of the affordances of mobile, network-enabled tools (Taylor, Takeuchi, & Stevens, in press). In that work, they illustrate distributed co-participation with the following example from a mother and daughter, "Leah":

> As an analytic practice, we decided to trace the movement of one Smithsonian story from Mom to Leah over the course of a day. At 7:30 AM, Mom found a story on the Smithsonian website that seemed relevant to Leah's Science Olympiad training on entomology. She read the story during her train ride to work and then sent it to Leah via email from her smartphone. Leah saw the story in her email inbox at school when she was able to check her phone during lunch, but she did not have time to read it closely because the phone was supposed to stay in her locker. Around 3PM on her walk home, Leah re-opened the story from her email and skimmed it. She then re-opened the story for a third time on her laptop at home and used some of the information contained in the article for a practice test she was making about insects for her Science Olympiad training. Mom and Leah did not talk about the article in person, but they were still co-participating in a family practice of reading science that was historically important to both of them, but for which they had little time to do in person. In this instance, mom and daughter sharing a popular science article occurred over an entire day, over three different devices, and in four locations.

In JME configurations (both side by side and distributed), children *and* adults are learning *together*, each providing different areas of experience and expertise. Children are often the experts at the tools, while adults provide deeper experience, expertise, and curatorial know-how around the content of the activity (Barron, Martin, Takeuchi, & Fithian, 2009; Ito et al., 2010). More research is showing how young people and their parents learn together with technology as well as how their respective roles get negotiated. In the Digital Youth Project, Ito et al. (2010) examined how, in new media ecologies, parenting practices and the material arrangements of home environments were shifting. Rather than parents serving as the sole knowledge brokers, roles and authority appeared more distributed, and *children* were sometimes observed influencing *their parents'* use of technology at home. This literature also suggests that adequate accounts of families' JME involve understanding how families reassemble space, time, and materials available at home in order to learn together with technology. Observing families going about their daily lives at home—using media and technology—we noticed how these configurations of space–time–materials reorganized routines in innovative ways, often in order to resolve some technological "resistance."

The Mangle of Technological Practice

As a way of understanding this reorganization of home life, we use Pickering's (1995) idea of the "mangle of practice" to talk about how technological engagement often involves tacking back and forth between human effort and material (technological) actions. According to this perspective, human activity is always bound up or "mangled" with devices we have invented, ostensibly to make tasks easier. However, often these tools resist our best efforts, requiring us to accommodate and innovate solutions. Pickering's metaphor of the mangle comes from a domestic tool used in the early twentieth century to wring or iron linens. We are drawing on Pickering's "mangle" for reasons that we will discuss below, but also to connect with the domestic, mundane qualities of using tools for home-based activities (e.g., ironing, cooking). We also see strong connections between the techno-scientific practices of the people Pickering originally studied to develop this concept (laboratory scientists) and the ways of pursuing or ironing-out problems that we observed children doing in their homes.

As in Pickering's studies of laboratory science, young people's work with technology unfolds through encountering resistance from the tools and then making accommodations. Young people make plans for, or have ideas and desires about, how they are going to use their time. If this activity involves technology (and it often does), the tools "respond" by doing something unplanned, mysterious, or puzzling; the technologies *resist* human interaction. Young people then make accommodations, refining or creating new plans based on their understanding of the tool's resistance. Home-based technological engagement, then, involves balancing the relations between the young people (tech users), the tools, and the other resources that are pulled into the "mangle," then ironed out to make the activity coherent.

An important component of Pickering's mangle is that the technological issues or problems develop *over time*. They are not given, but instead emerge in the course of going through the routine work at hand. Pickering writes:

> The contours of material agency are never decisively known in advance, scientists continually have to explore them in their work, problems always arise and have to be solved in the development of, say, new machines. And such solutions—if they are found at all—take the form, at minimum, of a kind of delicate material positioning . . .
>
> (1993, p. 564).

In the instance of young people using technology in their homes, the resistance they receive from their devices is never planned, never fully understood (initially), and making accommodations for this trouble unfolds over time, and sometimes over different places. We argue that Pickering's mangle offers a lens for seeing innovative learning opportunities in real-time, home-based digital media engagement. The mangle helps us (analysts) consider how young people (and often their parents) manage the mess of getting technologically connected. Sometimes fulfilling their desires with technology often fundamentally reorganizes household life.

Study Description

Our work began with "the idea that digital media and technologies are part of the everyday and more spectacular worlds that people inhabit" (Pink et al., 2016, p. 7). In other words, our explicit focus was on families' engagement with digital media, and we assumed that we would observe interesting moments taking place in ordinary home environments. We collected primarily video-based data of these observations, because we were interested in the ways these moments would unfold in-time and we wanted to be able to review these activities after-the-fact; we used our own digital tools to capture data (e.g., wearable and stationary cameras). We understood that our presence in the everyday settings and routines of our participating families was itself a "re-mediation" of daily life. This is one way we acknowledge that technology saturated the practices we observed in homes but never existed apart from them. Our methods captured how technology use was situated within ongoing routines and activities within the homes and families of young people, but because the methods themselves required extensive use of technologies, we also saw ourselves as taking part, to some small degree, in the mangle of household practices.

We designed a study in which different methods of collecting data on families' technology and digital media use might construct a more cohesive narrative of "typical" daily activity. In other words, we understood that conducting *only* video-based observations in the home during the focal participants' after school hours would miss important routines that are digitally mediated in the morning, on the commute to school, and in the hours before bed. Therefore, we also conducted interviews and over-the-phone surveys with focal children to fill in these gaps and to get a fuller picture of the range of media and technology they engaged with while in the study as well as where and with whom such engagement took place. For a complete description of our data collection methods, please refer to Study 4 in the Appendix.

This closeup look at how families organize ordinary routines was possible because we limited the number of families, allowing for in depth analysis of many hours of video. Reviewing all of these data, we identified and compared "cases" of digitally mediated, collaborative activities that were organized by, or produced, teaching and learning outcomes in the home. Cases were constructed from the various data sources described above. We identified seventeen such cases in which young people, along with their siblings, parents, or friends, were engaged in some joint teaching and learning activity with technology. Our analytic focus was on a few families and the minute-by-minute moments that take place during media engagement. We dissected these moments in order to find out how materials, people, space, and routine tasks got assembled in particular and idiosyncratic ways. Within and between these seventeen cases, we focused on interactions through which family members instructed and learned from one another based on a shared interest (e.g., how to prepare a pomegranate, how to excel in FarmVille, how to remember choreography to a new song).

This allowed us to identify typical patterns of how young people engage with digital media and technologies and how this engagement has implications for family and/or household routines. As with any study like this, we hope our analysis of the data is attentive to everyday learning in young people's homes in ways that adapt to changing media engagement and technological practice and advance a theory sensitive to these ongoing changes. Here, we provide material for a theory of learning with technology within the context of homes and family life that accounts for the complexity—the material maneuvering, the temporal emergence, the effort expended—of *getting connected* in the technological mangle (Pickering, 1995).

Meeting Technological Resistance: Collecting, in Action

We found that young people's learning with digital media often followed a pattern of collecting and connecting. Again, we use *collecting* to refer to young people assembling and organizing the necessary materials and resources (including people) into one place before being able to engage in a desired activity with digital media. We use *connecting* to refer to young people engaging in the digital media activity they were planning—or some version of it—before and during collecting. In what follows, we show how collecting and connecting looked in action, but also the nature of learning across these activities. In short, young people's learning during collecting was problem-based *in the service of* interest-driven learning during connecting. These findings highlight the often difficult and intensive effort children and their parents expend on constructing the *opportunity* to engage with digital media well before the desired activity even takes places.

Young people often had desires and made plans for how they were going to use their time. When these plans involved digital media, young people had to manage instances when the technology resisted their efforts. Pickering writes about resistance as "the occurrence of a block on the path to some goal" (p. 569). Examples of this technological resistance included young people wanting to: use devices that were insufficiently charged, access information on an Internet site that was behind a paywall, maintain a working wireless connection, and use an application that required adult credentials.

Collecting is when a young person, before being able to engage with digital media in the way that she desired, assembled and organized different tools, people, and information within a given space. It was not uncommon for collecting to also occur in the middle of engaging with digital media when the technology suddenly stopped working in the appropriate way. In our analysis, collecting was easily identifiable in moments of talk-in-interaction by one or all of the following characteristics:

- People's objectives and the tool's functionality were out of sync;
- People's understandings of the technological "trouble" were temporally emergent; young people never planned for or anticipated technological resistance and their understanding of how to fix the trouble developed over time; and
- A shared understanding of intentions and/or goals had yet to be accomplished between family members.

Getting in Sync

While collecting, young people diverted somewhat from their initial setup. They moved around the house, assembling the right cords, additional devices, batteries, people, and information in order for the intended activity to work. Collecting also included explaining and negotiating with family members so that these other stakeholders eventually shared an understanding of the young person's desires. Therefore, talk while collecting was often misaligned between family members; people were confused about what was going on, people asked many questions of one another, and people could be highly frustrated. Interleaved with getting the tool to cooperate was communication aimed at syncing up with family members or friends in terms of sharing an understanding of objectives and obstacles in the way of accomplishing those objectives. The following example is representative of these aspects of collecting that we saw across young people's technology use. In this and the following examples, all names are pseudonyms.

Natalie, a 10-year-old Black girl who lived with her mother and grandmother in the Midwest, was an avid user of technology in her home. She personified Mimi Ito et al.'s (2010) categorization of "messing around" with technology. Natalie sought opportunities to engage with digital media, frequently experimented and played around with new tools and activities (e.g., Makey Makey, an invention kit that can connect everyday objects to a computer), and arranged the appropriate conditions in her home to support her digital media activities. During one observation, Natalie made plans to Skype with her father in California, "so he can see me," she explained to the researcher. Natalie was familiar with using Skype on her mother's smartphone, but her mother was not home and had deleted the Skype application from her phone; Mom claimed it used too much data. Under these new conditions, Natalie tried to Skype from her laptop, a familiar device but an unfamiliar platform from which to use this application.

In order to accomplish a Skype connection on the laptop, Natalie first had to find the power cord and an available outlet in which to plug it (see Figure 4.1 for Natalie's different steps of collecting). After she successfully plugged in her computer, and trained her gaze back on the monitor, she realized that Skype required her to have an adult's birthdate to enter into the information field. (To create a Skype account, you need to be 18 years old.) In response to this discovery, Natalie called her grandmother (literally, on a phone even though her grandmother was in the house) to explain her need to create a Skype account. The following excerpt is taken from their disjointed phone conversation that eventually led to grandmother coming into the room.

Natalie:	Okay. Um. I have to get my parent's [inaudible] ((*runs across room, brings back cordless phone, dials phone number, sets phone on desk, phone rings, speakerphone on*))
Grandmother:	Hello?
N:	Nanny.
G:	Yeah?
N:	Um. Um, my dad told me to like Skype or FaceTime him today or whenever I can, so I'm trying to create an account and I need your permission if I can.
G:	Okay, want me to come up there?
N:	It's up to you.
G:	But-
N:	It's up to you.
G:	But you're doing, you're creating a Skype account?
N:	Yeah.
G:	I thought Skype was already on your mother's computer.
N:	No. Like, like I have to have a account TO Skype him.
G:	An account what?
N:	TO Skype him.
G:	Let me go see.
N:	Okay ((*looking at computer screen, speaks through clenched teeth*)).

By the end of this phone exchange, Natalie and her grandmother still did not share an understanding of Natalie's intentions, nor the technological resistance Natalie encountered. But grandmother had an interest in helping Natalie; she offered to leave her location in her bedroom to come to Natalie's side. Upon grandmother entering the living room, where Natalie was located, Natalie had an explanation at the ready for why she required assistance using Skype to talk with her father, as reported in the next excerpt:

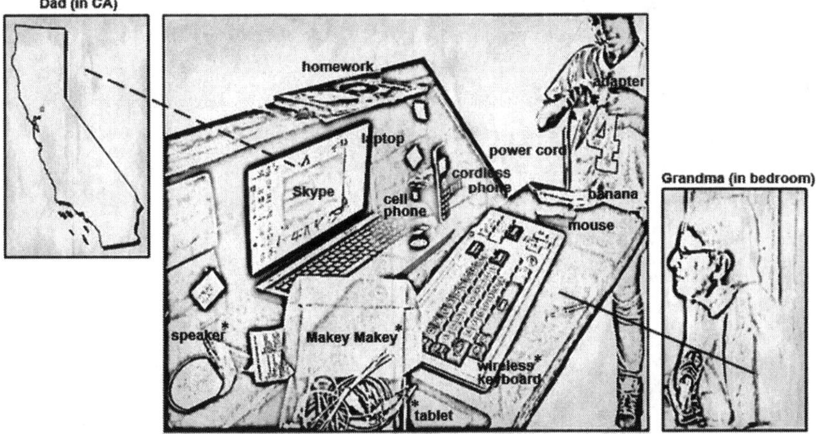

FIGURE 4.1 These are the resources Natalie used for trying to Skype with her Dad. Items denoted by an ⋆ remained on the desk during collecting, but were not used to Skype. We include the banana as it was a remnant of a previous activity involving Makey Makey, a kit that turns objects into touchpads and connects them with the Internet.

G: ((*coming into the room, off camera*)) You Skyped him before.

N: That was on my mom's phone. ((*stays facing computer while talking to grandmother behind her*))

G: I thought Skype was on the computer as an application.

N: It is. But this like, mmm ((*turns to look at grandmother*)) for example you know Instagram? Or Facebook?

G: Yes.

N: You know how you could download the app?

G: Yes.

N: Okay. Um. You know if you download the app and how it says you need to log in?

G: Yes.

N: That's how this is even though I already downloaded the application, I need to either create an account by logging-

G: Why can't you use your mother's account?

N: Because I don't know hers. And she deleted her Skype because she said it wastes data because she has Facetime.

G: Oh.

N: And I don't know if she's going to be back. Do you know when she's going to be back?

G: No, she has to run five miles today, so that's what she is doing. Okay, so what do you need from me?

Natalie needed her grandmother's status as an adult for a legitimate birth date to make a new Skype account. Grandmother was skeptical of giving out this information, so Natalie drew a comparison between creating a Skype account and an Instagram account, an application with which her grandmother was familiar. Natalie and grandmother then got in sync about Natalie's intentions, and Natalie obtained the necessary information to download Skype on her laptop. However, the technological resistance was just beginning for Natalie; after creating a username, she could not create an appropriately complicated password (for the software) and then remember that password to retype it (we all know this experience well). Then, to inform her father she was available to Skype, she tried to call him on his phone first. This effort was thwarted, too, as she had the wrong phone number. In this last excerpt, once again she called on her grandmother for more information—the correct digits with which to reach her father.

Researcher: What's the matter?

N: Okay, so: um: the first password was not really working out and then so I tried to make it more complicated and every time I try to make it more complicated um it didn't match. ((*typing*)) So: I try . . . Hmm. Okay, per-fect. Oh, shoot. [inaudible] ((*dials number on phone, phone rings*)).

G: ((*coming back into room*)) Is that the Skype?

R: That's the phone.

N: Oh, yeah, it's the phone ((*turns to face grandmother*))

G: I know that. I don't know how you do the Skype. Who are you calling? Your dad? ((*an automated voice on phone says, "Your call has been forwarded to an automated voice message"*))

N: ((*to grandmother*)) That's not his phone number.

R: (laughs)

N: Cause his phone number has a voicemail. What's his number? ((*looks at grandmother*)) I know it's (starts to say a number).

G: Okay, just a minute ((*in other room again*)) Obviously I'm your tech assistant.

R: (laughs)

N: No wuh

G: Yes.

N: ((*dials number again, holds phone to chin while it dials*)). Hm. (a man answers) Hi, is this Gino?

Man on phone: I'm sorry?

N: Never mind (high pitched) ((*sets phone down on desk, looking at computer screen*)) Yeah, I need the phone number. While

	I'm doing that . . .((*takes out homework pages from notebook on top shelf of desk*))
G:	(*from other room*) You have to dial (says the area code) on that phone [inaudible]
N:	I did it was the wrong number (high pitched).
G:	[reads phone number
N:	Hold on ((*repeats number aloud while she dials it on phone*)). Oh I put TWO nine one seven.
G:	No, it's FOUR nine.
N:	(*phone rings*). [whispers something inaudible] ((*goes back to her homework pages while the phone rings*))
G:	He doesn't have voicemail.
N:	He does. He must be on the phone with somebody. ((*continues working on homework without looking up*))
G:	Um-hm.
N:	Or he just don't know- or he just don't know who it is.
G:	He should, that's the house number.
N:	That's just real creepy. ((*dials number again*)). [calls to grandmother] It's four-nine-one-seven or four-nine-zero-seven?
G:	Four-nine-zero-seven.
N:	That's right. (phone rings). Okay. He's not answering-
Father:	Hello?

This example of Natalie trying to Skype her father shows that collecting was an intensive process of problem solving; as the nature of the problem unfolded, young people assembled and organized different media, people, and information over time in the service of connecting. Amid all of this effort, however, a young person's objective of getting connected became temporarily incoherent or invisible during collecting as both child and adult family member became deeply invested in the iterative grunt work of stabilizing the relations between devices, people, and goals.

In making the technological mangle coherent, young people not only learn how the technology is resisting their efforts and why, but also how to communicate and negotiate desires with other family members so that the various actors (e.g., grandmother, Skype, phone, father), and the relations between them, were stable enough to eventually achieve connection. In this way, collecting and connecting are not entirely distinct activities, but rather are interwoven. In order to collect resources, young people must establish connections with family members and tools. Once connections were stabilized, technology could (and often did) disrupt the flow of activity, calling on new collection strategies. This finding illustrates how collecting is replete with opportunities for learning; it is not the case that meaningful engagement with digital media must wait until connection is flowing smoothly, nor that young people passively consume technology and digital media. Furthermore, even when a task appears to be running smoothly, disruptions or resistance from technology remain an ongoing possibility.

Collecting across Time and Locations

Collecting, in the service of learning or engaging with an interest (e.g., learning to play a song on an instrument, learning how to seed a pomegranate), was temporally emergent, sometimes stretching across several days and places (e.g., home, YouTube, school, grocery store). In some instances, collecting was initiated when young people vocalized an interest to family members. These interests were usually long-standing, familiar ones of which a child wanted to explore a new facet but could not do so without significant assistance. Adults then became vital in helping young people assemble and organize the resources required to engage in that interest, or a specific aspect of it. Adults suggested resources and ways of acquiring them, and also helped mobilize and connect young people's interests across settings (e.g., Barron et al., 2009). The following example is representative of these aspects of collecting that we saw across young people's technology use.

The Ehrets, a family of two parents and two sons, were a middle class White family living in a Midwestern suburb. Like several other families we observed, Mom was central in collecting the necessary resources so the family could engage in digitally mediated interests together, especially around cooking and music. The two sons were particularly interested in watching cooking shows on TV and trying out new ingredients they saw being used, often seeking additional, just in time, advice on YouTube (e.g., how to seed a pomegranate). They also used YouTube for watching music videos from Mom and Dad's generation of artists.

In one instance, Mom guided the oldest son, Nate, across several days and locations to collect the necessary resources for learning Led Zeppelin's Kashmir on the cello. As a nascent cellist in the sixth grade orchestra, Nate's musical interest was piqued at the middle school concert when the eighth grade orchestra performed Kashmir to a rapt audience. In the following interview excerpt, Mom described this event as an example of "doing research" with technology around a particular interest she shared with her son, in this case, music.

Mom: We-re- you get the green light to use technology if it's teaching you something
If you're legitimately doing research
Or learning how to do something for the first time
Like even how to play an instrument
Like, we were –h
So, Nate had a cello concert at school
The big kids, the 8th graders, got to play Kashmir by Led Zeppelin

Researcher: (laughing)
Mom: And it was AWEsome
And all the parents were like, "Oh my god, this is so awesome!"
R: Awesome
Mom: And Nate came home, and he was like, "I should ask Ms. Shaw for the music"—
—and I'm like, "I bet it's online"
So we go online, we look for the notes, it's all like these pay websites, and I'm like,
R: Hm-hm
Mom: "Let's just ask Ms. Shaw tomorrow, she'll probably have sheet music to give you,
But I said, "In the interim
let's watch this-" so he watched this youth orchestra from England
Do this amazing Kashmir performance
And apparently it's like a trend.

This example is counter to popular notions of young people heading directly to digital resources and parents being more likely to seek out or use non-digital resources in moments of interest-driven teaching and learning. While Nate's initial impulse was to seek out non-digital resources from his teacher at school, Mom was the person to suggest using the Internet for locating the sheet music. However, in summoning the powers of the Internet, Mom and Nate encountered a technological bottleneck that many of our participants were unwilling to work through: the paywall.

Instead, the technological resistance re-directed the trajectory of the activity, as it often does. Even though they were unable to find and download the sheet music from the Internet (for free), Mom seemed to want to capitalize on a teachable moment with her son "during the interim." Using YouTube, they located several other examples of youth orchestras from across the world performing "Kashmir" to discover orchestral performances of Led Zeppelin's song as "a trend." As it turns out, Nate's initial impulse to seek out his teacher, in person, for the (non-digital) sheet music was the best option for learning how to play this song on his cello. This particular kind of technological resistance, paying for access, necessitated that Nate wait until the next day at school to collect the necessary resources. After the following day at school, Nate returned home with his cello to practice Kashmir with sheet music, and also reference the same YouTube videos he watched with his mother the previous day.

Parents, and other adults in the home, regularly suggested the use of digital tools to help their children find new information, connect to different people, and discover a new "genre" of activity. Parents also recognized the complications that might arise from suggesting digital tools but were willing to help their children work through these issues. As in the examples above, we regularly saw adults providing children with the right set of resources to achieve connection, even if that connection did not happen immediately.

Ironing out the Mangle: Getting Connected

Collecting blurs into connecting when young people need their parents, grandparents, and/or siblings, not necessarily for expertise, but for information (e.g., a birthdate, a password,) or permission (e.g., the green light to use a shared device, time to be engaging with technology). In this way, inviting family members into the mangle can lead to co-participation in the activity that was not initially planned for by the young person. Eventually, relations between the different components of the mangle stabilize, or connect up. Cords are plugged in, batteries are charged, passwords gain access, devices are exchanged, and family members are generally on the same page regarding the objectives for children's media engagement. The mangle is made coherent, and this coherence leads to a smoother picture of digital media engagement.

Intimacies across Space

Connecting is often an aligned and intimate arrangement, physically and/or discursively. When the connection is "in room," bodies are close to one another (and more stationary), typically around a screen. When the connection is online (e.g., doing homework with a friend over FaceTime on an iPod Touch), intimacy is still present, but is expressed through talk, and facial cues transmitted through the iSight camera, for instance. Conversations during connecting are familiar, personal, and much more relaxed than during collecting. During connecting, talk is related to an interest, and the topic of resisting tools and applications falls away, albeit temporarily. Not surprisingly, collecting re-emerges during connecting when the technology resists again, but because other relations have been previously stabilized (e.g., the person with the information and experience with the device is already in the room), these moments are quickly triaged so connecting can resume.

As an example, Kara, a 12-year old White girl living in the Midwest, was talking to a classmate, on her and her mother's shared iPod Touch, about a common homework assignment. Before this scene, however, Kara spent significant and harried time borrowing the device from her mother who had been using it in the kitchen to play Pandora. She then had to find the charging cable for the device, gather the appropriate worksheets, find her classmate's phone number, and organize herself and all of these materials in a quiet space (where her four siblings were not) around an available electrical outlet in which she could charge the Touch. Only then were Kara and her classmate able to interact about topics they were interested in: first homework assignments and then developing a new friendship by learning about each other. (Kara was a new student in this school and interested in growing her social network.)

The conversation below, between Kara and her classmate (who is off camera, but is visible and audible to Kara through the FaceTime application), shows how talk and interactions are intimate and driven by interest rather than by getting the technology to cooperate.

Classmate: [off camera, on Kara's phone] Wait, so how many siblings do you have again?
Kara: Four.
Classmate: So there are five of you?
Kara: Yeah. ((*nodding*))
Classmate: And you're the oldest?
Kara: Uh-huh. ((*nodding*))
Classmate: And they're all little?
Kara: Hm-hm. ((*nodding*))
Classmate: That's cool.
Kara: ((*smiling, laughing*))

Kara's classmate then puts her phone on the bed so she can get ready for basketball practice while still maintaining a conversation about family life with Kara. In quiet, private locations in their respective homes, the girls' talk maintains a sweetness and excitement that are characteristic of blossoming adolescent friendships.

As seen explicitly or implicitly in the examples described so far, connecting with family members and friends across different locations was an important objective for children and parents' digital technology use. In analyzing these activities, however, participants' enactments of collecting and connecting were distinct; relaxed intimacy, for example, was not a characteristic of collecting but was a common quality in how connecting was enacted. Young people were more than willing to expend tedious effort collecting the right resources so that they could pursue an interest in developing friendships and maintaining their relationships through digital media and technology.

Intimacies Interrupted

After getting synced-up, being connected was often interrupted by repeated technological breakdowns, only to necessitate collecting again. The flow of the activity shifted or was interrupted. Just because young people achieved connection, there was rarely if ever a guarantee that technological resistance would remain at bay.

In one final example, Katie and her brother, two White children living in a Midwestern suburb, got connected together through *Minecraft* play. As was typical for them, Katie and her brother played together across two different devices in their living room. Her brother played on his tablet on one sofa while she played with him wirelessly on her iPad on the adjacent sofa. After some initial collecting, Katie "finds" herself and her brother in the game world.

Katie: Hey [Brother], have you generated this world?
Brother: Yeah
K: Do you have to do something to make it on Wi-Fi?
B: ((*approaches her and leans over her tablet*)) No you just press start. ((*returns to his sofa*))
K: Oh. Here I am. Oh, that's you. Alright. Let's go get some stuff, right?
B: Yeah, I'll go off this way, you can go off that way.

After being connected with her brother for several minutes, Katie crashes the game by tapping the screen of the iPad over and over. Her game comes to an abrupt halt and she has to start collecting the correct resources to mitigate the technological resistance she now encounters. This involved getting her brother to pause his own game play and come over to Katie's couch to help her iron out the trouble.

K: ((*taps repeatedly on screen*)) There's something wrong with this iPad.
B: ((*approaches her and leans over her tablet*))
K: I was hitting the cow and now it's doing this. ((*reaches over for his tablet, types on its screen*))
B: ((*pulls his tablet away from her, returns to his sofa and sits down*)) You always glitch everything out like that. You always make it zoom in. You've got to shut it down and then-
K: How do you shut it down? Oh okay. No, it's still zoomed in.
B: ((*approaches her again, sets down his tablet on her couch, reaches for her iPad*))
B: ((*restarts iPad, scrolls across screen*))
K: ((*taps iPad screen, reaches for B's tablet*)) I'll just use this one.
B: No! ((*returns to his sofa with both tablets, continues restarting iPad*)) ((*walks over and hands iPad back to Katie's*)) Here.
K: Gracias.
B: Now after it shuts down you've got to turn it back on and it's [inaudible].

Brother helps Katie turn the game back on and they resume playing Minecraft until Katie's device starts giving her trouble again.

K: It's not turning on [Brother].
B: ((*approaches sofa*)) That's because you've gotta hold it.
K: ((*presses start button on side of iPad*))
B: You've got to HOLD it.
K: Oh whoa, okay. ((*gives him the iPad*))

B: ((*takes the iPad back to his sofa, presses start button*)) Now you wait for it to turn on. ((*sets the iPad next to Katie, returns to his sofa and picks up his tablet*)).
K: Wait? Oh my. Ha, it works! ((*selects game icon from menu screen*))
B: Down the back side of the mountain.
K: Oh, you're giving yourself away [inaudible]. ((*resumes game play*))

For Katie and her brother, there was an initial stage of collecting that involved gathering their tablet computers, arranging themselves on adjacent couches, and situating themselves and a wearable camera with respect to the researcher's camera. After several minutes, they were both online and had "found" each other in-game; sister and brother were literally connected to the Internet while also personally connected to each other in an intimate routine of many siblings (i.e., shared game playing). Once game play began, they were able to immerse themselves in collaborative activity. But collaborative activity was quickly disrupted when Katie zoomed in too quickly and the device resisted her efforts and froze. She then had to ask her brother for help on operating the tool. He stopped his game play, put his device down, walked over to her couch, and showed her what to do on the iPad. He returned to his spot and their play resumed.

Though it was certainly possible for children alone in separate rooms of the house to collect the personal resources or expertise necessary for stabilizing an activity, connecting was often aided by close physical proximity and copresence. Keeping collaborators on hand enabled kids to move quickly back into stable forms of activity and to stay in-sync and engaged. Thus, the temporary resistance of technology was tempered by siblings' reliance on each other as tools or tutors. In this way, as well as being a way of staying in-sync with technology, connecting took on affective dimensions when this allowed people to stay in tune with each other in a task.

During the connecting phase, young people's engagement with technology looked energetic yet relaxed, as represented in Kara's conversation above. They pursued digitally mediated interests that ranged from music to cooking, homework to basketball, and dancing to learning the fastest ways of cleaning one's room. Learning about these interests over smartphones, tablets, iPod Touches, gaming consoles, and laptops came at a cost, however, and consumed family members who were initially peripheral to the intended activity. These familial resources get pulled into the mangle of young people's technological practice. In this way, getting connected for one young person often sent a ripple of disruptions throughout the household and family members reorganized their time and their physical arrangements. Learning with digital media and technology was often a family endeavor that brought parents, caregivers, and siblings together in unexpected ways. Technological resistance gave everyone a chance to learn in collaborative interactions, bringing family members closer together rather than pushing them apart, or isolating them, from one another.

Conclusions

We have provided a new framework with which to understand young people's engagement with digital media and technology that accounts for the effort involved in making the technological mangle coherent. This effort is typically left out of discussions of how young people engage with digital media, treated as mundane "noise" or messiness *outside* of the learning process. However, we argue that the effort involved in making the mangle coherent—in collecting and stabilizing relationships between people, tools, and information within an appropriate space—is integral to learning with technology. In fact, considering and analyzing this collecting phase reveals that a different kind of learning happens with digital media and technology that is less interest-driven and more tools and resource-focused.

In our view, young people collecting and connecting through digital media and technology in and around their homes closely approximates Pickering's (1995) mangle of scientific practice in the laboratory. How young people came to struggle and to cope with emergent technological problems is not far from how scientists puzzle through the issues at hand, issues they cannot predict in advance of their activities. Once the activity gets going, the mysterious agencies of devices sometimes come to play key roles in how and whether the activity takes shape. This study demonstrates that young people are adept at negotiating with, troubleshooting, and making accommodations for the technology that resists their agency; they learn to stabilize relations between necessary resources to make good on their planned activities that focus on interests rather than the tools.

This analysis presents an interesting new set of questions about the interplay between interest-driven and problem-based learning, at least as these concepts apply to learning with technology. If collecting and connecting are not entirely distinct—but rather are fluid and emergent—then some problems may seep into interests, or conversely, interests may be interesting precisely because they entail technological problem solving. While we would not go so far as to claim that young people "liked" that their batteries died or that the Wi-Fi connection was spotty, there was rarely if ever a moment when frustration with technology was so intense that it ended the activity. To the contrary, problem solving in the mangle of practice seemed to deepen interest rather than deter desires. Knowledge practices often operate in this way, requiring sometimes invisible, yet immersive grunt work in order to produce something new or to bring closure to a defined task (Star, 1999). Seeing into children's technological mangle brought attention to this hidden dimension of learning—how addressing problems and following interests interact in practice.

We conclude with a reiteration that young people's often tedious efforts to learn with technology and digital media can bring family members together in collaborative, problem-solving arrangements. Ironing-out issues with technology is no doubt annoying. But it is also much more, too. Dealing with technological resistance is one of the most mundane cases of *homework* that families experience today. As such, almost all household members are implicated in this work, so must communicate, negotiate, and care for one another's objectives in getting the job done. We believe this perspective on technology in the household is an important one to counter the popular notions of our digital tools driving family members apart.

References

Barron, B., Martin, C. K., Takeuchi, L., & Fithian, R. (2009). Parents as learning partners in the development of technological fluency. *International Journal of Learning and Media, 1*(2), 55–77.

Cole, M., & Griffin, P. (1983). A socio-historical approach to re-mediation. *Quarterly Newsletter of the Laboratory of Comparative Human Cognition, 5*(4), 69–99.

Goodwin, M. H., & Goodwin, C. (2013). Nurturing. In E. Ochs, & T. Kremer-Sadlik (Eds.). *Fast-forward family: Home, work, and relationships in middle-class America.* Berkeley, CA: University of California Press.

Hjorth, L., & Hendry, N. (2015). A snapshot of social media: Camera phone practices. *Social Media and Society, 1*(1), 1–3.

Ito, M., Baumer, S., Bittanti, M., Boyd, D., Cody, R., . . . Tripp, L. (2010). *Hanging out, messing around, and geeking out: Kids living and learning with new media.* Cambridge, MA: MIT Press.

Leander, K. M., Phillips, N. C., & Taylor, K. H. (2010). The changing social spaces of learning: Mapping new mobilities. *Review of Research in Education, 34*(1), 329–394.

Paradise, R., & Rogoff, B. (2009). Side by side: Learning by observing and pitching in. *Ethos: Journal of the Society for Psychological Anthropology, 37*(1), 102–138.

Pickering, A. (1993). The mangle of practice: Agency and emergence in the sociology of science. *American Journal of Sociology, 99*(3), 559–589.

Pickering, A. (1995). *The mangle of practice: Time, agency, and science.* Chicago, IL: University of Chicago Press.

Pink, S. (2012). *Situating everyday life.* Los Angeles, CA: Sage.

Pink, S., Horst, H., Postill, J., Hjorth, L., Lewis, T., & Tacchi, J. (2016). *Digital ethnography: Principles and practices.* London: Sage.

Rideout, V., & Hammel, E. (2006). *The media family: Electronic media in the lives of infants, toddlers, preschoolers, and their parents.* Washington, DC: Kaiser Family Foundation.

Star, S. L. (1999). The ethnography of infrastructure. *American Behavioral Scientist, 43,* 377–391.

Stevens, R., Satwicz, T., & McCarthy, L. (2008). In-game, in-room, in-world: Reconnecting video game play to the rest of kids' lives. In K. Salen (Ed.), *The Ecology of Games, Connecting Youth, Games, and Learning* (pp. 41–66). Cambridge, MA: MIT Press.

Takeuchi, L., & Stevens, R. (2011). *The new co-viewing: Designing for learning through joint media engagement.* A report of The Joan Ganz Cooney Center at Sesame Workshop and LIFE Center. New York: Joan Ganz Cooney Center.

Taylor, K. H. (2013). Counter-mapping the neighborhood: A social design experiment for spatial justice. Doctoral dissertation. Retrieved from *ProQuest Dissertation and Theses.* (Accession Order No. AAT 3575572).

Taylor, K. H., Takeuchi, L., & Stevens, R. (in press). Mapping the daily media round: Methodological innovations for understanding families' mobile technology in use. *International Journal of Learning and Media.*

Wertsch, J. (1998). *Mind as action.* Oxford: Oxford University Press.

SECTION 2

Parent Engagement

Section Editor: Alexis R. Lauricella

5

DIGITAL MEDIA AS A PARENTING SUPPORT TOOL FOR HISPANIC FAMILIES IN THE UNITED STATES

Alexis R. Lauricella, Briana Ellerbe, and Ellen Wartella

We are at an important period in technological history. We have seen a vast boom in mobile, Internet-accessible technology, and recently seen access to new devices reach relatively even rates among various ethnic and income groups within the United States. Now the majority of all parents with young children have access to the Internet, through mobile phones, tablets, or computers (Rideout, 2013). Importantly, we are no longer seeing a digital divide as strongly associated with race/ethnicity (Rideout, 2013), meaning that Hispanic adults are as likely to use smartphones and social media sites as other ethnic groups (Lopez, Gonzalez-Barrera, & Patten, 2013). With the Hispanic population growing in the United States (Stepler & Brown, 2016) and also having higher rates of poverty (DeNavas-Walt & Proctor, 2014) it is important to understand how technology might be used within this specific population to provide increased social support, and especially parental support. The goal of this chapter is to examine the ways in which Hispanic parents obtain and seek out parenting support both off- and online. Given the dramatic rise in the rates of families of Hispanic descent and the novel role that digital media may play in supporting parents of young children, we seek to describe and discuss, both qualitatively and quantitatively, the ways in which Hispanic parents engage with their social network both on and offline.

Hispanic Families

In 2014, there were more than 55 million people of Hispanic descent (i.e., from Spanish-speaking, and particularly Latin American countries) living in the United States, making them the second fastest growing demographic in the United States after Asians (Stepler & Brown, 2016). Hispanic individuals now make up 17 percent of the nation's population (DeNavas-Walt & Proctor, 2015), 65 percent of whom were born in the United States (Krogstad, 2016), and Hispanic children make up 24 percent of all United States 0- to 17-year-olds (Federal Interagency Forum on Child and Family Statistics, 2015). Hispanic residents in the United States also have one of the highest poverty rates (DeNavas-Walt & Proctor, 2014) with 30 percent of Hispanic children living in poverty (Krogstad, 2014) and approximately one-third of families have incomes that are just barely meeting the child's basic needs (DeNavas-Walt & Proctor, 2014). Further, many Hispanic children live in neighborhoods with poor housing and high levels of crime (Bishaw & Fontenot, 2014). This situation may be attributed to several social, political, and economic factors, including parents' level of education, availability of jobs with a living wage, access to housing, and challenges that come with immigration, or ethnicity-related stressors (French & Chavez, 2010; Stepler & Brown, 2016). For instance, 61 percent of Hispanics over the age of 25 have a high school degree or less (Stepler & Brown, 2016), which in turn could limit the number of steady, well-paying jobs to which they have access.

Social capital is one critical factor that can offset the negative consequences of poverty (Denner, Kirby, Coyle, & Brindis, 2001). Existing research and scholarship suggest that families descending from Hispanic countries, particularly Mexico, have a strong sense of *familism* and a greater likelihood of living in proximity to extended family (though these traits are highly variable across families due to cultural, economic, or situational differences) (Keefe, Padilla, & Carlos, 1979; Sarkisian, Gerena, & Gerstel, 2007; Vega, 1990). Research documents the important benefits of familial proximity and support. When parents have close support systems, the association of unstable residential conditions with conflict among family members diminishes (Riina, Lippert, & Brooks-Gunn, 2016), parents experience better parenting outcomes (Crnic & Greenberg, 1990; Hashima & Amato, 1994), and in turn, children experience better academic and social outcomes (Dunst, Trivette, & Cross, 1986). In addition to in-person familial or communal forms of social capital, new digital opportunities provide additional methods for parents to obtain support and maintain social capital.

New digital tools have changed that way in which many people communicate and connect. Access to mobile technology has increased across all ethnic and income groups, allowing more families to have regular Internet access than ever before. Hispanic adults are as likely to own smartphones and use social networking sites as White and African American adults (Lopez et al., 2013). Social networking sites may be one way to increase social support for Hispanic parents. In particular, these new platforms may offer Hispanic families a unique way to connect with extended family members who may not live nearby (e.g., in their countries of origin) as well as provide opportunities for organizations, nonprofits, and companies to provide social support to Hispanic families through unique, nonconfrontational means.

Social Support

Social support encompasses a large category of ways in which individuals intend to be helpful to another individual. According to Glanz, Rimer, and Viswanath (2008), social support encompasses four major categories or types of behaviors: emotional, instrumental, information, and appraisal support (Glanz et al., 2008; House, Kahn, McLeod, & Williams, 1985). According to Glanz and colleagues (2008) emotional support is demonstrated through expressions of love, trust, empathy, and caring (Glanz et al., 2008). Instrumental support is demonstrated through the provision of a tangible aid or service to an individual. Informational support is demonstrated when an individual provides advice, suggestions, or information to support another individual. Appraisal support occurs when an individual provides information that supports the individual's self-evaluation, or self-esteem. This often occurs in the form of constructive feedback or affirmation (Glanz et al., 2008). Each type of support can come from a variety of sources, including offline networks such as parents and family members, friends, books, magazines, and professionals like pediatricians and teachers or from new online support networks like websites and social media sites. For the purposes of this paper, we examined three of the four types of support for parents and parenting specifically: emotional, instrumental, and informational support. We excluded appraisal support for this study because it is less directly connected to parenting support, which was the focus on our research.

Offline Parenting Support

Parenting young children is a challenging and often confusing task. As a result, parents of young children (under age 8) seek information, advice, and support from a range of sources, including friends and family as well as books, magazines, medical professionals, and websites (Wartella, Rideout, & Lauricella, 2014). Data from a nationally representative study indicate that parents were more likely to seek out individuals rather than text-based sources for parenting advice (Wartella et al., 2014). Almost 90 percent of parents report that they are "very" or "somewhat" likely to go to their spouse and 73 percent of parents say they go to friends for parenting advice. Parents reported other family members, including their mother (68 percent), father (45 percent), in-laws (47 percent), and other relatives (52 percent), as likely sources of parenting advice. Children's pediatricians (73 percent), teachers (57 percent), and faith or religious leaders (39 percent) were additional individuals that parents were likely to go to for parenting advice.

Online Parenting Support

While there is evidence that parents go to individuals including family, friends, and experts to obtain parenting advice and support, newer technologies and communication tools provide opportunities for parents to get advice and support from these individuals as well as others online. Parents report using online communication platforms including message centers, e-mail, and discussion boards to plan opportunities to meet in person (Hall & Irvine, 2009), but also to share parenting tips, advice, and support (Drentea & Moren-Cross, 2005). Other research indicates that parents actively seek out parenting advice and support through online discussion boards (e.g., Brady & Guerin, 2010; Fletcher, May, St. George, Morgan, & Lubans, 2011).

Recent data by Duggan, Ellison, Lampe, Lenhart, and Madden (2015) found that 71 percent of all parents use social media to get support from their friends and many parents (74 percent) report that they receive support from other individuals on social media as well. Their study demonstrated that more mothers (80 percent) report receiving support than fathers (65 percent). Support from social networking sites is relatively high, although support for parenting issues specifically was less common, with only 42 percent of all parents saying they received social or emotional support on a parenting issue from social media (Duggan et al., 2015). Further, most parents (79 percent) indicate that they get useful information from social media sites, but fewer (59 percent) report getting useful information about parenting specifically (Duggan et al., 2015).

More broadly, several recent reviews show that the majority of parents go online to look up parenting information and for social support, suggesting the Internet is a key resource for parents (Doty & Dworkin, 2014; Dworkin, Connell, & Doty, 2013). The Internet in general is a resource that parents use to locate parenting information and obtain support, but social networking sites offer a unique platform for such practices (Duggan et al., 2015). Facebook originated as a social networking site to connect college students and their peers, but in the past decade has become a site for people of all ages, and extends beyond personal connections. Millions of businesses, companies, and organizations now have their own Facebook pages through which they push messages to their audiences (Koetsier, 2013). Beyond established companies and organizations, Facebook also allows pages for "groups" of users that share similar interests. As a result, the social networking component of Facebook is embedded in a larger support and information system. For example, parents may be part of local area parenting groups or may "like" or "follow" parenting and child development organizations like Baby Center, Parents Magazine, Univision, or the American Academy of Pediatrics. Thus, parents who visit Facebook may receive parenting advice or information even if their original intention was to use Facebook for more personal and social connection purposes. While only 18 percent of parents of children under age 8 report going to social networking sites for parenting advice or information (Wartella et al., 2014), we suspect that parents may be obtaining parenting advice or information from these social network platforms more frequently. The advice or information may come directly from friends and others that they know on Facebook or it may come from organizations, nonprofits, businesses, or local community groups.

Sundstrom (2016) conducted qualitative interviews with mothers of newborns and found that parents frequently reported using online support networks and sources as a guide for information. She reports that mothers explained the use of social networking sites like YouTube as a resource for providing visual examples and tutorials about how to complete basic childcare skills like swaddling a baby or changing a diaper (Sundstrom, 2016). Parents also discussed the value of online sites for locating other people in similar situations who may provide support and guidance. This study also found that the majority (82 percent) of mothers had Facebook accounts and described the importance of connecting with friends online to obtain health-related information. Overall, the findings reveal how new mothers use technology for support as they address the health challenges related to the birth of a new baby, and illustrate the importance of including online social supports and social networking sites in research on parenting.

A handful of studies have specifically investigated parents' Facebook use, but they tend to focus on new mothers and their information seeking behaviors, rather than on the information they actually receive on Facebook. For example, Morris (2014) found that mothers of very young children (0–3 years old) post questions on Facebook to gain social support in general and more specifically to obtain tangible and informational support. Similarly, Holtz, Smock, and Reyes-Gastelum (2015) studied a specific Facebook group for new moms and moms-to-be and found that women primarily used the group for information seeking, information sharing, social support, and entertainment. However, few studies have specifically investigated whether and how parents of young children, particularly low-income or minority parents, obtain parenting advice or information on social networking sites.

Study Methodology

Data for this chapter were collected by researchers at the Center for Media and Human Development at Northwestern University and the Joan Ganz Cooney Center (JGCC) at Sesame workshop. At Northwestern University, the researchers collected broad quantitative data through an online survey, and at the JGCC, researchers collected more in-depth qualitative data through in-person interviews and observations. Data from both sites were combined to provide qualitative context for the quantitative data.

Survey Topics and Participants

The research team at Northwestern University designed an online questionnaire to assess parents' online and offline social support and use of social networking sites for parenting-related information. The questionnaire included items addressing respondents' parenting network, access to technology, social networking site use, and their levels of parenting support both online and offline. The instrument was available in both English and Spanish (see Appendix, Study 5 for more details).

The final sample included 163 participants of Hispanic origin with a household income of less than $70,000. All respondents identified as Hispanic. The majority were Mexican (78 percent), 6 percent Dominican, 5 percent Salvadorian, 2 percent Puerto Rican, 1 percent Columbian, and the remaining 7 percent were from other countries. The vast majority of participants were very low-income, with 71 percent of respondents reporting an annual household income of less than $30,000 and another 29 percent with an annual income between $30,000 and $70,000. Most (81 percent) respondents were female. Respondents ranged in age from 20 to 50 years old: 25 percent of respondents were 27 years old or younger, 50 percent were between 27 and 36 years old, and 25 percent were 37 years old or older. Educational attainment was relatively low: 34 percent of respondents did not have a high school diploma, 35 percent had a high school diploma or GED, and 32 percent had at least some college experience. More than two-thirds of the sample (70 percent) were not born in the United States.

Family Interviews and Observations

The JGCC study participants consisted of 15 families with at least one child between the ages of 6 and 9 from a range of countries of origin (e.g., Puerto Rican, Dominican, Mexican, Ecuadorian, and Salvadorian) and socioeconomic backgrounds. Parents varied in immigration and generational status (e.g., first to third generation born in the United States).

Researchers visited families in their homes one to two times every other week, over a span of 6–8 weeks, for a total of at least five visits. Data collection approaches included a technology inventory of working devices in the home, interviews with parents and children about media use in the home, and observations of families' activities, especially around media and technology use together. In the weeks that researchers did not visit families, the focal child of the study would receive a daily, 5-minute experience sampling phone call to inquire about what he or she might be doing with media in that moment and what other media-related activities he or she might have done or planned to do that day. All names were changed to protect the identities of the participants. (See Appendix, Study 8 for additional details.)

Findings

Findings from the combined studies indicate how Hispanic families engage with various types of social support both on and offline. First, we describe the importance and heavy reliance on local support networks by many Hispanic families. Next, we discuss the unique ways in which social support networks exist and are utilized by Hispanic families with young children by focusing on three important constructs of support: instrumental, emotional, and informational support, as discussed by Glanz et al. (2008). Finally, given the vast increase in access to digital technologies, we discuss the ways in which parents utilize digital technologies such as video chat (including FaceTime), and Facebook to maintain relationships and connections with their support networks both locally and internationally. This combination of large-scale survey data and rich case study data provides a detailed description of how Hispanics rely on both online and offline social networks for support as parents of young children.

Hispanic Parents' Social Support Networks

Hispanic families have strong and extensive offline social support networks. Nearly all parents surveyed in the Northwestern study reported having at least one person with whom they discuss parenting issues and almost half reported having five individuals to go to (see Table 5.1).

Types of Individuals Who Provide Support

Parents reported going to certain types of people for advice about specific issues, including their own parents, siblings, spouses, friends, co-workers, and experts (see Table 5.1). Respondents were asked to list up to five family members or friends with whom they most often discussed general parenting issues, and many parents (59 percent) reported that their spouse was a key person (e.g., Person 1 or 2) that they went to for parenting advice. Parents also relied heavily on their own parents and siblings.

Similar to parents in the larger survey, parents in the JGCC study frequently reported turning to multiple extended family members for support. This social support from extended family was particularly crucial as 10 of the 15 families were single-parent families. Many of these parents heavily relied on the support of their family, friends, and communities in the upbringing of their children. These primarily local and in-person supports ranged from live-in or nearby grandparents to close friends and neighbors. Renelle Vasquez, a mother of five, described her strong ties with her parents, aunts, uncles, and cousins who lived 2 hours north of her home. While visiting them required a long drive, she and her children made the trip often since among her children's closest playmates were their cousins up north.

In the survey, parents reported regularly seeking out information and resources from a variety of people in their support networks. Many parents (61 percent) reported that they go to family members at least once a week to talk about parenting topics. Almost half (48 percent) of parents talked with their child's teacher or childcare provider about parenting topics at least once a week. Just over one-third reported going to friends (38 percent) or pediatricians (35 percent) and only one-quarter (25 percent) used books or magazines at least once a week. Parents in the JGCC sample also regularly talked to family members and others about parenting topics, and also relied on other types of experts and services not included in the survey.

TABLE 5.1 Hispanic Parent Social Networks: Descriptive Statistics

Relationship	*Person 1 (N = 158)*	*Person 2 (N = 132)*	*Person 3 (N = 111)*	*Person 4 (N = 86)*	*Person 5 (N = 75)*
Partner/spouse (%)	42	16	8	5	5
My parent (%)	23	19	20	12	12
My sibling (%)	11	23	18	10	4
Relative (%)	2	14	3	1	16
Friend (%)	8	23	18	13	40
Co-worker (%)	10	1	23	43	1
Expert (%)	3	4	3	1	0
Parenting experience					
Parent (%)	86	78	76	70	75
Parent of young child (%)	56	36	37	48	73
Location					
Home (%)	49	23	5	7	8
City (%)	29	50	51	57	55
State (%)	8	9	13	12	12
Country (%)	5	6	6	7	5
Different country (%)	11	9	22	14	17
Communication tools					
In person (%)	81	73	59	67	67
Phone/text (%)	58	55	70	52	56
E-mail (%)	2	4	5	5	7
Social media (%)	7	10	10	7	15
Video chat (%)	4	6	6	7	7

Note. Proportions are calculated for each category and may not add up to 100% due to missing data.

Location of Support Network

While there are tools to support social relationships and support at a distance, frequently parenting support networks consist of family members living relatively close to, if not within the same home as, the parent (see Table 5.1). As mentioned above, parents in the JGCC study reported multiple extended family members including their own parents (children's grandparents), siblings, cousins, and aunts and uncles whom they see regularly. For example, Clarissa Claudio, a single mother, indicated that her 8-year-old son, Julius, spent much of his time with his maternal grandparents while she worked, and he also regularly visited aunts, uncles, and cousins who lived nearby.

Forms of Communication with Local Support Network

Hispanic parents are highly connected with their support networks through a variety of communication technologies (see Table 5.1). Parents reported regularly speaking in-person with the individuals listed as key members of their social network. However, phone and texting are consistent tools of communication used by Hispanic parents to connect with all members of their social network. Newer forms of technology like social networking sites, e-mail, and video chat are much less commonly used by Hispanic parents for connecting with their parenting support network. As described by some families in the JGCC sample, parents rely on key members of their family and friends for childcare support, often times reporting that children spend considerable amounts of time with grandparents, aunts, or uncles. As a result, parents are likely interacting with these people on a regular basis and often seeing them in person, thus limiting the need to rely on newer digital media as a primary tool for making connections.

Types of Parenting Support

Here we describe our findings in relation to three important types of support, starting with instrumental support, followed by emotional and informational support (Glanz et al., 2008).

Instrumental Support

Instrumental support is demonstrated through the provision of a tangible aid or service to an individual. Many parents receive instrumental support "often" or "always" from family (51 percent) and teachers (41 percent). Books/magazines (30 percent), friends (27 percent), and pediatricians are also key members of Hispanic family's instrumental support team (see Table 5.2).

Parents rely on family and friends to provide various forms of instrumental support, but the most frequently identified need in our survey of parents was childcare. When respondents were asked how regularly they received childcare support, 32 percent reported that they had someone who could take care of their child "all of the time" if they needed it. Another 30 percent reported that they had someone who could take care of their child "most of the time" if they needed it. Only 17 percent said that they had someone who could take care of their child "none of the time" or "a little of the time" if they needed it (see Table 5.2). In the JGCC study, parents discussed the important role of their parenting support network in providing childcare. As previously mentioned,

TABLE 5.2 Types of People Who Provide Different Types of Support "Often" or "Always"

	Instrumental Support	*Informational Support*	*Emotional Support*
Family (%)	51	48	73
Friends	27%	30%	605
Pediatrician (%)	22	30	28
Teacher (%)	4	43	46
Books/magazines (%)	30	35	26

Clarissa Claudio discussed her reliance on the children's grandparents for childcare when she was at work. She also depended on her parents to give her some much needed leisure time with friends. Similarly, Natalia Diaz reported that her children, Addy (age 8) and Daniel (age 2), spent a lot of time at their grandmother Lola's house nearby while Natalia balanced three jobs. The family had an extensive support network just within grandma's house, where the children's grandfather, great uncle, and great aunt also resided. Lola was a respected matriarch within their community, so Addy and Daniel interacted with and had the support of many of Lola's neighbors and friends as well.

In addition to leaning on support systems to look after children in a parent's absence, parents relied on their social networks to enrich their children's activities. Ana Martinez often sent her three children, Analise (age 9), Richie (age 7), and Deangelo (age 5), to church with her mother on Sundays, and also sent them with her neighbors on Wednesday evenings to an outdoor church service for youth in the neighborhood. While she often felt too busy to take them herself, she relied on her family and friends to make sure that her children attended church, as she felt church was important for their lives and development.

Emotional Support

Parents do not just receive support directly related to their children. The vast majority of parents surveyed reported that they had someone to go to "all of the time" or "most of the time" if they needed someone to relax with, to do something enjoyable with, or to take their minds of things. Reports of emotional support from family and friends was very high with 73 percent of parents reporting "always" or "often" feeling supported by family and 60 percent reporting "always" or "often" feeling supported by friends (see Table 5.3). While many parents regularly felt emotionally supported by family and friends, teachers were also reported as emotionally supportive by 46 percent of parents. Parents with large support networks also had people that they could go to for relaxation or to enjoy time out

TABLE 5.3 How Often Parents Received Various Types of Support

	None of the time	*A Little of the time*	*Some of the time*	*Most of the time*	*All of the time*
Instrumental support: watch your child (%)	7	9	22	30	32
Emotional support: take your mind off things (%)	5	6	9	37	43
Emotional support: get together for relaxation (%)	3	6	9	34	48
Emotional support: someone to do something enjoyable with (%)	2	3	11	32	51

of the house. For instance, Noelia Hernandez, who migrated from Mexico City to New York as a child, was part of three different formal groups where she socialized and has built a strong social network: a gender- and age-mixed soccer team, a folkloric dance group, and a local organization providing Mexican and Latino communities with educational wellness, economic, and leadership programs.

Informational Support

In the survey, parents reported receiving informational support regarding parenting issues from their family and teachers more so than their friends. Almost half of parents (48 percent) reported "always" or "often" learning how to do something involving their child from family members and teachers (42 percent) and another one-third (35 percent) regularly learned from books or magazines. In contrast, only 30 percent reported "often" learning how to do something involving their child from friends or from pediatricians. For other types of information, like how to care for a sick child, parents often sought help from family members (See Table 5.2).

Families in the JGCC study received specific types of information from different sources. Many parents reported that they went to teachers, pediatricians, librarians, and people in other community organizations to get information about media use, technology, and education. Parents especially held teachers in high regard for information about the education and well-being of their children. Renelle Vasquez encouraged her daughter Jolena daily to play math games that were recommended to her by her teacher. She also had a young son with autism, and was in constant communication with professionals as well as her sons' school for resources and advice.

Digital and Online Social Support

In the survey, many parents reported using a variety of technology tools to stay in touch with their social support network. Overwhelmingly, Facebook was the most frequently used social networking site, reported by 78 percent of parents. Fifty percent reported using Facebook daily or several times a day. There were no differences in Facebook use as a function of family income or whether the parent was born in the United States. Other social networking site use was very low, with only 29 percent of parents reporting using Pinterest, 25 percent using Instagram, and 13 percent using Twitter.

Findings from families in the JGCC study exemplified the important role that social media had in these Hispanic families' connections to family and friends. The Parades family frequently connected with extended family members in Ecuador through video chat, Facebook, and other communication apps, because of their limited ability to travel and visit them regularly. Similarly, Jessica Ortiz-Galarza discussed how e-mail and social media made it easier to reconnect with friends and family in Ecuador and other places after she moved to the United States as a young adult. She reported using Facebook, WhatsApp, and LINE (a communication app that offers free voice calls and messages) to keep these relationships alive from a distance. Sofia Edwards said that she had very few friends where she lives in New York, but keeps in touch with her family (parents and siblings) and childhood friends in Mexico City through phone, FaceTime, and to some extent Facebook. In this instance, a mother who had immigrated and felt a lack of social connections in her geographic location was still able to garner support from family and friends back home.

Beyond parents' use of media to connect with family and friends, many parents reported using Facebook and other social media specifically for their child so that family and friends could watch their children grow up online. Jessica Ortiz-Galarza and Renelle Vasquez created Facebook pages for their children, updating the pages regularly so that friends and family could keep track of the children's development and experiences.

Support from Facebook and other social networking sites could take various forms. Parents used social networking sites to keep other family members and friends informed about their family. This was a common theme in the case study families.

A more overt and direct way to use Facebook to obtain support is through using the platform as a tool to seek out parenting advice and support. More than half of parents reported that they posted to Facebook purposely to seek out instrumental support (53 percent), informational support (57 percent), or emotional support (54 percent). Parents who did use Facebook to seek various types of support generally reported that it was "somewhat helpful." Specifically, of parents who reported that they posted on social media for instrumental support (n = 84), 66 percent reported it was "somewhat helpful" and another 26 percent reported that it was "mostly helpful." Of parents who reported posting on social media for informational support (n = 83), 63 percent reported it was "somewhat helpful" and another 34 percent reported that it was "mostly helpful." Fewer parents reporting posting on Facebook for emotional support (N = 78), but of those who did, 69 percent reported it was "somewhat helpful" and another 22 percent reported that it was "mostly helpful".

A less overt but potentially more common way in which parents obtain support online is through observation of content that they had not purposefully searched for. Many parents report obtaining other types of support indirectly from social networking sites like Facebook. More than half of respondents (60 percent) reported that they regularly ("sometimes", "often", or "always") see information on Facebook that provides instrumental support, such as information about how to teach their children how to tie their shoes, potty training, and so forth. About two-thirds of the surveyed parents (66 percent) reported receiving emotional support from Facebook. Even more parents (69 percent) report getting informational support from Facebook, such as information about healthy nutrition, tips related to schooling, and other kinds of material.

Conclusion

This study of Hispanic families provides new evidence regarding the diverse and powerful social networks that support Hispanic parents in the United States. Through analyses of survey reports and qualitative data from families with varying backgrounds, we have presented evidence that parents consistently go to family members for parenting advice, but also rely on a range of online and offline support networks. One innovative way in which Hispanic parents are connecting and receiving support is through the use of Facebook and other newer digital platforms such as videochat, text messaging, and other apps.

This chapter used large-scale survey data to provide insights into how parents obtain parenting support from local and distal friends and family, and how new technologies may also provide them with new avenues to receive parenting support. The in-depth interviews with 15 Hispanic families provide specific examples of how some families negotiate the complex roles of parenting in an age where many parents are living further away from their immediate family and opportunities to obtain support have changed with increasing technology. Results from this mixed-methodological approach document the ways in which parents of young children in the United States develop networks of family members and close friends who live nearby and help with crucial instrumental support, such as childcare. They also maintain relationships with friends and peers at a distance, who provide both parenting-specific support and more general emotional support.

While this study did not look at the effects of social capital and social support directly, we found that social support is clearly present for lower income Hispanic families, although the ways in which parents obtain it may differ given personal circumstances. Given the historical sense of familism that has existed in Mexican families and others of Hispanic descent (e.g., Vega, 1990), it seems logical that Hispanic parents seek out help and support from family members (and of course, this is true of parents regardless of ethnic background). When family support is not viable, due to geographic distance or other variables, these parents find support from others, including friends, teachers, and community organizations. In addition, the Hispanic parents in our studies found other ways to stay connected and supported by family members, even those who lived far away and could not be visited often. New technologies, like Facebook, have provided families with opportunities to communicate and connect regularly with relatives and friends. Parents reported updating grandparents and friends from their home country with images and text updates about their children growing up in the United States using Facebook. Many of these parents also reported that they obtain or "find" support and ideas for how to better raise their children on Facebook even when they were not directly seeking that type of support.

As with earlier studies, the research reported here demonstrates that the emotional closeness and personal relationships that parents have with an individual are important criteria for seeking advice and emotional support from that person.

Moreover, parents are almost twice as likely to seek advice on a weekly basis from family members compared to friends or experts such as pediatricians or parenting magazines. Finally, technology is particularly useful to connect families and friends across time and space, such as documenting a child's growth and development on Facebook, or using social networking sites and the Internet to connect with family out of the country. Such family members can provide both emotional and informational parenting support and advice at a distance. In short, twenty-first century technologies, such as the Internet and social media, offer useful means for low-income Hispanic families to connect with family and friends, who remain their main sources of parenting advice. Technology serves as a means to sustain, reinforce, and extend the more traditional social networks in which Hispanic parents are embedded.

The results of this study are descriptive and do not allow us to make claims about cause and effect relationships, for example, between the kinds of social support available and improved parenting outcomes. With this in mind, we offer the following recommendations.

First, future research should continue to study ethnically diverse families and their use of new media platforms, specifically around social and parenting support. One promising approach is to document the storytelling networks of Hispanic families. The flow of community discourse, information, and narratives can be followed through a community's storytelling network of individuals, organizations, and media (Ball-Rokeach, Kim, & Matei, 2001). Through identifying and understanding such storytelling networks, researchers and educators can strengthen existing structures of social and parenting support, as well as create new forms of support. Additionally, more controlled experimental work should directly examine the impact of social networking sites on parents' perceived support, actual support, and other potential indirect benefits including enhanced social capital, employment options, and household income.

Second, it is important for those who work with these specific communities and populations to understand the ways in which technology may be supporting a diverse array of families in unique and powerful ways. Given how much time parents spend on social network sites, educators, pediatricians, teachers, community organizers, and librarians should seek to better understand their roles within networks of parental support and how they can reach parents using new technology.

Finally, interventions and other parenting support initiatives may want to use new technology and social networking sites as ways to reach parents directly and easily. Much like the work of Text4Baby and other texting interventions (e.g., Hurwitz, Lauricella, Hanson, Raden, & Wartella, 2015), reaching out and connecting with parents through these tools with parenting advice and information may be more effective and impactful than requiring parents to seek it out or obtain it in other ways.

In sum, Hispanic parents are not replacing their traditional family networks with online resources, but using both types of resources to help them as parents both on and offline. From these multiple sources, parents are getting informational, instrumental, and emotional support to aid them as parents. For practitioners who wish to better serve the needs of such parents, becoming more aware of these varied and existing sources of both online and offline support is the first step toward finding creative ways to strengthen and extend this support for all families.

Acknowledgments

We would like to thank Dr. Lori Takeuchi, the Principal Investigator of the JGCC Study, for her conception of and guidance of the study. We would also like to thank Rocío Almanza-Guillén, Jason C. Yip, Alan Nong, Anna Ly, and Kristen Kohm from the JGCC and Courtney Blackwell from Northwestern University for their help with data collection and analysis. We also want to thank the families that participated in the Northwestern University survey and the JGCC interviews. Finally, we want to thank our funders the Heising-Simons Foundation and the Bezos Foundation for their support with these projects.

References

Ball-Rokeach, S. J., Kim, Y. C., & Matei, S. (2001). Storytelling neighborhood: Paths to belonging in diverse urban environments. *Communication Research, 28*(4), 392–428.

Bishaw, A., & Fontenot, K. (2014). *Poverty: 2012 and 2013. American community survey briefs.* Washington, DC: US Census Bureau.

Brady, E., & Guerin, S. (2010). "Not the romantic, all happy, coochy coo experience": A qualitative analysis of interactions on an Irish parenting web site. *Family Relations, 59*(1), 14–27.

Crnic, K. A., & Greenberg, M. T. (1990). Minor parenting stresses with young children. *Child Development, 61*(5), 1628–1637.

DeNavas-Walt, C., & Proctor, B. D. (2014). *Income and poverty in the United States: 2013. Current Population Reports, P60–249.* Washington, DC: U.S. Government Printing Office. Retrieved from www.census.gov/content/dam/Census/library/publications/2014/demo/p60-249.pdf

DeNavas-Walt, C., & Proctor, B. D. (2015). *Income and poverty in the United States: 2014. Current Population Reports P60-249.* Washington, DC: U.S. Government Printing Office. Retrieved from www.census.gov/content/dam/Census/library/publications/2015/demo/p60-252.pdf.

Denner, J., Kirby, D., Coyle, K., & Brindis, C. (2001). The protective role of social capital and cultural norms in Latino communities: A study of adolescent births. *Hispanic Journal of Behavioral Sciences, 23*(1), 3–21.

Doty, J. L., & Dworkin, J. (2014). Online social support for parents: A critical review. *Marriage & Family Review, 50*(2), 174–198.

Drentea, P., & Moren-Cross, J. L. (2005). Social capital and social support on the web: The case of an internet mother site. *Sociology of Health & Illness, 27*(7), 920–943.

Duggan, M., Ellison, N. B., Lampe, C., Lenhart, A., & Madden, M. (2015). *Social media update 2014*. Washington, DC: Pew Research Center.

Dunst, C. J., Trivette, C. M., & Cross, A. H. (1986). Mediating influences of social support: Personal, family, and child outcomes. *American Journal of Mental Deficiency, 90*(4), 403–417.

Dworkin, J., Connell, J., & Doty, J. (2013). A literature review of parents' online behavior. *Cyberpsychology*, 7(2). http://dx.doi.org/10.5817/CP2013-2-2

Federal Interagency Forum on Child and Family Statistics. (2015). *America's children in brief: Key national indicators of well-being*. Retrieved from www.childstats.gov/americas children/tables.asp

Fletcher, R., May, C., St. George, J., Morgan, P. J., & Lubans, D. R. (2011). Fathers' perceptions of rough-and-tumble play: Implications for early childhood services. *Australasian Journal of Early Childhood, 36*(4), 131.

French, S. E., & Chavez, N. R. (2010). The relationship of ethnicity-related stressors and Latino ethnic identity to well-being. *Hispanic Journal of Behavioral Sciences, 32*(3), 410–428.

Glanz, K., Rimer, B. K., & Viswanath, K. (Eds.). (2008). *Health behavior and health education: Theory, research, and practice*. San Francisco, CA: John Wiley & Sons.

Hall, W., & Irvine, V. (2009). E-communication among mothers of infants and toddlers in a community-based cohort: A content analysis. *Journal of Advanced Nursing, 65*(1), 175–183.

Hashima, P. Y., & Amato, P. R. (1994). Poverty, social support, and parental behavior. *Child Development, 65*(2), 394–403.

Holtz, B., Smock, A., & Reyes-Gastelum, D. (2015). Connected motherhood: Social support for moms and moms-to-be on Facebook. *Telemedicine and e-Health, 21*(5), 415–421.

House, J. S., Kahn, R. L., McLeod, J. D., & Williams, D. (1985). Measures and concepts of social support. In S. Cohen, & S. L. Syme (Eds.), *Social support and health* (pp. 83–108). New York: Academic Press.

Hurwitz, L. B., Lauricella, A. R., Hanson, A., Raden, A., & Wartella, E. (2015). Supporting Head Start parents: Impact of a text message intervention on parent–child activity engagement. *Early Child Development and Care, 185*(9), 1373–1389.

Keefe, S., Padilla, A., & Carlos, M. (1979). The Mexican-American extended family as an emotional support system. *Human Organization, 38*(2), 144–152.

Koetsier, J. (2013, March 5). Facebook: 15 million business, companies, and organizations now have a Facebook page. *VentureBeat*. Retrieved from http://venturebeat.com/2013/03/05/facebook-15-million-businesses-companies-and-organizations-now-have-a-facebook-page/

Krogstad, J. M. (2014). Hispanics only group to see its poverty rate decline and incomes rise. *Fact Tank*. Retrieved from www. pewresearch. org/fact-tank/2014/09/19/hispanics-only-group-to-see-its-poverty-rate-decline-and-incomes-rise

Krogstad, J.M. (2016). 10 Facts for national Hispanic heritage month. *Fact Tank*. Retrieved from www.pewresearch.org/fact-tank/2016/09/15/facts-for-national-hispanic-heritage-month/

Lopez, M. H., Gonzalez-Barrera, A., & Patten, E. (2013). *Closing the digital divide: Latinos and technology adoption*. Washington, DC: Pew Research Center.

Morris, M. R. (2014). Social networking site use by mothers of young children. In *Proceedings of the 17th ACM Conference on Computer-Supported Cooperative Work & Social Computing* (pp. 1272–1282). New York: ACM.

Rideout, V. (2013). *Zero to eight: Children's media use in America 2013*. New York: Common Sense Media.

Riina, M., Lippert, A., & Brooks-Gunn, J. (2016). Residential instability, family support, and parent-child relationships among ethnically diverse urban families. *Journal of Marriage and Family*, *78*(4), 855–870.

Sarkisian, N., Gerena, M., & Gerstel, N. (2007). Extended family integration among Euro and Mexican Americans: Ethnicity, gender, and class. *Journal of Marriage and Family*, *69*(10), 40–54.

Stepler, R., & Brown, A. (2016). Statistical portrait of Hispanics in the United States. Retrieved from www.pewhispanic.org/2016/04/19/statistical-portrait-of-hispanics-in-the-united-states/

Sundstrom, B. (2016). Mothers "Google It Up": Extending communication channel behavior in Diffusion of Innovations Theory. *Health Communication*, *31*(1), 91–101.

Vega, W. A. (1990). Hispanic families in the 1980s: A decade of research. *Journal of Marriage and the Family*, *52*(4), 1015–1024.

Wartella, E., Rideout, V., Lauricella, A., & Connell, S. (2014). *Parenting in the age of digital technology: A national survey*. Evanston, IL: Center on Media and Human Development, School of Communication, Northwestern University. Retrieved from http://cmhd.northwestern.edu/wpcontent/uploads/2015/06/ParentingAgeDigitalTechnology.REVISED.FINAL_.2014.pdf

6

RESPONDING TO CLASSROOM CHANGE

How Low-Income Latino Parents View Technology's Impacts on Student Learning

Vikki Katz, Carmen Gonzalez, and Alexia Raynal

In schools across the United States, technology is being integrated into classroom learning at rapid rates. From digital curricula to one-to-one (1:1) laptop programs and computer-based standardized testing, there are high hopes that technological innovation can improve student learning and help close stubborn gaps in educational outcomes between lower and higher income students (McClure et al., 2017; U.S. Department of Education, 2017; Zheng, Warschauer, Lin, & Chang, 2016). Education scholars have found, for example, that at-risk students perform better on state competency examinations when their learning is supplemented through simulations, video-based activities, and a more interactive learning environment that is responsive to individual student needs (Darling-Hammond, Zielezinski, & Goldman, 2014).

Many of the initiatives that seek to integrate technology into the classroom are developed and assessed locally at the district or state level. The success of such initiatives depends on a variety of factors, from adequate supports and training for teachers, to quality hardware and connectivity (Katz & Levine, 2015). Because in-school technology initiatives are primarily concerned with changing the experiences that students have in their classrooms, the researchers and practitioners who develop, implement, and evaluate them spend less time thinking about how those same students are also children in families. As a result, we know relatively little about parents' perspectives on technology's role in their children's classroom learning—especially parents who are of lower income and minority backgrounds.

And yet, research shows that parents' perceptions of the opportunities and risks that technology offers their children are critical to the success of such initiatives. The cross-disciplinary literature on parental mediation confirms that ways in which parents restrict, discuss, and use media with their children is a major factor in how children experience and orient themselves to technology (Nathanson, 2015; Valkenburg, Krcmar, Peeters, & Marseille, 1999). Parents' own backgrounds and experiences with the Internet and Internet-connecting devices influence how they mediate their children's engagement with digital tools. And parents who have less income, formal education, and/or English language proficiency are most likely to be "under-connected" to digital technologies. Among these parents, immigrant Hispanics face the most acute challenges of all; almost half (44 percent) do not use a computer even occasionally, and 20 percent do not go online at all (compared with 4 percent of Whites and US-born Hispanics, and 2 percent of Blacks). Almost half (45 percent) have been online for less than 5 years, and only 40 percent say that they feel confident online. They are also less likely than other parents to help their children use computers or the Internet (66 percent, compared with 73 percent of Black, 81 percent of US-born Hispanic, and 83 percent of White parents; Rideout & Katz, 2016).

Qualitative research suggests that these limited personal experiences can make parents more fearful of the dangers their children might encounter online, because parents feel unsure of their abilities to protect their children from harm. For example, Tripp (2011) documents how low-income Mexican immigrant parents adopt highly restrictive mediation practices by limiting children's time online to homework and forbidding them to "look around" on the Internet. On the other hand, Katz (2014) describes the potential that Mexican-origin parents see in these technologies for enabling children's access to the kinds of opportunities that motivated them to raise their children in the United States in the first place. Parents' hopes, paired with their own limited experiences, may therefore lead to over- or underestimating risks their children might encounter online.

These prior studies confirm the importance of parents' influence on their children's technology experiences—and furthermore, that parental mediation decisions are affected by parents' own experiences with technology. Studies like the two summarized above (i.e., Katz, 2014; Tripp, 2011) examine how immigrant Mexican-heritage parents' mediation strategies affect children's technology experiences beyond school. In this chapter, we build on that foundation to investigate parents' perspectives on how technology impacts their children's in-school experiences.

Study Purpose and Methods

In our research, we focused specifically on Mexican-heritage families headed by immigrant and/or US-born. Mexican-heritage families experience greater social disparities than those from other US Hispanic groups (Brown & Patten, 2013), and therefore stand to gain more from school programs that enable greater access to learning opportunities. Children of Mexican immigrants (as opposed to those whose parents are US-born of Mexican heritage) face particularly acute challenges. They are more likely to grow up in poverty, and to have parents who have not completed high school and who report difficulties speaking English, than other US children (Child Trends, 2014; Johnson, Kominski, Smith, & Tillman, 2005; Lopez & Velasco, 2011). Eleven percent of all children growing up in the US today, and 40 percent of children of immigrants, have at least one Mexican-born parent (Child Trends, 2014).

Our analyses draw on data we collected through qualitative interviews with 170 Mexican-heritage parents in three US cities: Chula Vista, California ($N = 52$); Tucson, Arizona ($N = 58$); and Denver, Colorado ($N = 60$). All report household incomes that qualify their focal child (grades K-8) to receive reduced cost or free school meals (see more details on study methodology in Appendix). The school districts in these three cities all serve high-poverty, predominantly Mexican-heritage student populations, and all were engaged in a variety of technology initiatives. These included Connect2Compete (C2C), a public-private partnership that qualifies low-income families for subsidized ($9.95 per month) home broadband access (see www.everyoneon.org/about/c2c). Working in districts offering C2C ensured that respondents' families had access to at least one affordable option for broadband service at home.

Our analyses of these interview data are driven by the following questions:

1. How do low-income Latino parents respond to the introduction of technology into their children's classroom learning?
2. How do parents interpret the consequences of specific district and state-level technology initiatives for their children's educational trajectories?
3. What are the implications of parents' perspectives on technology and learning for educators and for the successful deployment of future technology initiatives?

Findings

In the sections that follow, we document emergent themes in our data with regard to: parents' general perceptions of how introducing technology impacts classroom learning; how they respond to broad-scale tech initiatives specific to their districts; and finally, how they work to extend children's learning at home.

How Technology Changes Classroom Learning

Parents shared their views on how classroom technology use generally influences their children's formal learning experiences. While specific technology initiatives were designed to meet each district's needs, parents' feelings about the integration of new devices, platforms, and programs into their children's schooling varied in similar ways across study sites. Some parents viewed these changes positively, others negatively, and many were too ambivalent or unfamiliar with either the devices themselves or the specifics of classroom instruction to take a strong stance.

We found, as Livingstone (2002) had, that parents generally worked to understand their children's childhoods through the lens of their own childhood experiences. In that sense-making process, parents identified specific affordances—which communication scholar Nancy Baym defines as "the social capabilities [that] technological qualities enable"—that technology presents for their children's learning (2010, p. 44). Three affordances that emerged most strongly in our analyses were personalization, interactivity, and skills development. How parents conceptualized these affordances provides insights as to how parents evaluate technologies' potential depending on the specific context and child in question.

Personalization

Proponents of technological innovations in the classroom have frequently emphasized its potential for enabling students to work at their own pace and engage with content in formats calibrated to their individual learning styles (Cuban, 2016). Interviewed parents recognized these same affordances for personalization, especially if their child had special needs or a learning style that they considered unique. For example, a mother of a fourth-grade boy in Arizona felt that her children benefited from audiovisual modes of learning. She described how an audiobook program helped her youngest daughter, who has special needs, to learn how to read. This feature was particularly helpful for this mother because she did not speak English and felt limited in her abilities to support her child's literacy development (note: when parents responded in Spanish, we have included both the original Spanish and an English translation):

> A ella le ayuda mucho [el audiolibro]. Mientras que la estoy mirando, lo está leyendo. Primero lo escucha, luego lo trata de leer ella, y luego ya hace como una oración.
>
> The [audiobook] helps her a lot. She reads it as I watch her. She listens first, then she tries to read it, and then she writes a sentence.

Similarly, a mother of a fourth-grade boy in Arizona reflected on how technology offered children tailored possibilities for personal expression and aids for improved comprehension:

> [El internet] les sirve mucho porque les ayuda a expresarse mejor. Si les dejan alguna tarea y no la pueden hacer, la misma computadora les [ofrece] diferentes formas de explicarles mejor. El papel, [en cambio], nada más les da un [tipo de] información.
>
> [The Internet] is very helpful to them because it helps them express themselves. If they can't complete their homework, the computer [offers them] different and better ways to explain things to them. [Whereas] paper only offers you one [kind of] information.

Parents frequently emphasized how platforms with multiple content formats offer learning modalities that meet their children's individual needs and expand their capacities.

On the other hand, many parents worried that classroom technology use threatened another highly valued form of "personalized learning": the quality of the teacher–student relationship. This concern was not limited to parents we interviewed. In the nationally representative survey we conducted with lower-income parents during the second phase of our study, one-quarter (26 percent) and three-quarters (75 percent) of US- and foreign-born Hispanics, respectively, either "agree" or "strongly agree" that they worry that their child's teacher knows less about their individual needs due to classroom technology use (compared with 23 percent of White and 24 percent of Black parents; see Rideout & Katz, 2016).

Convergent with those survey findings, our interviews revealed that immigrant parents were especially concerned that technology use could constrain the relationships their children developed with their teachers. Parents frequently emphasized how "essential" it is for teachers to work directly with students, as opposed to relying on technology. The mother of a fifth-grade boy in Arizona was concerned that "human interaction" with teachers could be replaced by mediated forms of instruction. This fear was echoed by parents who had difficulty imagining a classroom in which students' attention is focused on a device, rather than on the interpersonal exchanges happening around them. Using laptops during class, or submitting and receiving feedback on homework assignments online, were perceived as impersonal teaching formats.

Interactivity

Parents perceived technology's affordances for personalizing their children's learning as closely tied to its affordances for interactivity; that is, the considerable possibilities that devices offer for engagement with educational content. They framed their children's natural curiosities about, and desires to use, technology as an indicator of how introducing these innovations into the classroom could motivate children to learn. A father of a second-grade girl in Colorado, for example, felt that classroom technology use could tap into children's existing interests. He noted that his daughter is "more excited to learn and . . . type on the laptop" than she is about paper assignments, and that with it, she has become more confident to finish assignments on her own. Similarly, a mother of a seventh-grade boy in Colorado was optimistic that the state's impending transition to computerized standardized testing might benefit her tech-savvy son:

> A él le gusta utilizar las computadoras y entonces a lo mejor se va a animar más [con los exámenes digitales].
>
> He likes using computers, so maybe he'll be more excited about [digitized exams].

Parents often tied their children's attraction to technology's interactivity to their growing access to, and engagement with, multiple devices in their daily lives. The interactivity that digital technologies afforded was thus seen as a valuable way to sustain children's attention; the mother of a seventh-grade boy in Colorado said: "[My children are] more interested in whatever they're reading because it's online. It catches their attention for some reason."

Some parents started noticing changes in their children's learning when they began using technology in the classroom. A mother of a third-grade girl in Arizona described how her daughter had benefited from the one-to-one laptop program and digital curriculum in her district in the following way:

> [She] improved a lot in math and reading ever since it [became] more interactive. If they're forgetful, they can just go back to it without an excuse. It's good because they can pause it and restart it and rewind it instead of just missing information, and they can go at their own pace.

While the two affordances are closely related, this parent's observation highlights how interactivity is distinct from personalization. She describes the ability to stop and start content as a learning enhancement distinct from whether the content is tailored to her child's needs. This is an example of technology's affordances for interactivity, but not for personalization. Parents generally viewed both kinds of affordances as having potential to meet children where they are, and therefore holding promise for increasing student engagement.

While parents saw potential in how drawn their children were to technology's interactive properties, they held critical views about the skills that children develop through these platforms. The father of a third-grade girl in Colorado, +for example, was concerned with potential learning losses:

> A lot of times when kids are learning on the Internet or computers, they lose the common sense of actually learning it, physically learning it in the books, and actually having to be taught that from somebody speaking to them.

Parents' discomfort with their children losing the "common sense" of traditional modes of instruction was compounded by the game-like presentation of many interactive learning applications, which closely resemble entertainment media. These reservations also explain why some parents felt that the interactive affordances of new technology would adversely affect learning for children who are easily distracted, as a mother of a third-grade boy in California described:

> Lo más negativo es que ellos quieren estar cada vez más tiempo en el internet. Eso provoca que paren de hacer tarea enfocados. Uno avanza cuando está enfocado . . . cuando le dedica al 100% a pensar en la tarea. Pero están [distraídos] . . . Entonces tengo que estar reenfocándolos.

> The most negative part of it is that they increasingly want to spend more time online. That keeps them from focusing on their homework. One makes progress when one stays focused . . . when one is dedicated to thinking 100% about homework. But they are [distracted] . . . So I need to spend time helping them refocus.

Interactivity can therefore hold promise or be a pitfall for learning, depending on how parents perceived their children's particular characteristics. Broader research on educational media, and in particular educational games, reflects this same ambiguity regarding the cognitive effects of interactive learning platforms (Clark, Tanner-Smith, & Killingsworth, 2016). A recent nationally representative survey of more than 1,500 parents of children ages 2–10 reveals that parents believe that 44 percent of their children's screen time is educational—and that children who use educational media weekly learn a lot about cognitive skills, reading or vocabulary, and math from television shows, online videos, computer games, and mobile games (Rideout, 2014). This same study, however, found differences based on race and ethnicity, with Hispanic parents being less likely to say their child has learned from educational media—suggesting a possible shortage of educational media content for Hispanic children. Because learning with technology requires a certain degree of self-direction, it can be difficult for users to determine the effectiveness of interactivity as an affordance (Buckingham & Willett, 2013; Delen, Liew, & Willson, 2014).

Skills Development

Finally, parents also recognized the skill-building opportunities that technology use affords to their children. They saw great value in their children developing digital skills (e.g., effective web searching, touch typing), and felt that introducing technology into classroom instruction and homework assignments in the elementary grades was crucial to their children developing those capabilities. Parents also viewed digital literacy as increasingly important for children's career options, educational opportunities, and social mobility; as one Arizona parent said, "The sooner they start, the more power [they have]." Reflecting a similar framing, a father of a seventh-grade girl in Arizona said:

> I think it's definitely a good idea, especially with the technology moving as rapidly as it is, that [schools] get them used to navigating through a computer and how to use certain search engines . . . [If children] learn how to work a computer when they're younger, once they get older it will be easier for them to get a job that's going to be in that realm.

Technology initiatives offered by the school districts were thus appreciated by many parents because they were, at a minimum, exposing their children to digital tools that could help them develop skills needed for pursuing professional career options. A mother of a fifth-grade boy in Arizona, for example, commented:

> Yo creo que tienen ventaja, porque en otros distritos no tienen este programa [de computadoras portátiles], entonces es una ventaja porque para el futuro va a ser bien indispensable la computadora y la tecnología.
>
> I think that they have an advantage, because other districts don't have this [laptop] program, so I think it's an advantage because in the future computers and technology will be indispensable.

Parents' conceptualizations of why and how digital literacy is important for their children's education varied. When pressed for examples of how technology enables children's access to opportunities, the majority of parents failed to articulate a concrete connection. The literature suggests that their uncertainty is well founded; Warschauer and Matuchniak (2010) find that when teachers assume that low-income students lack home broadband access, they spend a disproportionate amount of class time developing drill and practice skills, as opposed to the research projects and simulations that promote higher order skills that teachers more frequently emphasize in more affluent schools. And some parents, especially those who did not have experiences with technology during their own schooling, worried about the displacement of other important skillsets such as handwriting, spelling, and grammar.

Even more fundamentally, parents worried that technology in the classroom makes it easy for children to find the answers, but obviates their need to learn problem-solving processes. For example, recently arrived immigrant parents were particularly concerned that their children would either lose their existing capacities to solve math problems manually or that they would never develop those skills. For immigrant parents, these concerns often stemmed from the cultural value placed on "traditional" forms of schooling and learning that do not involve technology. A mother of a fifth-grade girl in Colorado said:

> Por un lado está bien porque hacen [la tarea]. Pero por otro lado ellos también [deberían] pensar cómo hacerla o cómo desenvolver sus habilidades. [Las computadoras] les están diciendo todo. Y si ellos pensaran cómo hacer [su tarea], pues estaría mejor.
>
> In a way, it's great because they do [their homework]. But on the other hand, they should also think about how to solve it or how to develop their skills. [Computers] give them everything. And it would be better if they had to think about how to do [their homework].

One mother in Arizona detailed how her seventh-grade daughter's teacher avoids these issues by mixing online and offline components through an educational program known as blended learning. Blended learning makes this mother feel comfortable with classroom tech use because digital assignments still require her daughter to demonstrate reasoning abilities in nondigital formats: "The science teacher is always having them research anything that they're working [on] online. . . . But [this] teacher has them write [their findings] down on paper and bring it [to school]. So that works." Perhaps the most important thing to consider about this mother's testimony is that her favorable impression of blended learning will make her more open to the possibilities of incorporating technologies into classroom learning.

Parents' Perspectives on Local Technology Initiatives

We also asked parents about specific technology initiatives that were being introduced in their districts. Parents' responses provide deeper insights into their hopes and misgivings about the influence of technology on their children's educational trajectories. Their responses also reveal missed opportunities for improving communication between parents and teachers about technology-driven changes to learning environments; we address these in the chapter's conclusion.

Sunnyside, Arizona

In November 2011, voters approved an $88 million bond to the Sunnyside Unified School District (SUSD) that included $27 million for a range of technology initiatives. The centerpiece of those initiatives was the district's one-to-one program that loans students in grades 4–12 a personal laptop to use in class and at home. Students were expected to carry the laptops with them every day, take care of them, and follow the district's guidelines for appropriate use. The district simultaneously adopted a digital curriculum that teachers were unevenly, but increasingly, using during class periods and to assign and collect homework.

Getting the bond on the ballot was motivated by the urgent need to improve historically low test scores and graduation rates. Pam Betten, director of Sunnyside's 1:1 program, saw the program's purpose as being even more far-reaching: "If our ultimate goal is to have kids be successful when they leave school, and the world outside is changing, then we have to do something systemic to prepare them for that change" (Digital Promise, 2014).

The Sunnyside interviews were conducted midway through the 2013–2014 school year, which meant all interviewed families had had one or more school laptops on loan for at least 6 months; many were into their second or third year of the program. Parents generally appreciated the district's efforts to not only foster tech literacy from an early age, but to also provide students with the necessary equipment. The program's launch coincided with an increased number of assignments requiring online research, as a mother of a fifth-grade boy noted:

> What they're requiring [now] is for them to do research . . . there's times low-income parents don't have a way of buying them a computer, a laptop or any other electronic. They're providing [laptops] for them and it's good. Because if the [schools] request so many things and they can help with some of it, that's an advantage.

However, families were acutely aware of their financial liability if the school laptops were damaged, lost, or even stolen. A parent meeting and a signed "technology contract" was required before a laptop was loaned out. This contract outlined specific rules and consequences, some of which made parents nervous. For example, the mother of a seventh-grade girl had established clear rules for when the school laptop could be used at home; her concerns were based on parents being financially liable for any repairs beyond normal wear-and-tear:

> Once they do their homework, [the computer is] turned off, [put] back in the case, and you don't get it until you go back to school. If they need to research something else, we have a home computer or their iPod. I think if you break it, you buy it. So if you're going to use something, use your own. This is borrowed . . . I don't ever use the school laptop.

It is striking how many parents were afraid to use the computers, considering that one of the goals of sending the laptops home was to encourage family use. The chilling effect of the contract language on parents' use was compounded by personal and community experiences. Many parents had either incurred out-of-pocket expenses related to the school laptops and others volunteered that they had heard about other families having costly experiences with damaged laptops and charging cables.

As a result, parents appeared hyperaware of the rules surrounding the 1:1 program, but knew little about how their children were actually using the laptops, and why doing so would enhance their learning. The contract language had emphasized the risks of this particular technology integration extensively, but had failed to adequately highlight its potential rewards. The inadvertent result was that, in many families, the school laptop was off limits for anyone other than the student it was assigned to, and its use limited to completing homework assignments—a much narrower usage than the program designers had intended.

Denver, Colorado

Interviews in Denver were conducted at the start of the 2014–2015 school year—the first year in which all Denver Public School (DPS) students (grades 3–12) would be required to take standardized math and language art tests online (Engdahl, 2013).[1] Feelings about how this move would affect students varied enormously among state and district leaders. Joyce Zurkowski, Executive Director of Assessment for Colorado's Department of Education, told the *Denver Post* that a partial prompt for the policy change was that "today's digital natives are comfortable using technology and are more engaged learning online" (Gorski, 2014).[2] In the same article, Brian Fuller, DPS' Executive Director of Accountability and Technology, clarified that even though the district uses technology in the classroom, they have not resolved digital inequality between students: "You have students . . . who have their own technology they use every day, to some students who may never touch technology except in the classroom" (Gorski, 2014).

The benefits and potential pitfalls of online testing—especially for students facing digital equity challenges—was hotly debated by administrators, but we found that few very parents had any idea that the shift was even taking place. Because our interview questions were the first time that most parents had heard about this substantial change, we were able to capture their immediate, if largely uninformed, reactions.

Most parents' early responses were positive, but their evaluations were driven by how much their children "liked" computers, or by a belief that testing would be more engaging this way. For example, when pressed to explain why she "definitely" thought her fourth-grade daughter's class would perform better in online tests than they would in paper-based tests, one mother said:

> I don't know—a computer is more entertaining than sitting there with a piece of paper and a pencil. I feel like that's why they learn quicker and pick up on things more, just because it's more entertaining for them . . . They could interact more. It doesn't feel like a test so much.

Other parents worried that a digital testing platform would either distract children, encourage them to rush through the test, or to think less carefully before answering —precisely because the format was more engaging for them. For example, the mother of a fourth-grade boy said, "I kind of think [their performance] is going to be a little worse because they'll just click on whatever they can and be done with it, versus actually seeing it [i.e., considering the question carefully]."

Others were concerned that the logistics of examination administration could adversely affect students in a variety of ways, from online testing being harder for teachers to supervise, to issues with the technology itself. The mother of a fourth-grade girl said:

> I feel that there's more space for error. If something goes wrong with the computer, something can go wrong with the scores. That doesn't mean the kid had a bad grade. But if something went wrong in the process, [the administrators] are going to think . . . all these kids got bad grades.

Finally, a few parents raised equity concerns with regard to how their children would fare against their more privileged counterparts in the district in an online testing environment. When asked about the initiative, a mother of a fifth-grade boy said:

> I don't like the idea so much. I think they're not going to perform as good. A lot of the students [in this school] barely have access to the Internet. Some of them barely have a computer, and then all of a sudden [the district] just throws them in [to online testing].

And when asked how her own son specifically would be affected by the change, she said:

> I do think it's going to make a difference. I think if my son would be getting, let's say for example, 70, he's probably going to get a 50, a 45 [in the online version]. Because he's not too sharp on computers and, if it's timed, it's going to make it even harder, more pressure on them.

Local Initiatives and Technological Affordances

Parents' reactions to digital technology initiatives in Arizona and Colorado reflected their more generalized hopes and concerns about how these devices and platforms might contribute to their children's learning experiences.

Colorado parents highlighted both the benefits (i.e., that testing could be more engaging), and the costs (i.e., that students will rush through the examination) of a digital testing environment's interactivity affordances. They discussed concerns about how their children's skills development in that environment would measure against what they imagined the skillsets of more privileged students in the district would be—and therefore, whether the testing would be measuring their tech-related skills rather than their relative mastery of curriculum content. Arizona parents expressed pride that the school district was helping their children to develop skills required to succeed in an increasingly digital world. They also felt that their children benefited from access to the personalized feedback from teachers that digital platforms made possible.

However, our findings also show that parents in both districts had limited understandings of why these initiatives were being implemented and had not been meaningfully included in district decisions to deploy them in the first place. In Colorado, most parents did not even know that the testing protocols were changing; in Arizona, the punitive tone of the contracts parents had to sign for the laptops made families more apprehensive and distant, instead of actively engaged.

Efforts to Extend Learning at Home with Technology

Our final research question shifted our analytical focus from what parents thought of schools' technology integration efforts, to what parents did to support and extend children's formal learning at home. Parents reported helping with homework whenever possible, taking their children to the library for research materials or to use the computers, and bringing technology into their homes to enhance academic activities. Both immigrant and US-born parents in our sample (the latter group usually being children of immigrants themselves) were deeply committed to their children making the most of the considerable opportunities available to them by virtue of attending school in the United States. The mother of a fourth-grade girl in Colorado echoed what we heard from many other parents, saying:

> Aquí tienen muchas oportunidades, tanto para el estudio como para tener un mejor futuro . . . Yo les digo que este es el trabajo de ellos, estudiar. Esa es la herencia que nosotros como padres les vamos a dejar.
>
> They have a lot of opportunities here, ranging from education to having a better future . . . I tell them that this is their duty, to study. That's out inheritance, as parents, for them.

Almost uniformly, interviewed parents considered their children's access to digital technologies and the Internet crucial to their educational trajectories. It took considerable ingenuity for these parents, all of whom were raising children who qualified for subsidized school meals, to afford these technologies. Parents talked about waiting for tax returns (through the Earned Income Tax Credit for working poor families), combining children's birthday and Christmas presents to purchase one shared device, and forgoing needed car repairs and items that they needed themselves. After vital expenses like rent and electricity, parents prioritized paying for Internet access before paying other bills.

Parents who were unable to provide consistent home Internet connectivity felt frustrated by what they saw as escalating academic demands to do so, as the mother of a fifth-grade girl in Arizona described: "It used to be where on a daily basis she had homework on her laptop. That was a little stressful, because sometimes it was hard for me to give her Internet, for me to provide that." Similarly, the mother of a first-grade girl in Arizona discussed her own challenges:

> A veces es difícil, pero prefiero no pagar otras cosas que [no pagar] el Internet por las tareas. Antes, lo cortaban, y durábamos tres meses para volverlo a pagar. Ahora no, porque si no lo tengo, ¿cómo le voy a ayudar para las tareas?
>
> Sometimes it's hard, but I prefer not to pay for other things than [not to do so] for the Internet, because of homework. They used to disconnect our service before, and it would take us three months to pay for it again. That's not the case anymore, because if I don't have it, how will I help her with homework?

The sacrifices that parents described demonstrate their deep commitment to ensuring that their children can access digital leaning opportunities—even though, as we have discussed in the prior sections, they did not always fully understand what those opportunities were.

Beyond financial challenges, many parents were keenly aware that their own limited capabilities with technology prevented them from fully supporting their children's learning experiences at home. Such difficulties were most pronounced among parents who were immigrants, had limited English proficiency, and/or had not completed their schooling in the United States, as reflected by an immigrant mother with a fourth-grade son in Arizona, who said,

> Como yo no le sé mover [a la computadora], no sé si terminaron [la tarea] o no.
>
> Since I don't know how to use [the computer], I can't even tell whether they finished [their homework.]

Parents who were less proficient with technology were also more likely to say that they found the district's decisions to introduce technology into children's homework routines challenging. In some cases, parents felt that schools requiring technology use at home conflicted with their parenting styles, and particularly with regard to how children should spend their time outside school. When pressed to elaborate, this mother explained why she did not appreciate teachers encouraging young students' technology use at home without first consulting the parents:

> Yo al no leer y no escribir, yo no me doy cuenta de lo que está pasando. Muchas vecinas de aquí no estamos de acuerdo que les dieran laptops tan chiquitos . . . Porque no ponen atención mas que cómo estar en la escuela con las laptops. Vienen y se meten mucho.
>
> Since I can't read or write, I can't really tell what's happening. My neighbors and I do not agree with the school's decision to provide younger kids with laptops . . . because all they want to do now is finish school work in their laptops. They use them way too much.

Teachers' Support for Extending Learning at Home with Technology

On the other hand, parents who had more experience with digital devices highlighted how important teacher recommendations for specific apps, programs, and online games were to them. Usually, these recommendations either served a remedial function in subject areas where a student was weak, or provided opportunities to extend and deepen learning in areas where their child was especially strong. A mother of a fourth-grade girl in California described how her daughter's "reading level has gone up dramatically," partially due to the "websites that [her teachers] gave her so she could practice at home." Across our study sites, parents felt they had good rapport with their children's teachers. They were also generally willing to implement teachers' suggestions for devices, websites, and programs that their children could benefit from. We also found that parents who were familiar with digital platforms felt more comfortable encouraging their children to engage with educational technology, confirming a link that Lauricella et al. (2016) noted in a separate study.

Whether teachers' recommendations helped a student catch up or move ahead, parents trusted them as experts on educational media. A mother of a fourth-grade girl in Arizona appreciated her daughter's teacher recognizing when and how her daughter needed extra support outside of the classroom: "[Her teacher] will send reference websites that would help [my child get] better with math, which is what she's been struggling with. He'll do it more when she needs the reference and she's a little behind." Parents tended to view teachers' recommendations as signals that they (a) really knew the child's individual needs, and (b) shared parents' own deep investments in children's growth and success. These recommendations also familiarized parents with the ways that well-curated educational media can strengthen specific skills for their children. In turn, those experiences have the potential to mitigate parental uneasiness or confusion about how technology is changing their children's learning.

Making and maintaining these kinds of constructive parent–teacher relationships is dependent, however, on teachers taking initiative to seek out local resources and make recommendations that are responsive to parents' needs. In the absence of institutional supports, these are tenuous connections, because parents are dependent on the goodwill of individual teachers going beyond the call of duty, a dynamic that can change from one school year to the next (Katz, 2014; Small, 2010; Valenzuela, 1999).

Actionable Recommendations

If well-intentioned technology initiatives are not realizing their full potential to expand learning opportunities for low-income students, what can we do differently? Our goal in this chapter was to assess how parents are interpreting and responding to the increasing integration of technology into their children's formal learning. In this final section, we present practical for educators to increase parental engagement with technology initiatives, as an important step toward supporting children's learning in the digital age.

Our most fundamental recommendation for educators is to consider technology as a tool—not a replacement—for building strong relationships between home and school. Robust connections between parents and teachers have always benefited students, and technology offers exciting possibilities for new ways to stay in contact, exchange information, flag learning concerns, and so forth. But, as we have argued elsewhere (Katz, Levine, & Gonzalez, 2015), technology itself cannot resolve disparities in educational opportunities. Over-prioritizing technology can hurt relationships; the Arizona district profiled above is a cautionary tale in this respect. Their focus on protecting the laptops from damage—coupled with failing to consider parents' discomfort with being compelled to assume financial responsibility for a device, especially when the district had inadequately explained its learning value—strained relationships with parents in unintended ways. Here are some practical ways to stay focused on maintaining and improving parent–teacher relationships when introducing technology into the classroom.

1. *Treat parents as partners.* We found that parents already consider technology use critical for children's academic success and make considerable sacrifices to make it available to their children. Involving parents from the very start in designing and implementing technology initiatives can create a shared sense of ownership in those pedagogical changes. Partnering with parents also helps schools, by bringing to light potential issues with initiatives before implementation, or ways to improve them. In our California study site, the district decided to partner with interviewed parents to develop a smartphone application for district parents. Levinson (2014) profiled this collaborative process and how the district ultimately ended up with a tool that improved home–school communication and increased parents' trust in district initiatives with technology.
2. *Evaluate current tech initiatives from parents' perspectives.* Our findings show that parents have numerous (mis)perceptions about what technology is doing for their children's learning. Addressing parents' concerns is critical to making existing programs successful. Even though interviewed parents considered technology use crucial for developing children's twenty-first century skills, they worried that technology use would disrupt how and what children learn. These fears were especially prominent among parents who had limited experience with technology themselves. Teachers can counter these concerns by walking parents through how technology is used in the classroom to address worries about technology "taking away from teacher time," as a mother of a sixth-grade boy in Colorado said. Furthermore, modeling productive engagement with technology for learning can be especially helpful for parents who are less familiar with, and anxious about using, these devices with their children.
3. *In developing new initiatives, get crystal clear on program goals.* We observed multiple technology initiatives being implemented in the three districts where we conducted interviews. It was not always clear what learning gains these new programs were intended to accomplish. Clear curriculum goals and well-developed rationales for why new devices and platforms provide affordances for learning that traditional forms of instruction do not, is crucial for successful implementation. For program objectives to be clear to parents, they have to first be clear to teachers; prior research shows that teachers often also lack clarity in this regard (Pressey, 2013; Zielezinski, 2016).
4. *Only innovate as quickly as families can keep up.* As children proceed through school, parents who have limited education, English proficiency, or experience with the US educational system become less confident in their abilities

to guide their children's schoolwork. In Colorado and Arizona, we found that rapid adoption of digital homework submission had inadvertently deepened these challenges; parents who had previously been able to help students with math homework in traditional formats now struggled to help them with the same content when it had to be completed online. Adopting new programs or devices should not come at the expense of increasing intergenerational divides; leaving parents behind diminishes their abilities to support their children's learning, which ultimately disadvantages students' academic advancement (also see Katz & Levine, 2015).

5. *Evaluate and support connectivity at home.* Classroom technology initiatives are most likely to be effective if families can support and extend those learning experiences at home. Our national survey revealed that while 94 percent of lower-income families have an Internet connection, more than half are "under-connected" in some way, including service interruptions, slow connection speeds, and not having enough time online (Rideout & Katz, 2016). All districts should evaluate families' home connectivity and work with them to identify available low-cost connectivity options, or to lobby telecommunications companies to make such programs available. But, meaningful connectivity is about more than infrastructure. Our survey findings show that in the majority of families, parents help children, children help parents, and siblings help each other to learn with, and through, technology. Teacher recommendations to high-quality educational content and games are a way to validate existing family joint media engagement practices, and to enable them to extend those activities in ways that better support students' formal learning experiences.
6. *Support teachers to support families.* Pressey (2013) overviews five surveys of teachers, conducted by the Gates Foundation, Pew Center, Joan Ganz Cooney Center, Common Sense Media, and PBS. Across surveys, teachers' personal comfort with technology was a primary barrier to classroom use. Our findings reveal that parents considered teachers as trusted resources for educational media, and that these recommendations were signals to parents that teachers were invested in providing children with the personalized tools they need to learn best. As we noted in the chapter, teachers provided this assistance without district supports for their efforts; pooling resources so that each teacher does not have to learn the digital landscape themselves could enable more educators to effectively guide parents without unnecessarily adding to their workload.

Notes

1. Since a bond measure in the district had paid for testing devices in all schools, DPS was not allowing students to opt out of the online format, with the exception of students with disabilities or individualized education plans (Gorski, 2014).

2. The notion that young people are "digital natives" has been largely discounted by researchers, who feel this term obscures the considerable differences between more and less socially privileged schoolchildren (see Katz, 2016).

References

Baym, N. (2010). *Personal connections in the digital age.* London: Polity Press.

Brown, A., & Patten, E. (2013). *Hispanics of Mexican origin in the United States, 2011.* Pew Research Hispanic Trends Project. Washington, DC: Pew Research Center. Retrieved from www.pewhispanic.org/2013/06/19/hispanics-of-mexican-origin-in-the-united-states-2011/

Buckingham, D., & Willett, R. (2013). *Digital generations: Children, young people, and the new media.* New York: Routledge.

Child Trends. (2014). *Immigrant children.* Retrieved from www.childtrends.org/wp-content/uploads/2012/07/110_appendix1.pdf

Clark, D. B., Tanner-Smith, E. E., & Killingsworth, S. S. (2016). Digital games, design, and learning: A systematic review and meta-analysis. *Review of Educational Research, 86*(1), 79–122.

Cuban, L. (2016). *Draining the "semantic swamp" of personalized learning.* Retrieved from https://larrycuban.wordpress.com

Darling-Hammond, L., Zielezinski, M. B., & Goldman, S. (2014). *Using technology to support at-risk students' learning.* Stanford, CA: Alliance for Excellent Education and Stanford Center for Opportunity Policy in Education.

Delen, E., Liew, J., & Willson, V. (2014). Effects of interactivity and instructional scaffolding on learning: Self-regulation in online video-based environments. *Computers & Education, 78,* 312–320.

Digital Promise. (2014). *Bridging the digital divide for low-income students.* Retrieved from http://digitalpromise.org/2014/04/07/11-learning-24–7-at-sunnyside-unified-school-district/

Engdahl, T. (2013). Ready or not, online tests coming to Colorado. Retrieved from www.chalkbeat.org/posts/co/2013/08/20/ready-or-not-online-tests-coming-to-colorado/#.V3Vz8qJp5zw

Gorski, E. (2014). Colorado school districts debate move to online state tests. *Denver Post.* Retrieved from www.denverpost.com/2014/12/29/colorado-school-districts-debate-move-to-online-state-tests/

Johnson, J., Kominski, R., Smith, K., & Tillman, P. (2005). Changes in the lives of U.S. children: 1990–2000 (Working Paper No. 78). Washington, DC: Population Division, U.S. Census Bureau.

Katz, V. S. (2014). *Kids in the middle: How children of immigrants negotiate community interactions for their families.* New Brunswick, NJ: Rutgers University Press.

Katz, V. S. (2016). When children are their families' digital links. *Parenting for a Digital Future.* The London School of Economics and Political Science. Retrieved from http://blogs.lse.ac.uk/parenting4digitalfuture/2016/03/07/when-children-are-families-digital-links/

Katz, V. S., & Levine, M. H. (2015). *Connecting to learn: Promoting digital equity for America's Hispanic families.* New York: Joan Ganz Cooney Center at Sesame Workshop. Retrieved from www.joanganzcooneycenter.org/publication/connecting-to-learn-promoting-digital-equity-for-americas-hispanic-families/

Katz, V. S., Levine, M.H., & Gonzalez, C. (2015). Family partnerships are key to digital equity. *Education Week*. Retrieved from http://bit.ly/1UWA0o0

Lauricella, A. R., Cingel, D. P., Beaudoin-Ryan, L., Robb, M. B., Saphir, M., & Wartella, E. A. (2016). *The Common Sense Census: Plugged-in parents of tweens and teens*. San Francisco, CA: Common Sense Media. Retrieved from www.commonsensemedia.org/sites/default/files/uploads/research/common-sense-parent-census_whitepaper_new-for-web.pdf

Levinson, A. M. (2014). *Tapping In: Understanding how Hispanic-Latino immigrant families engage and learn with broadcast and digital media*. Doctoral dissertation, Stanford Digital Repository. Retrieved from https://purl.stanford.edu/bb550sh8053

Livingstone, S. (2002). *Young people and new media*. Thousand Oaks, CA: Sage.

Lopez, M., & Velasco, G. (2011, September 28). Childhood poverty among Hispanics sets record, leads nation: The toll of the great recession. Washington, DC: The Pew Hispanic Center. Retrieved from www.pewhispanic.org/2011/09/28/childhood-poverty-among-hispanics-sets-record-leads-nation/

McClure, E. R., Guernsey, L., Clements, D. H., Bales, S. N., Nichols, J., Kendall-Taylor, N., & Levine, M. H. (2017). *STEM starts early: Grounding science, technology, engineering, and math education in early childhood*. New York: The Joan Ganz Cooney Center at Sesame Workshop.

Nathanson, A. (2015). Media and the family: Reflections and future directions. *Journal of Children and Media, 9*(1), 133–139.

Pressey, B. (2013). *Comparative analysis of national teacher surveys*. New York: The Joan Ganz Cooney Center at Sesame Workshop. Retrieved from www.joanganzcooneycenter.org/wp-content/uploads/2013/10/jgcc_teacher_survey_analysis_final.pdf

Rideout, V. J. (2014). *Learning at home: Families' educational media use in America*. A report of the Families and Media Project. New York: The Joan Ganz Cooney Center at Sesame Workshop.

Rideout, V. J., & Katz, V. S. (2016). *Opportunity for all? Technology and learning in lower-income families*. New York: Joan Ganz Cooney Center at Sesame Workshop.

Small, M. (2010). *Unanticipated gains: Origins of network inequality in everyday life*. Oxford: Oxford University Press.

Tripp, L. M. (2011). "The computer is not for you to be looking around, it is for schoolwork": Challenges for digital inclusion as Latino immigrant families negotiate children's access to the Internet. *New Media & Society, 13*, 552–567.

U.S. Department of Education. (2017). *Reimagining the role of technology in education: 2017 National education technology plan update*. Washington, D.C.: Office of Educational Technology.

Valenzuela, A. (1999). *Subtractive schooling: U.S.-Mexican youth and the politics of caring*. Albany, NY: State University of New York Press.

Valkenburg, P. M., Krcmar, M., Peeters, A. L., & Marseille, N. M. (1999). Developing a scale to assess three styles of television mediation: Instructive mediation, restrictive mediation, and social coviewing. *Journal of Broadcasting and Electronic Media, 43*(1), 52–67.

Warschauer, M., & Matuchniak, T. (2010). New technology and digital worlds: Analyzing evidence of equity in access, use, and outcomes. *Review of Research in Education, 34*(1), 179–225.

Zheng, B., Warschauer, M., Lin, C. H., & Chang, C. (2016). Learning in one-to-one laptop environments: A meta-analysis and research synthesis. *Review of Educational Research, 86*(4), 1052–1084.

Zielezinski, M. B. (2016). What a decade of education research tells us about technology in the hands of underserved students. *EdSurge*. Retrieved from www.edsurge.com/news/2016-05-19-what-a-decade-of-education-research-tells-us-about-technology-in-the-hands-of-underserved-students

7

WHAT MAKES MEDIA EDUCATIONAL?

Learning from Latino Parents and Children

Sinem Siyahhan and June Lee

Since the 1960s, communication and education researchers and media designers have been interested in developing educational media for children and evaluating its impact (Schramm, Lyle, & Parker, 1961). While earlier efforts focused on educational content delivered through radio, books, and television, there has been an exponential growth in educational digital media production in the last two decades, along with the increasing ownership of computers, gaming consoles, cell phones, and tablets among families in the United States (Common Sense Media, 2013, 2015; Ito, 2009). At the same time, our understanding of learning has shifted from an "acquisition" model of learning, which focuses on the delivery of knowledge, to a "participation" model of learning, which emphasizes co-construction of knowledge (Jenkins, Clinton, Purushotma, Robison, & Weigel, 2006). This shift has blurred the lines of entertainment and educational media as well as challenged the very definition of educational media by foregrounding the context of media use (who uses media with whom when and how) as opposed to the content of media.

Let us demonstrate the blurring lines of entertainment and educational media with an example from video games. *Math Blaster*, a series of video games that teach children basic math skills such as addition, subtraction, multiplication, and division, is intentionally designed and marketed as educational by the producers of the series and is widely used in schools. On the other hand, the popular sandbox game *Minecraft*, where players mine for resources and craft tools and structures in a virtual world, is often considered entertaining but not necessarily educational. The game is neither intentionally designed nor marketed as an educational product such as *Math Blaster*. The game has no overt ties to academic content addressed in schools, although children often develop design and building skills, as well as enhance their problem-solving abilities and creativity as they collaborate with others playing *Minecraft* (Duncan, 2011). Despite its popularity, or perhaps because of it, the game has raised concerns among many parents and teachers who question its value. The extensive news coverage of *Minecraft* and how it can support learning suggests the need to convince skeptics of its educational benefits for children (e.g., Thompson, 2016). While authors such as Thompson (2016) offer detailed accounts of the potential of *Minecraft* game play for learning, *Minecraft: Education Edition* (MinecraftEdu), an educational version of the original game, was created by teachers for classroom use to "fine tune" the game for use in school and to control children's gameplay.

Furthermore, the cultural model of educational media for children in the United States is shaped by White middle-class values and norms around "good parenting" (Ito, 2009). Parents are expected to intentionally create a variety of opportunities for children to succeed academically and develop a competitive edge later in life. Enrichment activities like reading to children before bed, enrolling children in after school activities, and setting up play dates are a few examples of what "good" parents do to promote their children's academic achievement (Lareau, 2003). Within this value system, media is another tool parents can use to cultivate their children's trajectory of academic and life success (Buckingham & Scanlon, 2001; Nixon, 1998). As such, the content delivered to children through media is privileged over the context of children's media use. Any medium that delivers content that is closely aligned with school is labeled as "educational" since they keep children on the path to school and life success. The less obvious the alignment between the content of a medium and school, the more a medium is considered "entertaining," and thus perceived as a distraction from academic learning and a waste of time for children.

Although Latinos are the largest and fastest growing minority ethnic group in the United States and account for more than 40 percent of student enrollments in some states (Fry & Gonzales, 2008; US Census Bureau, 2012), we know little, if any, about how Latino families make sense of and navigate the complex landscape of educational media. In this chapter, we focus on the perceptions, values, and experiences of Latino parents and children regarding television and video games—the two most frequently consumed media among children and youth (Rideout, Foehr, & Roberts, 2010). Research suggests that Latino children are less likely to use technology for educational purposes, particularly in Spanish-speaking households (Fuller, Lizzarago, & Gray, 2015). In what follows, we first present quantitative data from the national survey of Latino parents about their perceptions of their children's use of educational media (Appendix, Study 1). We then share interviews conducted with 16 predominantly low-income Mexican American mothers and children (ages 4 through 17) to understand how they define educational media in the context of television and video games (Appendix, Study 3).

Our goal is to illuminate what Latino parents and children think of as "educational" media. By augmenting survey data with rich interviews with parents and children, we also address the limitations of survey research that often, and most likely unintentionally, perpetuates views of Latino and low-income families as "deficient" when it comes to educational media use. Specifically, we explore the following questions in this chapter: (1) How do parents perceive television shows and video games their children consume? (2) What are the similarities and differences between the way parents view television shows versus video games? (3) How are children's perceptions of television shows and video games similar or different from their parents?

Background

In her recent book, *Engineering Play*, Mimi Ito (2009) traces the emergence of "educational media" back to books, the oldest media children consume. She argues that books written for children were didactic, religious, and moralistic in their approach until the mid-nineteenth century. However, with the incorporation of playfulness and imagination in books like *Alice in Wonderland*, the idea that books can not only educate but also entertain children has gradually gained momentum and seeded the idea for what we now refer to as *edutainment*. Similarly, although early computer programs focused on drill-and-practice of academic content, computer software for children incorporated visuals, narratives, and playfulness by the late 1970s and early 1980s.

By the late 1990s, the edutainment media sector had grown its market share significantly (Shuler, 2012). However, it also became more age-segregated with a focus on early childhood and school readiness to address the concerns of White middle-class parents about learning and achievement in school (Ito, 2009). The media landscape of the home at the time typically involved a television, a VCR, video game equipment, and a computer (Woodard & Gridina, 2000). The digital divide between high- and low-income families also started to emerge during this time. Although low-income families tended to own a television and video game equipment, they were less likely to own a computer or have access to the Internet (ibid), a trend that persists to this day (Common Sense Media, 2013).

What was considered the "edutainment era" was short lived. Although the demand for children's television shows continued to grow, the market share of educational software and video games plummeted in the early 2000s. Since then, the video games industry has focused its attention on producing video games for entertainment purposes, becoming a business that generates more than 20 billion dollars in revenue annually (Entertainment Software Association, 2016). However, with the ubiquity of mobile apps, edutainment media is making a comeback. At the time this chapter was written, a quick search of the "education" category in the App Store identified 5,261 apps. Many of these apps focused on school-related content such as language learning, reading, and math. That said, educational media continues to make up a small portion of the market compared to entertainment media (Shuler, 2012).

Negative Perceptions of Entertainment Media

In the United States, the relationship between entertainment and education is often perceived as mutually exclusive: a television show or video game that is entertaining cannot be educational at the same time. Public discourse around children's media use overemphasizes the need for parents to take responsibility for setting rules, restricting access, and carefully monitoring their children around media. The American Academy of Pediatrics (AAP), an organization that parents rely on for parenting recommendations around media, provides guidelines for "a healthy media diet" for families (AAP, 2016), perpetuating the need for parents to exercise restrictive parenting styles around their children's media use. Such an approach to children's media use, particularly around television and video games, is hardly new.

Since its inception, television has been the primary medium children consume at home (Common Sense Media, 2013), exceeding other digital and nondigital media such as books and video games. The effects of television viewing on children have been a concern among parents, educators, researchers, and policy makers for as long as television has existed (Fisch & Truglio, 2001). In 1949, the Columbia Broadcasting System (CBS) sponsored Rutgers University faculty to conduct one of the first studies on the effects of television (Riley, Cantwell, & Ruttiger, 1949). Although the study found positive social effects of television watching for families, throughout the following decade many research studies focused on the negative effects of television watching on children (Wartella & Reeves, 1985). Since the 1950s, many congressional hearings and public debates were held regarding the adverse effects of television on children, and much advocacy work was aimed at regulating children's television. For instance, the Children's Television Act in 1990 was intended to increase the amount of educational children's programming on television. The Telecommunications Act in 1996 required the installation of electronic monitoring on television sets for parents to block inappropriate content for their children. These developments reinforced the idea that television content should be created specifically to optimize positive effects for children, and that parents should take an active role in protecting children from potentially detrimental or inappropriate content. Throughout the decades, the sharper distinction between educational and entertainment television has informed the view of the public about what counts as educational.

Similarly, public perception of commercial video games has been negative for many decades (Squire, 2002). Educators typically did not consider video gaming as an opportunity for learning unless the games had clear ties to academic content (Squire, 2003). A few educational video games, such as *Reader Rabbit*, *Math Blaster*, and *Oregon Trail*, entered the classroom in the 1980s, along with increased interest in computers as instructional tools. However, with the end of the "edutainment" era in the early 2000s, the presence of video games in the classroom faded. Although some commercial video games such as *Sim City* and *Civilization* piqued the interest of educators, they never made it into the classroom at scale.

Like television, the content of video games was the primary basis for restricting its use among children. In response to the violent and sexual content of video games, the Entertainment Software Rating Board (ESRB) adopted an age and content rating system to categorize video games in 1994 to restrict their purchase and access by minors (Chakraborty & Chakraborty, 2015). This rating system is one of the resources parents use to decide whether a video game is appropriate for their children.

Since the mid-2000s, there has been an exponential growth in the number of studies that investigate how learning occurs around commercial video games. Research suggests that children and youth develop problem-solving, systems thinking, spatial reasoning, literacy, and leadership skills while playing video games, including those with violent content (Gee, 2003; Green, Li, & Bavelier, 2010; Lisk, Kaplancali, & Riggio, 2012; Steinkuehler, 2004). Despite the growing evidence that entertainment media such as video games can promote children's learning, many parents associate controlling media or unplugging as "good parenting" in the United States (Ito, 2009). However, there are socioeconomic and ethnic differences with respect to how much parents restrict their children's media consumption. For instance, low-income Latino children watch television more than their upper-class White peers (Rideout, Lauricella, & Wartella, 2011). Similarly, Latino children use mobile technology more than White children (ibid). These findings combined with the messages parents receive from organizations like AAP position low-income Latino parents as "deficient" compared to middle-class White parents and other parents who may share different sets of norms and values around parenting and media.

The Relationship between Media, Technology, and Learning

Many educators and scholars believe that media of high quality and created with an educational focus may help to "level the playing field" and enhance underprivileged children's ability to succeed in school. As a case in point, the last 30 years of research on *Sesame Street* suggests a positive relationship between the amount of time that children 3–5 years of age watched the show and how much they learned about shapes, colors, and body parts. These findings were consistent across multiple studies in different countries (Fisch & Truglio, 2001). However, the role of digital media in children's learning and academic attainment continues to be a controversial topic in the field of education (Clark, 2001; Tamim, Bernard, Borokhovski, Abrami, & Schmid, 2011). The debate stems from the fact that conducting experimental studies around media effects on learning is notoriously hard. A small number of experimental studies and meta-analyses in this area suggest there are little or no effects of media on children's learning and educational outcomes (Tamim et. al., 2011). The lack of experimental studies makes it difficult to draw conclusions about causal links between media and children's educational outcomes.

According to Clark (2001), the teaching or instructional method accounts for learning gains with media, not the media itself. For example, a child who plays games on *Math Blaster* learn fractions because of the feedback they receive about their progress solving math problems as opposed to unique characteristics of the game (e.g., visuals, narrative, rules, etc.). Children who receive feedback from a teacher about their progress in solving the math problems would gain the same amount of knowledge because providing feedback to learners is an effective teaching strategy regardless of the medium through which it is delivered. More recently, scholars have suggested that it is important to understand *how* media supports learning, calling for a shift in focus from the delivery of content to understanding the context in which learning takes place with media (Kozma, 1994; Reiser, 2001). Their argument is that people do not mindlessly absorb information from the environment but are active agents in making sense of the world together with others across different situations. Therefore, rather than trying to understand whether children learn more from watching *Sesame Street* versus reading a book, researchers need to explore how different learners engage with the various affordances of these two media across time and space to optimize learning.

Recent studies that investigate the context of learning inform a more nuanced understanding of the relationship between media and education by highlighting when, how, and with whom children learn around media. For instance, research on *Sesame Street* suggests that children learn more when they watch the show with their parents who engage them in conversations and help them make sense of the information (Fisch, 2014). Similarly, most children's video gaming involves socializing with peers and siblings with whom they engage in collaborative problem solving while playing video games (Lenhart et al., 2008; Stevens, Satwicz, & McCarthy, 2008). The location of media devices such as television, computer, and handheld devices in the home mediate what, how much, and with whom children consume media, and in what ways this consumption supports learning (Plowman, McPake, & Stephen, 2008; Siyahhan & Gee, 2016; Takeuchi & Stevens, 2011). Despite growing research on the affordances of media for learning, we know little about how parents and children conceptualize the relationship between media, technology, and learning.

Generations, Media Use, and Changes in Our Understanding of Learning

Generations are often defined by the media technologies they use while growing up (Vittadini, Siibak, Reifova, & Bilandzic, 2013) because they create common practices, experiences, and understandings among people of the same generation and promote the construction of a shared identity (Buckingham, 2006). The amount of time children spend consuming media, as well as the number of media technologies available to them, increased dramatically over the last several decades (Gutnick, Robb, Takeuchi, & Kotler, 2010). Research suggests that there are differences between generations with respect to the kinds of media technologies they use and how they use them (Zickuhr, 2011).

Many have argued that Millennials or the Net Generation (those who are born roughly after 1982) approach media and learning that is fundamentally different than their parents (Prensky, 2001; Thomas & Brown, 2011). The Internet and digital devices provide opportunities for youth to connect with others and expand their knowledge, skills, and interests in ways that were not possible before (ibid). Furthermore, they engage youth in self-directed learning and help them develop lifelong learning habits such as persistence, resilience, and adaptability that one needs to develop not just for school, but also for life (Fisher, 2001). Thus, in the new media landscape children are not passive absorbers of information but active participants in learning.

For instance, in *Minecraft*, children first exercise self-directed learning by pursuing a goal and a challenge of their choosing in the open world of the game. If they play the game with friends, children need to negotiate the decision of what to build in the game with others. They can watch YouTube videos of other people building in *Minecraft* to get inspired. Building in the game takes time and patience as well as learning through trial-and-error. When confronted with a challenge in the game, children can post a question on a discussion board for *Minecraft* players, ask a friend, or another player online. Although children's experiences with and around media may not fit within the traditional acquisition model of teaching and learning, it is unclear if and how their views of what makes media educational are different than their parents.

Data Collection and Analysis

Data for this chapter comes from two different studies: (1) a nationally representative online survey using probability-based sampling, and (2) a small sample field study (see Studies 1 and 3 in the Appendix for details). On the national survey, parents were asked to rate how educational they found the following television shows and video games: *Sesame Street, Dora the Explorer, Mickey Mouse Clubhouse, SpongeBob SquarePants, Angry Birds, Minecraft*, and *Just Dance*. Parents rated these television shows and video games using a 5-point Likert scale as: (1) very educational, (2) somewhat educational, (3) not too educational, (4) not at all educational, and (5) not familiar enough (to evaluate). In this chapter, we refer only to the Latino parents' responses to this question (n = 682). Simple frequencies, percentages, and means were calculated for survey responses.

The field study participants consisted of 16 Mexican-American mothers who had at least one child between the ages of 4 and 6 years old, and at least one child between the ages of 7 and 18 years old living at home. We interviewed mothers and children separately about their perceptions of these television shows and video games, as well as about what makes media educational more broadly. Interviews were conducted at families' homes and lasted about 30–45 minutes.

For our analysis, we initially used open coding to identify themes across the data. We then categorized these themes into higher level codes. Our primary focus was on the nature of the beliefs that we found in the data as opposed to how often these beliefs were expressed. However, we do identify the relative frequency that different beliefs were articulated in our discussion of findings below. All names used with direct quotes are pseudonyms.

Findings

We will begin with a discussion of parent's perceptions of popular television shows, followed by their perceptions of popular video games. We then move to a discussion of children's beliefs about educational media in general.

Parents' Perceptions of Popular Television Shows

Many of the Latino parents in our research were very familiar with popular television shows. On the online survey, 91 percent of Latino parents were familiar with *Mickey Mouse Clubhouse*, 95 percent were familiar with *SpongeBob SquarePants*, 97 percent were familiar with *Sesame Street*, and 98 percent were familiar with *Dora the Explorer*. All parents whom we interviewed were also familiar with these televisions shows.

On the online survey and during the interviews, the majority of parents reported that they perceived *Sesame Street* and *Dora the Explorer* "very educational" and "somewhat educational" for their young children (see Figures 7.1 and 7.2). However, the interviews revealed that parents valued these two shows for different reasons. Many parents perceived *Dora the Explorer* as educational because it reinforced bilingualism and provided opportunities for dual language immersion. It was important for parents who themselves spoke primarily Spanish that their young children became fluent both in English and Spanish. They perceived the show as a vehicle for accomplishing this goal that they set for their children. Camila, aged 39, explained:

> It [*Dora the Explorer*] taught them English because with they speak solely in Spanish. All Spanish in the household, so when they started going to school—it's the fact that it is bilingual, you know. That it switches from English to Spanish, I really liked it for them to watch something like that.

On the one hand, parents who moved to the United States as adults and spoke primarily Spanish were concerned about their children falling behind their peers in school with respect to reading, writing, and speaking English. On the other hand, they valued their children maintaining strong connections to their homeland and Mexican culture through language. By the same token, parents perceived Mexican telenovelas (soap operas) as educational for their young and older

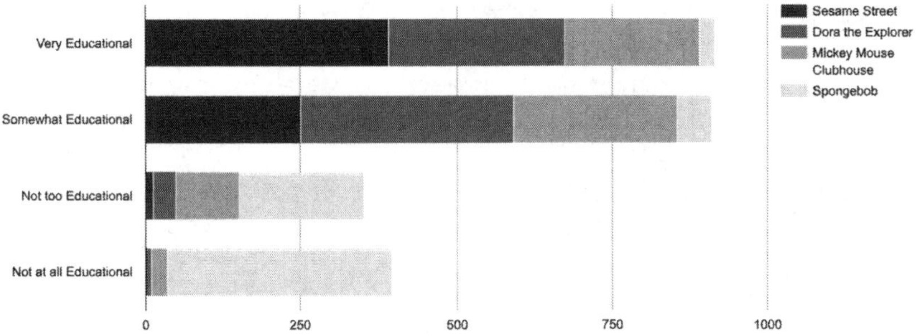

FIGURE 7.1 Parents' reports of *Sesame Street, Dora the Explorer, Mickey Mouse Clubhouse*, and *SpongeBob SquarePants* on the national survey

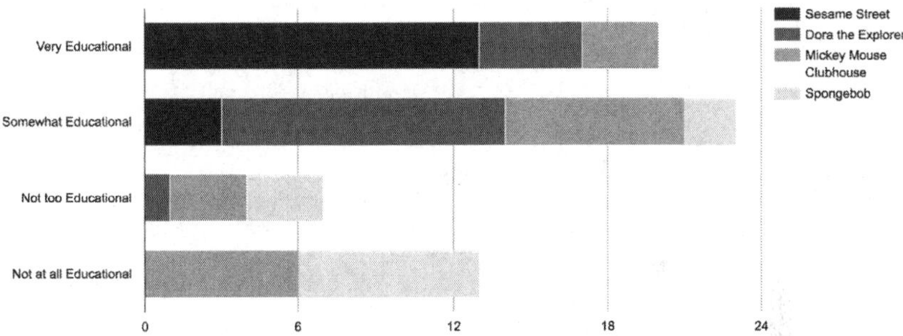

FIGURE 7.2 Parents' reports of *Sesame Street, Dora the Explorer, Mickey Mouse Clubhouse*, and *SpongeBob SquarePants* during interviews

children. They watched telenovelas together with their children to mutually reinforce cultural and familial ties (also see Chapter 9 in this volume). Similarly, parents perceived the popular Mexican sitcom *El Chavo Del Ocho*, broadcast between 1971 and 1980, as educational. They found episodes of the show on YouTube for their children to watch as a means of maintaining cultural and generational connections—parents watched the show while growing up and wanted to share it with their children.

Another television show many parents watched while growing up was *Sesame Street*. They drew upon their own learning experiences and memories of the show when evaluating its educational value for their children. They believed *Sesame Street* helped their children learn school-related content and skills important during early childhood. Parents most frequently reported that children learned colors, shapes, letters, and counting from *Sesame Street*. Although parents perceived *Dora the Explorer* as educational for its connection to their own culture, they found *Sesame Street* educational for its connection to other cultures and promotion of multiculturalism. Mariana, aged 38, explained:

> . . . for example, [my kids] see there in *Sesame Street* that there's China, there's other cultures . . . many other cultures. So, what I think, is that they will begin to understand that we are in a world, especially in the United States, where there will not be just people that think like them.

Parents perceived *Mickey Mouse Clubhouse* and *SpongeBob SquarePants* as the least educational among the four television shows (see Figure 7.1). Parents suggested that *Mickey Mouse Clubhouse* was mostly entertaining with some opportunities for school-related content learning (e.g., counting numbers) and social learning (e.g., friendship). *SpongeBob SquarePants* was by far the least favorite television show among parents whom we interviewed because of the language used by the characters in the show. Only two parents found *SpongeBob SquarePants* "somewhat educational" and suggested that the show promotes friendship and loyalty. Many parents were concerned about the show's negative influence on their children's social behaviors and mannerisms. Luciana, aged 40, stated:

> Like I mentioned, I don't really speak English. However, a mother who is also a teacher told me he [SpongeBob] says a lot of mean words, dumb things, and then you find your kids burping or things like that, so I don't think it is a good show.

Overall, parents perceived a television show to be educational when the show addressed content covered in school and supported children's school readiness. A television show was also educational if it promoted competency in both Spanish and English and strengthened children's ties to Mexico. Finally, parents perceived a television show as educational when it modeled appropriate social behaviors (i.e., manners) such as not talking back to their parents, respecting the elderly, helping others, being a good friend, and not burping in front of others. An entertaining television show was often described as "dumb," "funny," and "exciting" by parents. Some parents commented that educational television shows have predictable storylines and therefore are not as entertaining as other television shows. Several parents mentioned that their children got bored easily when watching educational television shows, and grew out of watching an educational television show such as *Sesame Street* by the time they were 3 years old. On the other hand, parents observed that television shows they considered entertaining sustained children's attention and interest for long periods of time.

Parents' Perceptions of Popular Video Games

Parents were less familiar with video games than television shows. On the national survey, 74 percent of parents were familiar with *Angry Birds*, 67 percent were familiar with *Just Dance*, and only 56 percent of parents were familiar with *Minecraft*. We found a similar trend in our field study. Eleven of the 16 parents were familiar with *Angry Birds*, 8 parents were familiar with *Just Dance*, and only 4 parents were familiar with *Minecraft*.

Overall, a small percentage of Latino parents found any of the video games "very educational" or "somewhat educational" on the national survey (see Figures 7.3 and 7.4). Many parents found *Angry Birds*, *Minecraft*, and *Just Dance* "not too educational" or "not at all educational." Because parents who participated in the field study were not familiar with these games, it was difficult for them to identify their educational value. Of the 11 parents who were familiar with *Angry Birds*, only two parents perceived the game "very educational" or "somewhat educational." Of eight parents who were familiar with *Just Dance*, six of them found the game "somewhat educational." Finally, of four parents who were familiar with Minecraft, two of them found the game "somewhat educational," and two of them found the game "not at all educational" (see Figures 7.3 and 7.4).

The two parents who perceived *Minecraft* as somewhat educational said that the game allowed children to use their imagination and creativity as they built

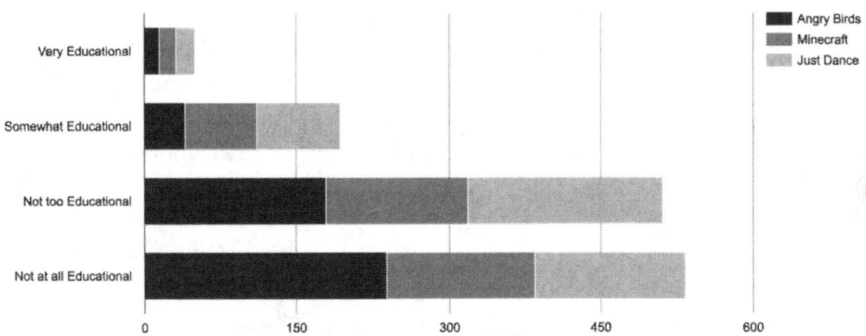

FIGURE 7.3 Parents' reports of *Angry Birds*, *Minecraft*, and *Just Dance* on the national survey

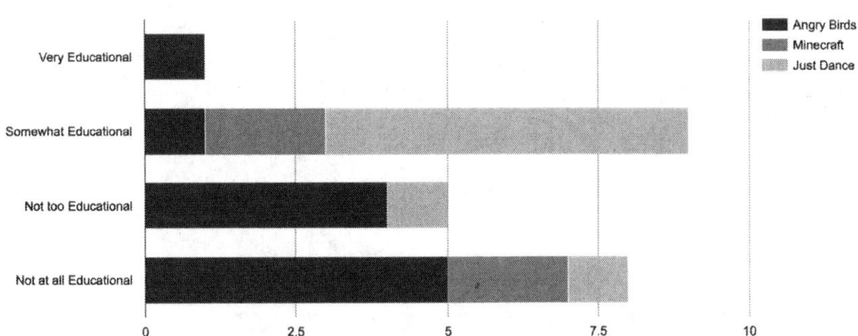

FIGURE 7.4 Parents' reports of *Angry Birds*, *Minecraft*, and *Just Dance* during interviews

structures and artifacts. Parents also mentioned that the game teaches patience to children because it takes a long time for them to build in the game. The two parents who found the game "not at all educational" found it difficult to see how spending building things was benefiting in any way. *Just Dance* was most often perceived as somewhat educational by parents. The physical activity that involved playing the game made the game educational, as Sara, aged 37, explains:

> Well, it's exercise, I mean, I'm thinking that it's only exercise . . . although they also learn coordination, as they are dancing . . . they move this hand and then the other. So maybe a little bit, it could be that they learn coordination.

Another game that parents found educational was *Magic Piano*, a game that allows players to play notes on the piano. Parents perceived a game to be educational when the game connected to real world practice. In the case of *Just Dance* and *Magic Piano*, the real-world practice involved doing a physical activity while playing. However, some parents mentioned FIFA (Fédération Internationale de Football Association) soccer video games as educational because children could learn about soccer as a game, learn to strategize as they played against the game system, observe how nonplayer characters played the game, and then go outside and practice the skills that they observed on their own.

Many parents found *Angry Birds* not educational for their children because of its repetitive game mechanic of throwing birds at different targets. Another game parents mentioned that shared the same qualities was *Flappy Bird*, a game with the goal of keeping a bird flying and dodging obstacles. One parent found dress-up and finger nail coloring games, so-called "pink games," educational for her daughter because they involved color matching and learning about real world tasks. Overall, parents seemed to use the same criteria for games that they used for television shows to determine their educational value for children. Parents found games that taught math and reading and supported their children's school learning to be educational.

Children's Reports of Educational Media

In this section, we also will start with perceptions of television shows, followed by perceptions of video games.

Television Shows

All children from ages 4–17 used the word "funny" when describing why they did not consider some of the television shows and video games that they consume educational. It was more difficult for younger children (ages 4–7) to articulate why they liked a television show or a video game, and whether they learned anything from them. Some of the television shows young children considered entertaining but not educational were *SpongeBob SquarePants*, *Tom and Jerry*, *Phineas and Ferb*, and *Curious George*. Older children watched the following shows that they thought were entertaining but not educational: *Loiter Squad*, *Bones*, *Duck Dynasty*, *Family Guy*, *Yu-Gi-Oh*, and *Dragon Ball Z*. These television shows were entertaining because they involved jokes and slapstick and made children laugh. Children also thought shows that are entertaining involved fantasy—things that would not happen in real life. Adrianna (aged 16) said, "I think entertaining is just like make believe stuff. They'll make up stuff like superpowers. They are not real. It's not educational."

There were fewer television shows that children considered educational. These include *Sesame Street*, *Mickey Mouse Clubhouse*, and shows on *National Geographic*, *Discovery Channel*, and *Animal Planet* because of their connection to the school. Rosie (aged 11) also considered *Shake It Up* educational "because they show you some steps when they dance." Dariana (aged 13) found *Cake Boss* educational because she wanted to be a pastry chef and learned the trade by watching the show. Finally, Valeria (aged 16) found *The Fosters* educational. She stated, "I learn what's right . . . like morals . . . um like family is everything and don't push away like your loved ones, and it just shows me like how people are. Like what to expect like being in foster care . . . like how it is."

No one reported a television show or video game as both entertaining and educational except Sebastian (aged 8) and Mariella (aged 17). Sebastian thought that *SpongeBob SquarePants* was entertaining, but he also learned trustworthiness and how to be a good friend from the show. He also found *Fairly Odd Parents* both entertaining and educational. He stated, "It teaches you what you don't do wrong and what to do. Like if you wanted to do something, you better not do it, like if someone tells you not to do it, then let's not do it." Mariella found *House of Cards* both educational and entertaining because she was "really into politics" and enjoyed the storyline, and at the same time, understood what was happening in the show because of the AP Government class she took.

Video Games

Some of the video games children considered entertaining but not educational were *Flappy Bird*, *Subway Surfer*, *Sonic the Hedgehog*, *Lego Star Wars*, *Don't Touch the White Tile*, *Angry Birds*, *Call of Duty*, and *Plant vs. Zombies*. Children found these games not educational because of the repeated player actions in these games. When we asked why these games were not educational, children said things like: "you only kill zombies," "you shoot people," "you just push the button," and "you just fly." Many children also found the following games not educational for the same reason: *Call of Duty*, *Minecraft*, *Grand Theft Auto*, and *FIFA*. From children's perspective, a video game was also entertaining when competition and challenge were involved.

Irving (aged 14) found *Call of Duty* educational "because in history class we learned about war and because they are war games . . . like, it talks about parts of war like the Soviet Union and the Nazis." Oswaldo (aged 8) found *Minecraft* educational "because it teaches me to be a builder and now I know how to do stuff." He also thought that *Grand Theft Auto* was educational because "It helps me drive better, it helps me when I grow up. I'll be a good person." Juan (age 5) found *FIFA* educational because he learned "tricks" about playing soccer.

Many children associated educational video games with school learning. For instance, Alberto (aged 9) found *Word Search* game educational because "it helps my brain think where the words are" He said: "a video game is educational when you get to do school stuff . . . where you have to use your reading skills and math." Tomas (aged 7) thought that educational video games "teach shapes and colors." Children also described an educational game as "when you learn something they you can actually use" and "things that give you, like things, that can add to how you live your life, that probably can do, can accomplish . . ." (Angel, aged 13). For instance, Kevin (age 12) found *Mario Kart* educational because "it teaches, like, how to be an engineer, like how you can tear apart a vehicle and add muscle." Osvaldo (age 8) found the *Princess Salon* and *Eye Makeup* game that his sister was playing educational because "they teach her to be a barber."

None of the children reported a game that was both entertaining and educational. When we asked children if a game can be both educational and entertaining, younger children responded "no." Older children, on the other hand, could not think of a game that was both entertaining and educational. Carolina (aged 7) was the only child who described her experience playing video games as involving teaching and learning. She said, "You learn . . . things, like in *Flappy Bird* my brother taught me how to press your hand, like your thumb on the tablet or phone and it goes higher; you let it go, and it goes down." Carolina explained that she learned the game in the process of playing it.

Discussion

We started this chapter with the argument that the lines between educational and entertainment media have blurred. Traditionally, the educational value of media has determined by the content (what is being consumed) as opposed to the context of media use. This perspective continues to dominate public discourse and research around parenting and media. On the one hand, parents perceive media as a tool to cultivate the development of their children and are encouraged to "feed" their kids with quality content by experts to this end. On the other hand, they are responsible for protecting their children from the adverse effects of media use. However, a growing body of research suggests that the context of media is essential in unlocking the potential benefits of media for children's learning. For instance, although a game like *World of Warcraft* may have violent content, it can also promote collaboration, problem-solving and leadership skills

(Steinkuehler, 2004). Given the complex landscape of educational media, it is important to understand how parents and children perceive and make sense of media that they consume.

Research on educational media, school readiness, and parental engagement often positions Latino low-income parents as less concerned than other parents with their children's school readiness and success. Our data shows that Latino low-income parents are aware of the skills their kids need to succeed in school and perceive media, particularly television shows, as a tool for their children to develop school-related skills such as reading and math like their White and middle-class peers. At the same time, these parents have additional concerns about their children developing language proficiency both in English and Spanish and maintaining cultural ties to their home country and culture. However, parents expressed these concerns only around television shows. They valued video games that helped their children develop school-related skills, yet none of the parents mentioned a video game that was educational because of its cultural ties. This is perhaps because parents were less familiar with the video games their children played. It is also possible that the topics and content covered in televisions shows are culturally more diverse than video games.

By and large, parents and children have a shared understanding of what counts as educational media. Regardless of the medium, the connection of the media content to what is learned in schools was the most frequently cited reason by both parents and children for their judgments of media as educational. The second most frequently cited reason was the connection of the media to life lessons about social norms and morals such as manners, respecting elderly, and being a good friend. The only difference between parents and children was the connection of educational media to their cultural heritage. None of the children mentioned finding a television show or a video game educational because of its ties to their Mexican heritage. Both parents and children associated fun, laughter, and excitement with entertainment media. Parents observed that educational television shows had predictable storylines and therefore were not as entertaining as other television shows. Children also mentioned that entertainment media involved fantasy and "make believe." They also associated "challenge" with video games that entertained as opposed to overtly educational games.

Both parents and children struggled to identify media that was both educational and entertaining and it seemed these two categories were mostly perceived as mutually exclusive, especially for video games. Parents attributed an educational value to watching novellas with their children because of their desire for their children to stay connected to their home culture. However, identifying the educational value of video games was more difficult. For instance, a small percentage of Latino parents on the national survey and Mexican-American parents and children who participated in the field study considered the popular game *Minecraft* to be both educational and entertaining. Perhaps the potential educational benefits of video games continue to be less obvious as compared to television, despite the growing number of studies showing video games' potential for supporting learning.

Implications and Future Directions

Our chapter has significant implications for the cultural framing of media and future directions for design. First, many have speculated that as the first generation that grew up playing video games became adults, negative perceptions of video games would change in our society and worldwide. However, our findings suggest that children do not realize learning takes place while they play video games and many of them do not consider their experience to be educational. One could argue that their perceptions perhaps are shaped by their parents who often perceive gaming as a waste of time. Given this trend, the likelihood that children who grow up playing video games will view such games as educational when they are adults with their own children seems low. This suggests the need for deliberate efforts to broaden parents' understanding of video games and how parents can support their children's learning with games.

Second, there continues to be a disconnect between research on media and learning and the perceptions of parents and children who privilege content over context when considering the educational value of media. At the same time, parents and children spend the most time with entertainment media. One reason for the lack of engagement with educational media at home is the limited number of television shows and video games that are intentionally designed to teach content. There is a need for more educational content to be produced across different devices to support children and families with diverse backgrounds. That said, even if there are more educational television shows or video games that promote content learning, it is unclear if children would spend more time with them. As parents in our study suggested, educational media sustain children's interest for relatively short periods of time. Therefore, only relying on producing content that is traditionally considered educational is insufficient to unlock the potential of media for enhancing the learning of all children. Entertainment media continues to make up much of the market and shape the experiences of children. We need to develop strategies that can engage the entire family critically with the entertainment media and create opportunities for family learning conversations around how what they watch or play informs learning in other aspects of their lives.

Finally, designers of educational television shows and video games need to consider the multicultural society we live in and how media supports or contributes to family values, norms, and ways of being. As our findings suggest, some television shows parents and children found educational modeled situations parents and children can relate to in their everyday lives and reinforced values that they hold as a family. Furthermore, parents perceived a television show to be educational when it made connections to their own cultural heritage. Although representations of different cultures on television shows has increased in the last several years, video games have been particularly slow in reflecting our society's diversity in positive ways. If the limited number of television shows and video games that parents and children mentioned as educational is any indication of the need for designing better content, we must be responsive to the different ways parents and children define educational media to improve their learning experiences. As such, media producers need to pay attention to cultural connections and social learning as much as academic content when designing media experiences that are meaningful and transformative for all children and families.

References

American Academy of Pediatrics (AAP). (2016). *Media and young minds*. Retrieved from http://pediatrics.aappublications.org/content/pediatrics/early/2016/10/19/peds.2016-2591.full.pdf

Buckingham, D. (2006). Is there a Digital Generation? In D. Buckingham & R. Willett (Eds.), *Digital generations* (pp. 1–13). Mahwah, NJ: Lawrence Erlbaum Associates.

Buckingham, D., & Scanlon, M. (2001). Parental pedagogies: An analysis of British "edu-tainment" magazines for young children. *Journal of Early Childhood Literacy*, *1*(3), 281–300.

Chakraborty, J., & Chakraborty, N. (2015). Public policy and violence in video games. *Interactions*, *22*(1), 64–67.

Clark, R. E. (Ed.). (2001). *Learning from media: Arguments, analysis, and evidence*. Greenwich, CT: Information Age.

Common Sense Media. (2013). *Zero to eight: Children's media use in American*. Retrieved from www.commonsensemedia.org/research/zero-to-eight-childrens-media-use-in-america-2013

Common Sense Media. (2015). *The common sense census: Media use by teens and tweens*. Retrieved from www.commonsensemedia.org/sites/default/files/uploads/research/census_researchreport.pdf

Duncan, S. C. (2011). Minecraft, beyond construction and survival. *Well Played*, *1*(1), 1–22.

Entertainment Software Association (ESA). (2016). *Industry facts*. Retrieved from www.theesa.com/about-esa/industry-facts/

Fisch, S. M. (2014). *Children's learning from educational television: Sesame Street and beyond*. New York: Routledge.

Fisch, S. M., & Truglio, R. T. (Eds.). (2001). *G is for growing: Thirty years of research on children and Sesame Street*. Mahwah, NJ: Erlbaum.

Fisher, G. (2001). Lifelong learning and its support with new media. In N.J. Smelser & P.B. Baltes (Eds.), *International encyclopedia of social and behavioral sciences, 13*, 8836–8840. Amsterdam: Elsevier Science.

Fry, R., & Gonzales, F. (2008). *One-in-five and growing fast: A profile of Hispanic public school students*. Washington, DC: Pew Hispanic Center.

Fuller, B., Lizárraga, J. R., & Gray, J. H. (2015). *Digital media and Latino families: New channels for learning, parenting, and local organizing*. New York: The Joan Ganz Cooney Center at Sesame Workshop.

Gee, J. P. (2003). *What videogames have to teach us about learning and literacy*. New York: Palgrave Macmillan.

Green, S. C., Li, R., & Bavelier, D. (2010). Perceptual learning during action video game playing. *Topics in Cognitive Science, 2*, 202–216.

Gutnick, A. L., Robb, M., Takeuchi, L., & Kotler, J. (2010). *Always connected: The new digital media habits of young children*. New York: The Joan Ganz Cooney Center at Sesame Workshop.

Ito, M. (2009). *Engineering play: A cultural history of children's software*. Cambridge, MA: MIT Press.

Jenkins, H., Clinton, K., Purushotma, R., Robison, A. J., & Weigel, M. (2006). *Confronting the challenges of participatory culture: Media education for the 21st century*. Chicago, IL: John D. and Catherine T. MacArthur Foundation.

Kozma, R. B. (1994). Will media influence learning: Reframing the debate. *Educational Technology and Development, 42*(2), 7–19.

Lareau, L. (2003). *Unequal childhoods: Race, class, and family life*. Berkeley, CA: University of California Press.

Lenhart, A., Kahne, J., Middaugh, E., Macgill, A. R., Evans, C., & Vitak, J. (2008). *Teens, video games, and civics: Teens' gaming experiences are diverse and include significant social interaction and civic engagement*. Washington, DC: Pew Internet & American Life Project. Retrieved from www.pewinternet.org/Reports/2008/Teens-Video-Games-and-Civics.aspx

Lisk, T. C., Kaplancali, U. T., & Riggio, R. E. (2012). Leadership in multiplayer online gaming environments. *Simulation & Gaming, 43*(1), 133–149.

Nixon, H. (1998). Fun and games are serious business. In J. Sefton-Green (Ed.), *Digital diversion: Youth culture in the age of multi-media* (pp. 21–43). London: UCL Press.

Plowman, L., McPake, J., & Stephen, C. (2008). Just picking it up? Young children learning with technology at home. *Cambridge Journal of Education, 38*(3), 303–319.

Prensky, M. (2001). Digital natives, digital immigrants. Part II: Do they really think differently? *On the Horizon, 9*(6), 15–24.

Reiser, R. A. (2001). A history of instructional design and technology: Part I: A history of instructional media. *Educational Technology Research and Development, 49*(1), 53–64.

Rideout, V., Lauricella, A., & Wartella, E. (2011). *Children, media, and race: Media use among White, Black, Hispanic, and Asian American children*. Evanston, IL: Center on Media and Human Development, Northwestern University.

Rideout, V. J., Foehr, U. G., and Roberts, D. F. (2010). *Generation M2: Media in the lives of 8- to 18-Year-Olds*. Menlo Park, CA: Henry J. Kaiser Family Foundation.

Riley, J. W., Cantwell, F. V., & Ruttiger, K. F. (1949). Some observations on the social effects of television. *Public Opinion Quarterly, 13*(2), 223–234.

Schramm, W., Lyle, J., & Parker, E. (1961). *Television in the lives of our children*. Stanford, CA: Stanford University Press.

Siyahhan, S., & Gee, E. (2016). Understanding gaming and gender within the everyday lives of Mexican-American family homes. In Y. Kafai, G. T. Richard, & B. Tynes (Eds.), *Diversifying Barbie and Mortal Kombat: Intersectional perspectives and inclusive designs in gaming* (pp. 59–71). Pittsburgh, PA: ETC Press.

Shuler, C. (2012). *What in the world happened to Carmen Sandiego: The edutainment era—Debunking myths and sharing lessons learned*. New York: The Joan Ganz Cooney Center at Sesame Workshop.

Squire, K. (2002). Cultural framing of computer/video games. *Game Studies, 2*(1), 1–13.

Squire, K. (2003). Video games in education. *International Journal of Intelligent Simulations and Gaming, 2*(1), 49–62.

Steinkuehler, C. A. (2004). Learning in massively multiplayer online games. In Y. B. Kafai, W. A. Sandoval, N. Enyedy, A. S. Nixon, & F. Herrera (Eds.), *Proceedings of the 6th International Conference on Learning Sciences* (pp. 521–528). Santa Monica, CA: ISLS.

Stevens, R., Satwicz, T., & McCarthy, L (2008). In-game, in-room, in-world: Reconnecting video game play to the rest of kids' lives. In K. Salen (Ed.), *The ecology of games: Connecting youth, games, and learning* (pp. 41–66), Cambridge, MA: MIT Press.

Takeuchi, L., & Stevens, R. (2011). *The new coviewing: Designing for learning through joint media engagement.* New York: The Joan Ganz Cooney Center at Sesame Workshop.

Tamim, R. M., Bernard, R. M., Borokhovski, E., Abrami, P. C., & Schmid, R. F. (2011). What forty years of research says about the impact of technology on learning: A second order meta-analysis and validation study. *Review of Educational Research, 81,* 4–28.

Thomas, D., & Brown, J. S. (2011). *A new culture of learning: Cultivating the imagination for a world of constant change.* Lexington, KY: CreateSpace.

Thompson, T. (2016). The Minecraft generation. *New York Times.* Retrieved from www.nytimes.com/2016/04/17/magazine/the-minecraft-generation.html

United States Census Bureau. (2012). *Population by race and Hispanic origin: 2012 and 2060.* Retrieved from www.census.gov/newsroom/releases/img/racehispanic_graph.jpg

Vittadini, N., Siibak, A., Reifová, I. R. E. N. A., & Bilandzic, H. (2013). Generations and media: The social construction of generational identity and differences. In N. Carpentier, K. C. Schrøder, & L. Hallett (Eds.), *Audience transformations: Shifting audience positions in late modernity* (pp. 65–88). New York: Routledge.

Wartella, E., & Reeves, B. (1985). Historical trends in research on children and the media: 1900–1960. *Journal of Communication, 35*(2), 118–133.

Woodard, E. H., & Gridina, N. (2000). *Media in the home.* Philadelphia, PA: Annenburg Public Policy Center of the University of Pennsylvania.

Zickuhr, K. (2011). *Generations and their gadgets.* Washington, DC: Pew Internet & American Life Project.

SECTION 3

Family Engagement

Section Editor: Amber Levinson

8

CHILDREN OF IMMIGRANTS' EXPERIENCES IN ONLINE INFORMATION BROKERING

Jason C. Yip, Carmen Gonzalez, and Vikki Katz

> Nina (girl, aged 13, Ecuadorian): Sometimes my mom needs really, really specific [information] and I find exactly what she wants. Like, if I've got to do it in English and she's speaking to me in Spanish, so I've got to. . . . You know, it's hard for me to know (and) look for exactly what she wants and translate to Spanish.

The above excerpt is from a set of interviews we conducted with Hispanic youth who search for and translate online information for their parents who are English language learners (ELL). Nina is one of the 10 youth we interviewed to understand how children bridge their families' access to online information. In multiethnic countries such as the United States, many immigrants face linguistic, cultural, and technological barriers to accessing information. To cope with these obstacles, parents who are not fully proficient in English often depend on their bilingual children to act as intermediaries to interpret and translate information (Katz, 2014b; Orellana, 2001). These youth often act as *brokers* as they facilitate their parents' connections with technology and information (Katz, 2014b).

Communities in the United States continue to experience demographic changes that make youth brokering a likely family strategy for connecting with vital information resources. One in five children in the United States is growing up in a home where at least one parent is foreign-born (Passel & Cohn, 2008), and 61 percent of children of immigrants have a parent who has difficulty speaking English (Shin & Kominski, 2010). In 2012, there were 25 million ELL individuals (9 percent of the national population) ages 5 and above in the United States (Pandya, Batalova, & McHugh, 2011). This reflects an 80 percent growth in the number of ELL individuals between 1990 and 2010 (from 13 million in 1990, to 25 million in 2010).

While prior studies have documented how youth brokers interpret a wide range of information (e.g., cultural, linguistic) for their ELL parents (e.g., Katz, 2014b; Orellana, 2001), we know less about how they utilize information communication technologies (ICTs) and digital literacy skills in their brokering practices. As ELL populations steadily increase, state and local governments are seeking strategies to communicate important information more effectively with these often-marginalized populations (Aizer, 2003; Lopez-Soto & Cebula, 2006). Since the evidence to date suggests that children are often crucial intermediaries between their families and their English-speaking environments, understanding the challenges they may face in doing so is important for us to consider. Our motivation for this study was not only to document possible constraints that children experience as brokers, but also the potentially creative learning strategies that they develop to negotiate high-pressure situations as they access vital information for their families.

Prior research on children's brokering activities suggests that the children who are most successful in their efforts (according to families' definitions of success) are those who are able to connect what they learn in one experience or setting, to subsequent times when they are called on to broker. The phenomenon known as *connected learning* refers to learning processes that are driven by personal interests, encouraged with peer and family support, and help learners connect their out-of-school pursuits to formal academic and career possibilities (Ito et al., 2012). Specifically, connected learning research places a strong emphasis on the role that digital media design and engagement plays in how youth pursue and connect formal and informal learning opportunities. Our focus on how learning opportunities are embedded in family goal achievement, and how such processes are tied to academic and career pursuits, builds on the connected learning body of knowledge.

Youth brokers often facilitate information for ELL parents and reinforce home-school connections (Orellana, 2001), but we know less about how digital tools and skills are involved in their goal achievement practices. We argue that youth brokers are relying on online information search as they tackle problem-solving tasks for their ELL families. By becoming more familiar with the challenges that youth brokers face during the online searching that they conduct on behalf of their families, and what strategies they develop to support their families' information needs, we are seeking to develop more informed strategies to promote connected learning as part of supporting family learning and wellbeing.

For this exploratory study on *youth online information brokering*, a term we use to denote the collaboration between children and parents in the search, translation, and brokering of information found in online spaces, we focused on Hispanics because they are the fastest growing minority group in the United States (US Census Bureau, 2012). Hispanics also account for 66 percent of the overall ELL population in the United States, totaling 16 million individuals in 2010 (Pandya et al., 2011), and report youth brokering as a common phenomenon (e.g., Katz

& Gonzalez, 2015; Orellana, 2001). Our investigation expands work in the fields of information sciences and communication, by examining youth online brokers' processes and experiences as they navigate complex online information. We limited our investigation to youth between 11 and 14 years old because prior research indicated that middle school marks the beginning of parents' intensive dependence on children's brokering skills (Hall & Sham, 2007). Our investigation was guided by three broad questions:

- What roles do youth (ages 11–14) play as online information brokers for their parents?
- What strategies and challenges shape learning roles in online information brokers?
- What are the affordances and limitations of digital technologies in brokering and learning?

Review of the Literature

Lower socioeconomic (SES) parents with limited English-language proficiency often depend on their children to search and interpret online information, since important resources (e.g., healthcare, education, social services) are predominately available in English (Katz, 2014a, 2014b). However, when online information is translated into non-English languages, ELL parents may face accessibility issues related to limited literacy, education, cultural knowledge, and/or access to ICTs and requisite skills to use them effectively (e.g., Ku & Matani, 2001; Ono & Zavodny, 2008). For instance, websites translated into Spanish typically use only one dialect of the language, despite Spanish having 20 distinct dialects (Thompson, 1992). This makes reading and understanding Spanish translations from English difficult for many consumers. As such, the responsibility of translating web content frequently falls into the hands of the children of these ELL families.

Available Resources

Although community institutions can be resources for translation help, information brokering is often an in-home activity (Katz, 2014a; Orellana, 2001). Public libraries can offer help related to information search, but low-income immigrant families may access such resources infrequently because of social isolation, busy work schedules, or mistrust of public institutions (Gehner, 2010). In healthcare settings specifically, researchers have documented how professional interpreters can facilitate information exchanges between non-English-speaking patients and English-speaking providers (Butow et al., 2011; Hsieh, 2007; Willen, 2011). However, interpreters may be unavailable, particularly in institutions providing low-cost free services that are often overcrowded. In this case, children of immigrants assume the role of information brokers in actual interactions with providers, as well as by searching for treatment information, insurance options, and local providers, which is usually done online (Katz, 2014a).

Youth Information Seeking and Problem Solving

Despite growing up in the digital age, US youth (not only those in immigrant families) are seldom aware of more advanced search features and may still be learning how to engage with ICTs by developing typing and search query skills (Foss et al., 2012, 2013). Studies of children (ages 6–11) and adolescents (ages 11–17) in native-born US families indicate that youth often have difficulty searching for information online and understanding information that they find (Druin et al., 2009; Foss et al., 2012, 2013). The challenges of online search and comprehension are more acute in lower SES immigrant families (Himma, 2007). Youth in these families have even more difficulty searching, finding, evaluating, integrating, and communicating information they find online than do youth from more affluent families (Leu, Forzani, & Kennedy, 2015). These search challenges may be due, at least in part, to limitations in reading comprehension and less sustained exposure to information literacy programs in schools (Leu et al., 2015).

Another limitation of the existing literature with regard to youth in immigrant families is that researchers tend to presume that youth search primarily for topics related to their own lives, rather than considering how search may be driven by family needs. For instance, Duarte Torres and Weber (2011) found that the majority of youth search queries focused on interests such as Harry Potter, Justin Bieber, Club Penguin, video games, and other popular culture topics. In a survey in Greece, Aslanidou and Menexes (2008) found that most young people (ages 12–18) conducted Internet searches at home related to their personal interests either very often (34.9 percent) or always (40.6 percent). It is likely that youth from higher income families use ICTs for their own purposes and personal interests because their parents have more technological literacy, access to resources, and are generally less dependent on their children for help in this context (Druin et al., 2009; Foss et al., 2012, 2013).

Researchers who have focused on youth in lower income and immigrant families reveal that these young people are more likely to use technologies collectively with their parents and families than their more privileged counterparts (Katz, 2010, 2014a, 2014b). This may reflect the wholly different positioning that youth in these families occupy when they serve as important sources of parental support. Adults often give youth participants *imposed queries*; that is, questions provided by someone else for the searcher to answer and resolve (Gross, 1999, 2006). For example, a teacher may ask a student to search for information for a classroom assignment. We have little evidence for how imposed queries from ELL family members affect youth's online information behavior. As a result, we have limited understandings of how these families engage in online information problem-solving tasks for critical issues such as immigration, health, and educational concerns. In order to identify the barriers that they encounter in those efforts, we believe that an in-depth examination of how youth brokers engage in online activities will permit us to more meaningfully inform efforts to address digital inequality and mitigate the broader social inequalities that are tied to access and connectivity.

Youth Learning through Online Information Brokering

Although brokering can be quite a difficult task for youth, researchers from education, sociology, and communication have documented important opportunities for positive learning outcomes. When children are motivated to develop expertise on topics that relate to their families, their brokering roles generate new learning opportunities (Eksner & Orellana, 2012). For youth, the act of brokering depends on high-level development of cognitive and social skill sets (Hall & Sham, 2007), and some researchers claim that language brokering and biculturalism in youth is positively related to Hispanic adolescent students' academic performance (Buriel, Perez, Terri, Chavez, & Moran, 1998). However, on the flip side of the coin, researchers have found that youth brokering of high priority information is stressful, leading to high-risk health behaviors, depression, and anxiety (Kam, 2011; Kam & Lazarevic, 2014).

Orellana's (2001) use of sociocultural theory in her longitudinal studies of children's brokering has been a considerable contribution toward understanding youth brokers' and parents' skills development. The direct investment in youth efforts to address their families' needs can help them engage in civic opportunities, support character development, and build stronger ties with their families (Orellana, 2001). For instance, Katz (2014a) notes that youth brokers often needed to translate complex health and medical information from doctors. Children who framed these interactions with doctors as educational and informative learning experiences found it easier to mitigate any discomforts resulting from youth managing interactions between their parents and health providers. Eksner and Orellana (2012) demonstrate the ways that language brokering with parents contributes to youth's knowledge of the social world, skills development in their home language and in English, problem-solving skills toward meaning-making, and other learning opportunities. Katz (2014a, 2014b) examines media brokering and how children facilitate their parents' understanding through media artifacts (e.g., print, online media) and mediated communication (e.g., phone calls, Internet). While prior studies frame cultural, language, and media brokering as important to youth brokers' developmental and learning trajectories, little is known about how online information search and brokering relate to those experiences.

Methods

Context and Participants

The 10 youth who participated in this study match the following criteria. First, they self-identified as the child of a Hispanic immigrant. Second, they have at least one parent with limited facility in verbal or written English. Third, they were between the ages of 11 and 14. Finally, each of the youth reports helping his/her parent(s) understand and navigate online content and ICTs. Table 8.1 provides relevant demographic information; all names are pseudonyms.

This study was conducted in Brooklyn, New York. In the middle school where teachers helped us to recruit participants, 72 percent of the student body was receiving free- or reduced-cost meals, and 59 percent were of Hispanic heritage. In this study, we were looking to identify children of immigrants; therefore, anxieties related to residency status prevented a broad sampling of the school's students.

TABLE 8.1 Demographic Information of the Youth Brokers

Name and Age	*Country of Origin*	*Family Characteristics*
Amanda (age 13)	Spain (mother)*	Two sisters (ages 5 and 9) and mom
Bella (age 14)	Dominican Republic	Three older sisters and one older brother (all not living at home, ages not available); lives with mom
Betty (age 12)	Dominican Republic	One brother (age 23), one sister (age 21), mom and dad
Don (age 11)	Dominican Republic	One brother (age 23), three sisters (ages 23, 20, and 18), mom and dad
Fernando (age 13)	Dominican Republic	One sister (age 18, not living at home), mom and dad
Jennifer (age 11)	Ecuador (mother) and Mexico (father)	One brother (age 8), one sister (age 6), mom and dad
Marina (age 12)	Dominican Republic	One sister (age 18), mom and dad
Nina (age 13)	Ecuador	One brother (age 17), mom
Ricardo (age 13) and Raphael (age 13) (twins)	Mexico	Three brothers (ages 7, 14 and 18), mom and dad, aunt and older cousin (18)

* We included this participant because her family identified themselves as Hispanic. She did not report where her father is from, but volunteered that she has strong family connections to the Dominican Republic.

Research Design and Data Collection

The questions in this study are adapted from an information search protocol from Bilal (2002) and Foss et al. (2013). We conducted 10 one-on-one interviews and search tasks with youth brokers in four sessions in an afterschool setting. After individual interviews, participants participated in a moderated group discussion about their brokering experiences. Four of the five researchers on this project spoke Spanish proficiently or fluently and were able to engage in Spanish dialogue with the youth.

Interviews and Search Tasks

We used a semistructured interview protocol (Merriam, 2009) to allow us to focus on our research questions, but with enough flexibility to identify emergent issues. We asked questions about family demographics, ICT usage, and general search behavior. Next, for 40 minutes, we asked youth to engage in a series of search tasks that were self-generated, imposed, simple, and complex. *Self-generated* tasks focus on searches with fewer constraints (Bilal, 2002; Gross, 1999). *Imposed* tasks provide limitations for children to search for information they would not normally search for (Gross, 2006). *Simple* tasks are baseline search tasks to make sure children can do basic searches (Bilal, 2002). Finally, *complex* tasks provide a challenge and allow us to see how persistent and resourceful children are at searches (Bilal, 2002). Based on these criteria, we asked participants to engage in the following tasks using school laptops:[1]

1. If your parent needed information on the public schools in this area, what information would you look up for them? (*Imposed and simple task*)
2. Can you show me how you find information for something your parents have asked you to search before? (*Imposed task*)
3. Can you show me how you find information for a problem you think your parents might have today? (*Self-generated task*)
4. If one of your parents was not feeling well or had been sick for a few days and wanted to know why, what information would you look up for them? (*Imposed and complex task*)

During these search tasks, we had the participant narrate how they were conducting the search and their opinions on the task. We video recorded screen interactions as the children explained their search tasks. During this time, we asked children to search as if their parents were present to simulate what being at home was like.

Group Interviews and Field Notes

After the search tasks, we had all participants engage in a 20-minute group discussion about how they search for information for their ELL parents. We conducted these group discussions to better understand what aspects of the search and brokering activities we had just observed are experienced similarly among youth online brokers, and which they experience differentially. The group conversations also provided a comfortable atmosphere for youth to share personal information they would not necessarily share individually (Eder & Fingerson, 2002). After each session, we generated individual summative memos of our experiences and contributed to efforts to interpret the collected data. Each group discussion (four total) included all the youth who had just completed their interview sessions (two to three youth per group) and two to three researchers.

Data Analysis

The data for this study consisted of individual and group interview transcripts, transcripts of the video recordings, and detailed field notes. We developed themes and categories to capture children's search and learning experiences for their ELL parents (Strauss & Corbin, 2007). Two researchers looked for themes, such as parental interaction, affect, search challenges and frustrations, and strategies for brokering. We categorized, sorted, and compared the themes to further develop categories for analysis. We then systematically compared and contrasted the themes between the researchers. Next, we made connections between the themes and its subcategories more explicit. We used selective coding to see if additional categories were needed. This sorting, comparing, and contrasting was performed until we reached theoretical saturation and that no new codes or categories were generated.

Findings

We present our findings based on our research questions. First, we outline the learning roles children and their families take on in the online brokering process. Second, we highlight the different challenges and creative strategies that online youth brokers engaged in. Finally, we examine the affordances and limitations of ICTs for learning in the process of online youth brokering.

Child and Family Roles in Online Brokering and Learning

Youth brokers in this study indicated that their parents' requests for information were a product of the specific kinds of challenges their family faced. Although we did not interview parents, we were able to ask youth brokers what kind of online searches their parents commonly assigned to them. We characterized one set of tasks as "non-urgent searches"; that is, searches that are important, but low in priority. These searches include maps and directions, online shopping, access to entertainment (e.g., videos, music), news, and recipes. Youth also indicated "urgent searches"; these are high priority and relate to complex life issues such as health and medicine, school choice, and immigration issues. For all these searches, children take on a myriad of roles in learning and teaching with their parents. For example, youth brokers act as *synthesizers* and must quickly glean and explain complex information. Some of these summaries have to be provided in Spanish, even though the broker locates the information is in English. For instance, we asked Betty (aged 12) to describe how she would explain information about school rankings to her mother (imposed and complex task); she did so in Spanish as the interviewer played the role of her mother:

Betty: Mira mami, estos son los mejores escuelas que hay en la ciudad. Mira, estos son las Matemáticas y el Ingles. Y mira, como están haciendo entre las escuelas. Ellos hacen mejor que los otros en una escuela como esta, 4.0 y este 3.7. Quiere decir que esta es mejor que esta.

Betty: Look mom, these are the best schools that there are in the city. Look this is Math and English. And look at how the schools are doing. They are doing better than others in a school like this one, 4.0 and this one 3.7. That means that this one is better than this one.

Although all 10 participants engage in online brokering for their parents, they did not all have the same skills for translation and synthesis. Some youth online information brokers (e.g., Don and Marina) had developing Spanish skills and mostly relied on a combination of online translation tools (i.e., Google Translate™) and their limited Spanish fluency. Other youth brokers were so fluent in Spanish that they acted not only as translators, but as more engaged *editors*. For example, Fernando (age 13) would spend time correcting longer Google Translate™ outputs for his parents to read (which could take up to an hour). These strong literacy skills in both languages were most important when youth had to broker urgent online information. In some families, however, expectations were high regardless of the urgency; Bella (age 14) noted, "We don't get recognition [for brokering well] because it's something we're supposed to do, if you're in a Dominican family. No, I'm serious; you're supposed to do it, you have to be the kid and translate."

Parents were not only depending on their children for online information brokering, they needed their children as *technology specialists*. Many parents were learning about technology from their youth brokers, as they searched online together. For instance, Ricardo (aged 12) explained how he was helping his mother understand how to access her paycheck online: "I was helping her log on and then . . . As I was helping her, I didn't know what her password was and stuff . . . So I told her where to put it, then. So my mom didn't know where to put it anywhere." Other youth brokers explained that while they were searching for online information, they often found themselves teaching their parents how to address technical issues with the devices they were using. Interestingly, Betty indicated it was her mom that first taught her how to use the computer to search online; some ELL parents have the requisite technology literacy to develop their children's basic understandings of digital tools. As their children progress with the technology, parents may in turn ask for help with more advanced functionalities.

The family unit itself takes on an *inquirer* role in social learning; that is, parents and other family members provide imposed queries (Gross, 1999) to the youth brokers, which often forces the youth out of their comfort zone, and challenges them to seek solutions. For example, the youth brokers in this study needed to search for things like *Remicade* (a drug) that may cause cancer, phyllodes tumors, immigration policies in online news sources, and school choice issue. These high-priority imposed queries, while incredibly difficult, push youth to be exposed to new online information they may not normally search for on their own personal interests. Unlike homework assignments from teachers, which can be ignored or forgotten, these online brokering tasks are social and emotional obligations that cannot be easily dismissed. They therefore constitute a unique opportunity for less structured, but highly motivated, learning to occur around technology.

Challenges and Strategies in Online Brokering for Learning

Although learning together through online brokering processes can help strengthen family bonds (Katz, 2014b), there are many challenges to learning in these experiences as well. The first challenge is dealing with *family pressures*; youth brokers indicated varying levels of stress while working with their parents. Although technology for search is becoming more mobile (i.e., smartphones, tablets), our participants indicated that their parents still preferred large displays from laptops and desktops so that they could sit together with their children as they brokered. However, Nina noted the frustration of having her mother next to her: "For me, sometimes I want to, like, find the right thing [online], but . . . I take a long time reading and then [my mom is] like, 'Okay, can you please hurry up?' or something. I'm like, 'I'm trying to find the correct information for you, so relax!' " Some youth felt their parents sat and monitored their search practices out of a sense of nervousness. Amanda (aged 13) explained, "If their instincts tell them we're doing something wrong, they go crazy; like, 'No, we're doing something wrong. That's not the right way.' But you don't know what it means, so why are you saying that?" Despite these minimal tensions that some participants noted, they more clearly emphasize their shared sense of commitment, persistence, and collaboration with parents to address family needs.

A second challenge to learning we observed was developing the requisite *digital literacy skills* to broker online effectively and efficiently. Digital literacy refers to the cognitive, motor, emotional, and sociological skills necessary to interpret and synthesize a wide range of digital information from multiple sources (e.g., Eisenberg, 2010). For challenging online information searches, youth had difficulty with query formation, filtering pertinent information, determining information reliability, and other known problems with searching and youth (Druin et al., 2009; Foss et al., 2013). For instance, we encountered two "rule-based" searchers (Fernando and Bella) who did not trust Wikipedia™ for reliable information (Foss et al., 2012, 2013). However, excluding Wikipedia™ from all their searches could, in some cases, result in missed opportunities for better online brokering. These technical challenges were overlaid by struggles to comprehend and explain technical words and phrases in some cases. As they narrated their searches, participants identified medical terminology, immigration policy terms, school choice, and even common, everyday terms (e.g., "preservative," "inseam") that they found difficult to understand and translate. While even fluent speakers of English could have trouble deciphering complex terms, these youth brokers were acutely aware that their parents were depending on their developing search skills to connect them with important, complicated information online.

Youth brokers often depended on people in their social networks to help them when searches were too challenging, including their other parent (if he or she spoke more English), older siblings, aunts, cousins, neighbors, and teachers. Participants did not mention friends as part of their support network. This is consistent with prior findings that children seldom discuss brokering with each other, either to protect their families' vulnerabilities or maintain their peer relationships as separate from their family responsibilities (Katz, 2014a).

To be as resourceful as possible, some of the youth described taking on *social mediation* roles to find the help they needed as they searched for and interpreted information for their families. The online brokers relied heavily on their social networks to support such tasks. Participants received help from their other parent, older siblings, extended family members, and even teachers and neighbors. However, online brokering can become more challenging when supportive family members are not consistently present. Some participants talked about older cousins (i.e., Jennifer, Raphael, and Ricardo) or siblings (i.e., Fernando) who had left for college, and left a void in their brokering support systems. These participants still contacted these resources as frequently as possible for assistance. Fernando described the difficult transition in his interview: "It's way harder because [my sister] is, like, the one in the house that knows how to translate. So, like, I know I can speak Spanish. I just can't be translating, because translating is really hard for me."

Urgent searches, especially when that urgency is sustained over time, are even more challenging without consistent sources of support. For instance, Fernando relayed that his mom had had a host of health problems that necessitated ongoing care: "My mom, since she is in a really critical condition, she really needs medical help. She goes to Peace Hospital [pseudonym] and . . . that hospital has been the one that has cured her . . . most of the time they only speak English [there]." Fernando recalled having to find information on a particular medicine for this mother:

> Well, my mom told me to search it [Remicade, a drug] up in the computer, 'cause that's the injection that they're gonna, that they're telling her that she should have. But like, she doesn't know if she should, 'cause they said that [the drug] might give her cancer.

To find more information, Fernando searched using the query, "Remicade effects on the immune system." When he examined the search results, Fernando went directly to Google Scholar™, thinking the scholarly information there would be more reliable. He arrived at an esoteric scientific journal as the first result on the page. Although he believed that the information was reliable, he did not understand the information or was unable to translate it. Fernando's example is a case in which a librarian or teacher could be an invaluable resource. However, none of the participants indicated that librarians were part of their support system, and few spoke to teachers. The sensitive nature of the information involved in cases like Fernando's can amplify their difficulties by reducing the chances that they reach out beyond their intimate circles for support.

While these participants detailed serious challenges to learning through brokering under pressure, they also came up with creative, less language-dependent strategies to help synthesize and convey complex information. Brokers often relied on hand gestures, which Jennifer (age 11) called "charades." Other children drew pictures supplemental to their explanations. Bella noted the difficulty in explaining what "preservatives" in food were and needed to draw out pictures of this concept. Finally, some children used physical objects to help their families out in online search. Marina, when she found a recipe online, translated the ingredients to her mother by finding and gathering the physical ingredients that were available. In order to describe what an "inseam" was for a school uniform website, Amanda needed to get a real pair of pants from the closet to show her mother. In these examples, we find that even though online brokering occurs in the digital space, learning and communicating digital information is still embedded in physical spaces and context-based (Lave & Wenger, 1991).

Affordances and Limitations of Technologies for Youth Online Information Brokering

Understandably, access to technologies for brokering also have their limitations for learning. While the larger screens helped to being the families together, youth brokers complained that dealing with their parents' frequent requests and pressure was not necessarily an incentive for online brokering. For instance, Bella described that she and her mother could be at the computer for an hour going from site to site: "We end up in stupid places because she wants to keep branching out somewhere." The user interface design of the technologies also did not support information accessibility for the youth brokers. For example, we noted that Google Translate™ and Dictionary.com™ do not use visual representations as a way to support understanding of the text, which can make multimedia learning more challenging (Mayer & Moreno, 2002). Finally, the youth in this study expressed fears and concerns about technology breaking. They explained about the anxiousness over computer viruses and explicit popup ads. These fears have been documented extensively in lower SES Hispanic families (Katz & Gonzalez, 2015), and often prevent families from trusting their children to access online information. For instance, Fernando described explicit popups as making online brokering more difficult, especially when his parents are sitting with him: "And I didn't click that [explicit pop-up ad] and it just gets me mad. And then they [parents] just, then they get mad. And they sometimes just take the computer away. It's not my fault when the ad appears."

Conclusion

Vygotsky (1978) theorized that, through social play, children and youth learn to develop higher order skillsets beyond their individual capabilities. Digital media scholars also argue for more attention to youths' personal interests and play in order to understand how youth are learning (e.g., Ito et al., 2012; Jenkins, Clinton, Purushotma, Robinson, & Weigel, 2006). Education scholars are also more closely examining the role of parents in co-learning with children through play and digital technologies (e.g., Barron, Martin, Takeuchi, & Fithian, 2009; Takeuchi & Stevens, 2011).

This exploratory study demonstrates that digital technology also contributes to youth learning through supporting family needs. Participants in this study described close interactions with their parents around various technologies. They reported that their parents sat down with them to access information for their family's wellbeing. While these interactions were frustrating, there were opportunities for youth to interact with their parents more directly. In stressful or urgent situations, youth online brokers made creative adaptions. They relied on their social networks, found non-digital solutions to communication issues (e.g., using gestures, developing analogies, drawing pictures, finding physical objects), and quickly synthesized and translated complex information (which they may not have fully understood) into their parents' language. Youth brokers in this study were motivated to demonstrate what they could accomplish for their ELL families. For instance, Betty emphasized in the group interview that she was eager to show off her abilities in search and translation, especially when her parents did not think she knew Spanish well enough.

In conclusion, the findings of this exploratory study highlight the need to examine brokering and family responsibilities in the context of digital literacy and connected learning. Our findings suggest that as more information (both urgent and non-urgent) is digitized and accessible online, youth brokers will face a flood of complex information decisions (e.g., query formation, information reliability) that will require deeper learning and connections to different domains. Online information brokering is not simply a collaborative effort between an ELL parent and youth broker. We believe schools, libraries, community organizations, and other local institutions need to partner with families to support digital literacy and connected learning practices in youth. For instance, youth brokers' searches for health solutions for their ELL families could be augmented with science learning from schools, digital literacy skills from libraries, and local community supports.

We also believe that the youth brokering process will be become more dependent on the integration and fluency of cultural, linguistic, and digital literacy skillsets. As such, access to technology for brokering online is not enough. This study advocates for a view of technology for *meaningful connectivity* for learning. While all the youths in this study had access to technologies for online brokering, our findings suggest a need for a closer examination beyond a binary view of the digital divide. Meaningful connections emphasize both the access to the technologies and the support to develop skills for learning. We recommend future studies examine the learning experiences of online youth brokers and their ELL families in the contexts of their homes over longer periods of time, and consider the broker's gender (Orellana, 2001), birth order (Orellana, 2001), bilingual proficiency (Katz, 2014b), and parental education (Katz, 2014b). Country of origin may also be a factor; our sample included Hispanic youth whose families originated from different Hispanic countries, though participants were similar in terms of age, place of residence, and access to home-based Internet and related devices.

Acknowledgments

We want to thank Michael Levine and Lori Takeuchi at the Joan Ganz Cooney Center for supporting this work. We thank Rocio Almanza and Alexia Raynal for volunteering on this project. We thank the youth, teachers, and staff at the local school that participated in this study. This study is a part of the Families and Media Project and supported by funding from the Heising Simons Foundation and the Bezos Family Foundation.

Note

1. While searching on their own home devices adds to authenticity of the task (see Foss et al., 2012, 2013), we chose to use school laptops because bringing their own devices to school was logistically more challenging.

References

Aizer, A. (2003). Low take-up in Medicaid: Does outreach matter and for whom? *American Economic Review, 93*(2), 238–241.

Aslanidou, S., & Menexes, G. (2008). Youth and the Internet: Uses and practices in the home. *Computers & Education, 51*(3), 1375–1391.

Barron, B., Martin, C. K., Takeuchi, L., & Fithian, R. (2009). *Parents as learning partners in the development of technological fluency*. Retrieved from www.mitpressjournals.org/doi/abs/10.1162/ijlm.2009.0021

Bilal, D. (2002). Children's use of the Yahooligans! Web search engine. III. Cognitive and physical behaviors on fully self-generated search tasks. *Journal of the American Society for Information Science and Technology, 53*(13), 1170–1183.

Buriel, R., Perez, W., Terri, L., Chavez, D. V., & Moran, V. R. (1998). The relationship of language brokering to academic performance, biculturalism, and self-efficacy among Latino adolescents. *Hispanic Journal of Behavioral Sciences, 20*(3), 283–297.

Butow, P. N., Sze, M., Dugal-Beri, P., Mikhail, M., Eisenbruch, M., & Jefford, M. S. (2011). From inside the bubble: Migrants' perceptions of communication with the cancer team. *Supportive Care in Cancer 19*(2), 281–290.

Druin, A., Foss, E., Hatley, L., Golub, E., Guha, M. L., Fails, J., et al. (2009). How children search the internet with keyword interfaces. Proceedings of the 8th International Conference on Interaction Design and Children (pp. 89-96). New York: ACM.

Duarte Torres, S., & Weber, I. (2011). What and how children search on the web. *Proceedings of the 20th ACM International Conference on Information and Knowledge Management* (pp. 393–402). New York: ACM.

Eder, D., & Fingerson, L. (2002). Interviewing children and adolescents. In J.F. Gubrium, & J.A. Holstein (Eds.), *Handbook of Interview Research: Context & Method* (pp. 181–202). Thousand Oaks, CA: Sage.

Eisenberg, M. B. (2010). Information literacy: Essential skills for the information age. *Journal of Library & Information Technology, 28*(2), 39–47.

Eksner, H. J., & Orellana, M. F. (2012). Shifting in the Zone: Latina/o child language brokers and the co-construction of knowledge. *Ethos, 40*(2), 196–220.

Foss, E., Druin, A., Brewer, R., Lo, P. Sanchez, L. & Golub, E. (2012). Children's search roles at home: Implications for designers, researchers, educators, and parents. *Journal of the American Society for Information Science and Technology, 63*(3), 558–573. http://doi.org/10.1002/asi.21700

Foss, E., Druin, A., Yip, J., Ford, W., Golub, E., & Hutchinson, H. (2013). Adolescent search roles. *Journal of the American Society for Information Science and Technology, 64*(1), 173–189.

Gehner, J. (2010). Libraries, low-income people, and social exclusion. *Public Library Quarterly, 29*(1), 39–47.

Gross, M. (1999). Imposed queries in the school library media center: A descriptive study. *Library & Information Science Research, 21*(4), 501–521.

Gross, M. (2006). *Studying children's questions: Imposed and self-generated information seeking at school.* Lanham, MD: Scarecrow Press.

Hall, N., & Sham, S. (2007). Language brokering as young people's work: Evidence from Chinese adolescents in England. *Language and Education, 21*(1), 16–30.

Hsieh, E. (2007). Interpreters as co-diagnosticians: Overlapping roles and services between providers and interpreters. *Social Science & Medicine, 64*(4), 924–937.

Himma, K. E. (2007). The information gap, the digital divide, and the obligations of affluent nations. *International Review of Information Ethics,* 7(9), 3–4.

Ito, M., Gutiérrez, K., Livingstone, S., Penuel, W., Rhodes, J., Salen, K., et al. (2012). *Connected learning: An agenda for research and design.* Chicago, IL: MacArthur Foundation.

Jenkins, H., Clinton, K., Purushotma, R., Robinson, A., & Weigel, M. (2006). *Confronting the challenges of participatory culture: Media education for the 21st century.* Chicago, IL: MacArthur Foundation.

Kam, J. A. (2011). The effects of language brokering frequency and feelings on Mexican-heritage youth's mental health and risky behavior. *Journal of Communication, 61*, 455–475.

Kam, J. A., & Lazarevic, V. (2014). Communicating for one's family: An interdisciplinary review of language and cultural brokering in immigrant families. *Annals of the International Communication Association, 38*(1), 3–37.

Katz, V. S. (2010). How children use media to connect their families to the community: The case of Latinos in Los Angeles. *Journal of Children and Media,* 4(3), 298–315.

Katz, V. (2014a). Children as brokers of their immigrant families' health-care connections. *Social Problems, 61*(2), 194–215.

Katz, V. (2014b). *Kids in the middle: How children of immigrants negotiate community interactions for their families*. New Brunswick, NJ: Rutgers University Press.

Katz, V. S., & Gonzalez, C. (2015). Community variations in low-income Latino families' technology adoption and integration. *American Behavioral Scientist, 60*(1), 59–80.

Ku, L., & Matani, S. (2001). Left out: Immigrants' access to health care and insurance. *Health Affairs, 20*, 247–256.

Lave, J., & Wenger, E. (1991). *Situated learning: Legitimate peripheral participation*. Cambridge: Cambridge University Press.

Leu, D.J., Forzani, E., & Kennedy, C. (2015). Income inequality and the online reading gap. *Reading Teacher, 68*(6), 422–427. http://doi.org/10.1002/trtr.1328

Lopez-Soto, E., & Cebula, R. A., III. (2006). *Promising practices: The importance of outreach to underserved populations*. Retrieved from http://digitalcommons.ilr.cornell.edu/edicollect/1212/

Mayer, R. E., & Moreno, R. (2002). Aids to computer-based multimedia learning. *Learning and Instruction, 12*(1), 107–119.

Merriam, S. B. (2009). *Qualitative research: A guide to design and implementation*. San Francisco, CA: John Wiley & Sons.

Moje, E. B., Ciechanowski, K. M. I., Kramer, K., Ellis, L., Carrillo, R., & Collazo, T. (2004). Working toward third space in content area literacy: An examination of everyday funds of knowledge and discourse. *Reading Research Quarterly, 39*(1), 38–70.

Ono, H., & Zavodny, M. (2008). Immigrants, English ability and the digital divide. *Social Forces, 86*(4), 1455–1479.

Orellana, M. F. (2001). The work kids do: Mexican and Central American immigrant children's contributions to households and schools in California. *Harvard Educational Review, 71*(3), 366–390.

Pandya, C., Batalova, J., & McHugh, M. (2011). *Limited English proficient individuals in the United States: Number, share, growth, and linguistic diversity*. Washington, DC: Migration Policy Institute.

Passel, J. S., & Cohn, D. (2008). *US Population Projections: 2005–2050*. Pew Research Center, Washington, D.C. Retrieved from www.popline.org/node/199218

Strauss, A. L., & Corbin, J. (2007). *Basics of qualitative research: Techniques and procedures for developing grounded theory*, 3rd ed. Thousand Oaks, CA: Sage.

Shin, H. B., & Kominski, R. A. (2010). *Language Use in the United States: 2007*. Washington, DC: US Census Bureau.

Takeuchi, L., & Stevens, R. (2011). *The new coviewing: Designing for learning through joint media engagement*. The Joan Ganz Cooney Center at Sesame Workshop. Retrieved from www.joanganzcooneycenter.org/Reports-asc.html

Thompson, R.W. (1992). Spanish as a pluricentric language. In M. G. Clyne and W. de Gruyter (eds.), *Pluricentric languages: Differing norms in different nations* (pp. 45–70). Berlin: Mouton de Gruyter.

US Census Bureau. (2012). *The 2012 statistical abstract—U.S. Census Bureau*. Retrieved from www.census.gov/compendia/statab/

Vygotsky, L. S. (1978). *Mind in society: The development of higher psychological processes*. Cambridge, MA: Harvard University Press.

Willen, S. S. (2011). Do "illegal" Im/migrants have a right to health? Engaging ethical theory as social practice at a Tel Aviv open clinic. *Medical Anthropology Quarterly, 25*(3), 303–330.

9

DADDY LOVES DORA AND MAMA LOVES DRAMA

Ethnic Media as Intergenerational Boundary Objects

Lori M. Takeuchi and Briana Ellerbe

Every once in a while, 8-year-old Benny sits down to watch the evening telenovelas with his mother and father. Not so much because he enjoys or even understands them—telenovelas are, after all, not produced with young children in mind. But it is one way to spend time with his parents, especially since he sees so little of his father during the workweek. Despite the novelas' mature content, Benny's mother appreciates when he joins them because of the additional exposure it gives him to Spanish conversation. As he grows older, she grows increasingly concerned about Benny losing his ability to understand Spanish. Benny and his parents may have separate reasons for coming together around telenovelas, but the end result is a family enjoying the evening together.

Benny is one of the 15 children we followed for 6 weeks as part of the Modern Families Study, a regional study of the Families and Media Project that sought to understand how low- and mid-income Latino families with children use media and technology in their everyday lives. Benny was not the only one who watched telenovelas with his parents or grandparents. Five other children from our Modern Families did and, with the exception of one 12-year-old girl, none found the dramas to be quite as gripping as the adults they watched with. Nevertheless, all six chose to be in the room while their parents or grandparents viewed telenovelas.

Upon witnessing a rash of whole-family viewings of World Cup soccer matches, we realized that the phenomena transcended soap operas, at least among our Modern Families. We detected a more general pattern of parent-child co-viewing around *ethnic media* than around mainstream US media, with ethnic media being defined as "media that are produced by and for (a) immigrants, (b) racial, ethnic, and linguistic minorities, as well as (c) indigenous populations living across different countries" (Matsaganis, Katz, & Ball-Rokeach, 2010, p. 6). This was notable because within our 15 case families, adults, and children tended to consume media separately. When they did so jointly, however, Spanish-language movies and news, adult dramas, soccer games, and other Latino-themed programs were often their content of choice. What was it about these shows that brought the families in our study together around a common screen? And what might family members be learning in their interactions with and around these programs?

This chapter aims to explore the phenomenon of intergenerational co-viewing around ethnic media, which to date has not been studied to the extent of co-viewing around mainstream US media. It does so by examining two Latino-themed television programs—*Dora the Explorer* and the telenovela *La Rosa de Guadalupe*—and why and how the families in our study interacted around them. Are there thematic or formal features they hold in common that add to their intergenerational appeal? What role do contextual and individual factors play in shaping these situations of joint media engagement? And what does learning look like in these two situations? The answers to these questions, we believe, can provide useful information to educators, media producers, and other practitioners who want to maximize children's out-of-school time for the learning and healthy functioning of the entire family unit.

Before presenting the case studies, we describe the role of ethnic media in immigrant and ethnic minority family life, and introduce the concept of the *boundary object*, particularly as it relates to intergenerational joint media engagement. Following this background, we describe our methods and then delve into the cases. The chapter concludes with a cross-case comparison highlighting common features of the shows we examined, with the aim of shedding light on previously unexplored learning moments that are bringing adults and children together in meaningful conversation, play, and other modes of interaction.

Background

Ethnic Media and Latino Audiences in the United States

The Hispanic-Latino population is the largest ethnic group in the United States, and by 2010 census measures comprised 17.4 percent of the total population (Colby & Ortman, 2015). Despite the diversity of cultures represented within the Hispanic-Latino designation, nearly all hold the Spanish language in common. This has presented a boon to Spanish-language broadcasters and networks serving US markets, where the Latino population collectively represents $1.3 trillion of purchasing power (Wallace Weeks, 2014). Media giants like Univision and Telemundo air Spanish-language programming that is produced in the United States as well as in Central and South America, and consumed by Mexicans, Ecuadoreans, and Cubans alike. Of course, not all US Hispanic-Latinos watch Spanish-language or Latino-themed shows; mainstream US media are just as, if not more, prevalent in Hispanic-Latino family life given their comparable ubiquity. The extent to which a particular individual or family consumes ethnic media depends on a variety of factors, including generation, primary language, country of origin, settlement region, age, and gender (Bendixen & Associates, 2005; Pardo & Dreas, 2011). Within the Hispanic-Latino population, for instance, 78 percent of primarily Spanish-speaking households watch TV in Spanish, compared to 50 percent of Spanish-English speaking and just 3 percent of mostly or English-only households (Pardo & Dreas, 2011). Hispanic-Latino women are also more likely than men to consume ethnic media, as are individuals older than age 60 (Bendixen & Associates, 2005).

For immigrants that do access ethnic media, these resources can play important *orientation* and *connective* functions (Adoni, Caspi, & Cohen, 2006). They provide critical information on how to navigate US systems, laws, and norms of behavior, find work, and connect with the local immigrant community. Ethnic media also powerfully connect immigrants to their lives left behind: to hear Spanish spoken in one's native dialect or cheer on the home country's futból team can instill a sense of comfort and belonging in a family still adjusting to a foreign environment. These very same programs can serve equally important, albeit different, functions for the children and grandchildren of immigrants (Durham, 2004). For instance, they expose youth to images and impressions of their ancestral heritage beyond what they learn from their parents and grandparents and, in doing so, help youth further refine their identities as members of a particular ethnicity (Matsaganis et al., 2010). Many immigrants fear that their US-born children and grandchildren will "lose" their culture growing up in America (Rumbaut & Portes, 2006; Takeuchi & Ellerbe, in preparation); others fear their children will never achieve or fail to maintain fluency with the mother tongue (Adair & Tobin, 2008; Kondo-Brown, 2006; Roca & Colombi, 2003). And for good reason—Spanish fluency within US Hispanic-Latino families has been shown to die out by the third generation (Portes & Rumbaut, 2006; Rumbaut, Massey, & Bean, 2006). Fortunately, there is a strong association between linguistic practices and cultural ideas, and ethnic media that are presented in the mother tongue can help reinforce lessons in native values, practices, and norms of behavior in children, especially with the guidance of an adult who can further model and encourage these practices (Park, 2006).

Ethnic Media as Intergenerational Boundary Objects

Adults and children are drawn toward media that speak to their particular life stages. This is why there are TV shows produced for children (e.g., cartoons) and TV shows produced for adults (e.g., soap operas), not to mention dedicated broadcast times (e.g., late night) and channels (e.g., Nickelodeon) to accommodate these viewing preferences. Audience-specific programming, along with the falling costs and shrinking form factors of the devices themselves, contribute to an age-based separation of television viewing in families today. Just 52 percent of parents of 2- to 10-year-olds watch TV with their children (Rideout, 2014), even though the average American adult watches 2.8 hours of TV per day (Bureau of Labor Statistics, 2016). Parents that watch with their children do so for 49 minutes per day and, as their children grow older, they co-view less often and for less time (Rideout, 2014).

While TV shows that adults and children equally enjoy are rare for the developmental reasons mentioned above, there have been a number of outstanding intergenerational programs over the years, starting with *Sesame Street*, which was carefully engineered to encourage parents to sit down and watch with their preschoolers (Fisch & Truglio, 2000). *The Brady Bunch*, *The Cosby Show*, *The Simpsons*, *American Idol*, *Black-ish*, and the recent swath of youth cooking competitions also deserve recognition for their multiage appeal. But in the 15 Latino families we studied, parents and children more often reported or were observed watching Latino-themed media together. Unlike the mainstream programs mentioned above, neither *La Rosa de Guadalupe* nor *Dora the Explorer* were produced with the intent of pleasing all-age audiences. As such, these programs acted as *boundary objects* (Star & Griesemer, 1989), a term that various disciplines (Akkerman & Bakker, 2011; Leigh Star, 2010) have appropriated to describe objects that link common activity across different domains of experience and expertise. Boundary objects hold different meanings or functions in each world, but can bridge gaps and facilitate communication between them. Some can even incite and inspire individuals to traverse domains, which can result in new understandings or growth.

Beyond just developmental differences, the dissimilarities between the childhoods of immigrant parents and their children can be particularly acute, and ethnic media can serve to bridge these experiences. What a mother and her tween-age daughter take away from a particular telenovela episode, for instance, is likely to differ significantly, given their own histories with love, betrayal, and life's other hardships. But their opposing interpretations and reactions to the drama can provide the basis for meaningful mother–daughter conversations, which in turn can steer the daughter to cross boundaries into new identities: as a moral individual, as a Honduran-American, and as a young woman. It is when parents and children engage with and around these boundary objects that they forge a family identity in their present locale and maintain a family narrative across generations. Ethnic media offer unique opportunities for sharing, enjoying, learning, and helping one another in the context of negotiating the family's values, norms, practices, and language. As Matsaganis et al. point out, "Ethnic media's role in negotiating and reinforcing ethnic identities is one of the many, often interrelated, functions that ethnic media can serve" (2010, p. 75). The present examination adds to this thinking by contextualizing identity formation within the framework of parent–child interactions. Though a parent and a child may be drawn to a shared event for different purposes and experience the content in different ways, what results is further solidification of the parent's and child's ethnic identities *in relation to one another*, as well as the family's ethnic identity more generally. This is why we believe these intergenerational boundary objects are worth special study, particularly those that relate to a family's ethnic heritage.

Methods

The two cases featured in this chapter are drawn from the Modern Families study conducted by the Joan Ganz Cooney Center. We followed 15 Hispanic-Latino families with at least one child between the ages of 6 and 9 for 6–8 weeks each, visiting them in their homes and other locations in the community. Although we focused on the media and technology practices of one focal child per family, these activities involved their siblings, parents, peers, and other family members and, accordingly, we treated the entire family as the unit of analysis. We spent our visits interviewing family members using a set of semi-structured interview protocols and observing them doing what they ordinarily do, which we captured using audio and video recording devices and field notes. The focal children were also called on the phone between weekly visits to log what they did with media and technology that day, with whom, and for how long. Further details on the Modern Families study's methods may be found in the Appendix, Study 8, and case family names used below are pseudonyms.

The cases featured in this chapter comprise two parts: (a) an examination of the history of the TV-based boundary object, including producers' intentions for the show, and (b) an analysis of how the program served to support intergenerational learning and interaction within a particular family. Although in both the *La Rosa de Guadalupe* and *Dora the Explorer* cases the data were drawn from interviews with parents reflecting on the roles these programs played in their children's development—as opposed to observations of the adult and child actually interacting around the shows—we also employ observational evidence to help make sense of the family's reactions to the show. The information required for the historical examinations were compiled by referencing published academic sources as well as Internet sources, the latter of which yielded more on the producers' intentions. We believe this twofold case approach to be unique: by juxtaposing a producer's objectives alongside a particular family's use of the show, we can hone in on how certain features may elicit certain responses. Too often, media studies focus exclusively on producers' intentions *or* consumers' uses and gratifications; here we look at how these intersect. With such information we can better understand the nature of intergenerational boundary objects so we can begin to take greater advantage of these often overlooked media moments.

We acknowledge that our exploration of two programs favored among the 15 families we studied is insufficient to capture a complete understanding of the role of ethnic media-based boundary objects in US Hispanic-Latino families. However, the deep and thorough analysis we present here is intended to complement our much broader analysis of the co-viewing activities of 185 Latino families living in four metropolitan areas in the United States (Takeuchi & Ellerbe, in preparation). The purpose of the latter investigation was to identify and classify the range of genres, devices, activities, and purposes involved in intergenerational engagement around ethnic media, and rendered a taxonomy that may be extended to also include Asian-, African-, and European-heritage families and the specific nationalities and ethnicities therein. Taken together, our deep and broad methodological approaches paint a fuller picture of how these intergenerational boundary objects foster family learning, connection, and identity.

The Cases

Case 1: Daddy Loves Dora

Chris Gifford, Valerie Walsh, and Eric Weiner conceived of *Dora the Explorer* in 1999, which began its 14-year run on Nickelodeon in 2000. Animators drew Dora Marquez as a large-eyed, brown-haired, sienna-complexioned, sporty 7-year-old of unspecified Latin descent. English may have been her primary language, but Dora spoke Spanish to communicate with friends and family and negotiate the tricky situations she often found herself in (Díaz-Wionczek, Lovelace, & Cortéz, 2009). Every episode followed a fairly standard narrative arc that presented Dora with a challenge that she—with help from her friends and audience members—tackled through a series of three steps. Dora enlisted the efforts of viewers by speaking to them through the screen and pausing for them to respond, making for a more interactive experience than most shows of its type (Hamilton, 2013).

Although *Dora the Explorer's* characters often spoke Spanish words and phrases, the main objective of the program was not to teach English-only viewers Spanish or, for that matter, Spanish-only viewers English. Rather, the curriculum aimed to develop preschoolers' problem-solving skills by having Dora model and encourage strategies such as observing, deconstructing complex problems, and asking for help. Spanish language (linguistic) skills were presented as a means to solve those problems, as were map-reading (spatial) and motor (physical) skills. In this way, the producers intended for Dora to demonstrate the use of *multiple* intelligences (Gardner, 1993) to tackle life's challenges (Díaz-Wionczek et al., 2009).

Producers set Dora's escapades in the context of a "a magical world replete with Latino touches—Spanish language, Latino-themed music, *dichos* (Latino sayings and proverbs), Dora's warm, embracing Latino extended family (*familia*), and Latino settings with people who reflect Latin America's racial and ethnic diversity" (Díaz-Wionczek et al., 2009). In fact, the producers were careful to not associate Dora or the show with any particular Latin nationality. Rather, through their portrayal of a "pan-Latino" world, the show exposed non-Latino children to cultural practices and traditions different from their own, and promoted strong Latino role models—which continue to be underrepresented in American TV and film (Mastro & Behm-Morawitz, 2005)—among all of its young viewers.

Dora the Explorer was one of the most popular educational TV programs for children during its eight season, 172-episode run spanning 2000 through 2014. The series aired on the Nickelodeon network's Nick Jr. station as well as on CBS during its Saturday morning Nick Jr. block. Spanish-dubbed versions of the program ran on both Telemundo and Univision. *Dora the Explorer* consistently scored top spots in 2- to 5-year-old children's television ratings and at the height of the show's popularity in 2004 attracted upwards of 21 million viewers per week (Frey, 2004). Since 2002, *Dora the Explorer* licensed merchandise, which has included everything from books and backpacks to cookies and cosmetics, has earned $11 billion revenue for Nickelodeon (Chozick, 2010).

Unlike *Sesame Street*, *Dora the Explorer* was not intentionally designed to get parents to sit down and watch alongside their children. Even so, Dora scored high parent approval ratings. A nationally representative survey of 1,577 parents of 2- to 10-year-olds conducted in 2013 found that 88 percent of parents considered *Dora the Explorer* to be either Somewhat (53 percent) or Very (35 percent) Educational, compared to the 96 percent of parents who believe *Sesame Street* to be Somewhat (38 percent) or Very (58 percent) Educational (Rideout, 2014). This is impressive given that *Dora the Explorer* has far fewer published studies demonstrating the effectiveness of its lessons than *Sesame Street*, a show whose educational efficacy has been demonstrated in more than a thousand of studies since 1969 (Fisch & Truglio, 2000).

Kenny Ortiz (44) and Jessica Galarza (38) have been together for a decade and have two children, 9-year-old Junior and 5-year-old Katie. Kenny is Puerto Rican, was born on the Lower East Side and raised with two brothers by his single mother, who moved from the island as an adult. Jessica grew up in Ecuador and immigrated to Queens with her parents and sister as a young adult. Jessica is more fluent in Spanish than she is in English, Kenny is the reverse, and they speak a mix of both languages with each other. The children speak English, but can understand the Spanish that their parents occasionally and their grandparents always speak to them.

The Ortiz-Galarzas are avid users of media in all varieties and forms. Board games, video games, DVDs, puzzles, and children's books line the overstuffed shelves of their living room, the central feature of which is a 60-inch flat screen TV. The living room is set up such that family members often use their personal devices (i.e., cell phones for the parents and tablets for the children) together while sitting on the couches facing the TV, which is almost always on and tuned to Nickelodeon, the Cartoon Network, HGTV, or a telenovela. Since the single bedroom holds two beds to accommodate all four family members, it is not a place anyone spends much time in, other than to sleep; the living room, therefore, functions as a space for both "alone" (e.g., homework) and "together" activities (family movie night).

Because Kenny has been employed off and on for the past couple of years, he's been the children's primary caretaker during nonschool hours. In an interview, we asked him whether there were any TV shows that he encouraged the children to watch. Without hesitation, he answered:

Kenny: *Dora the Explorer*. That's where he [Junior] learned a lot. He doesn't want to watch it any more. She'll [Katie] watch it sometimes. She used to watch it *all* the time.

Interviewer: Why do you like Dora so much?

Kenny: Oh [Katie] loves . . . [Dora] teaches all the time. And she's uh, she's Spanish. She's Spanish. So she speaks in some Spanish and she teaches *everything*.

Dora Marquez is not from Spain. But Kenny says he likes Dora "because she's Spanish[1]," suggesting a connection to a larger pan-Latino community that transcends specific ethnicities (Sáenz & Morales, 2015), one that is intentionally depicted in *Dora the Explorer* (Díaz-Wionczek et al., 2009), and one that his own family—a union of Puerto Rican and Ecuadorian blood and culture—certainly represents. Kenny also likes Dora "because she speaks in some Spanish." Kenny and Jessica do speak to Junior and Katie in Spanish—Jessica more so than Kenny—and in our other interviews with them, they expressed some remorse over their children not being more fluent. And Dora does more than just speak Spanish; she implores her watchers to repeat—and sometimes even shout—Spanish words and phrases at the screen to help solve the challenge at hand.

Finally, Kenny likes Dora because "she teaches *everything*." Kenny is among the 88 percent of American parents who consider *Dora the Explorer* to be either somewhat (53 percent) or very (35 percent) educational (Rideout, 2014). Nine-year-old Junior—who was standing nearby and halfway listening to us interview his dad—helped Kenny recall a recurring skit that his dad found particularly educational:

Kenny: There's like little games in there where they have little puzzles or something you gotta figure out.

Junior: A troll bridge, a troll bridge . . .

Kenny: And you've always gotta solve a problem from the toll bridge.

Junior: No, *troll*, troll bridge. He does riddles.

Kenny: Yah, that's what I was looking for.

The Grumpy Old Troll was featured in 16 episodes over six seasons of *Dora the Explorer* (Wikia, 2016) and Kenny's fondness of and familiarity with the troll indicate his presence in the room while his children watched the show. He may never have intentionally sat down to view the show with his children—recall that the producers did not intend to provide an intergenerational experience—but if he happened to be in the living room during the daily *Dora* broadcast, Kenny picked up on and evidently participated in some of the show's recurring antics. Such unintentional co-viewing has been reported in other studies where cramped quarters force family members to co-engage with media, simply because there are few spaces in the home available for individual media consumption (Horst, 2010; Takeuchi, 2011).

Case 2: Mama Loves Drama

Telenovelas, which have roots in Cuba, Brazil, and Mexico (Pérez, 2005; de Sá Pires, 2014), have become widely available across the globe and in the United States (McCabe & Akass, 2013; Miller, 2010). Despite their worldwide popularity, non-devotees of the telenovela might be tempted to refer to them as "Spanish soap operas" or "soaps of Latin America." However, this oversimplified definition falls short of recognizing differences between telenovelas and mainstream United States soap operas. For example, unlike the eternal plotlines of *General Hospital* or *Days of Our Lives*, telenovelas feature a limited number of episodes. Consequently, telenovela audiences often expect the story arcs to be wrapped with total knowledge of the characters' end situations (Acosta-Alzuru, 2003). Many viewers have love–hate relationships with the genre, either enjoying or despising its extensive melodrama (Singhal & Rogers, 1999). Some disapprove of the ways in which the stories tie to classism and an emphasis on social mobility, or sexist tropes and limited gender roles (Gomez Parga, 2014; Pearson, 2005).

While there exists a perception of telenovelas as melodramatic or superficial, they have deeply rooted social and political histories. There have been recent movements in places like Brazil and Venezuela to use the telenovela as a platform for addressing controversial social and cultural issues and to portray events taken from national news in the storylines (Acosta-Alzuru, 2003; Gomez Parga, 2014; de Sá Pires, 2014). In Mexico, there has also been a trend to represent messages surrounding tougher issues such as home violence or AIDS (de la Pérez, 2005). Since the late 1960s, several of Mexico's telenovelas have attempted to be educational, largely due to writer and producer, Miguel Sabido. Sabido aimed to use television for social change and saw great potential in the melodrama of telenovelas to promote "good" behavior and discourage "bad" behavior, which was largely influenced by Albert Bandura's social learning theory (Singhal & Rogers, 1999). He created several telenovelas, especially in the 1980s and 1990s, that promoted social themes such as family planning, responsible sexual relationships, and parenthood.

February 5, 2008 brought the premiere of *La Rosa de Guadalupe*, a Mexican drama created by Carlos Mercado Orduña for Televisa, the largest mass media network in Mexico (Trinidad, 2015). Many consider *La Rosa* to be a telenovela, though it has aired significantly longer than typical telenovelas and does not follow reoccurring characters. It also airs internationally, and began its broadcast in the United States in 2009 on Univision and its local affiliates. Its online presence includes hundreds of full episodes to watch on the streaming service Hulu, and several episode clips can be easily viewed on YouTube.

The premise of *La Rosa de Guadalupe* is rooted in the Mexican patron saint, the Virgin of Guadalupe. The national symbol has a shrine at Tepeyac Hill, where she is said to have appeared to Juan Diego in 1531 in an effort to bring more widespread belief in Catholicism (Wolf, 1958). Her image is ubiquitous in Mexico, as she is seen as the one who united the Spanish and the indigenous people in Mexico and, as such, a sacred representation of Mexican nationalism, the Catholic religion, and ethnic identity (Gomez Parga, 2014). In each episode, characters pray to the Virgin of Guadalupe as they struggle with conflict, confusion, and decisions. They rely on her to perform miracles in their situations, which are often based on current events and news stories in Mexico (Altamirano, 2012). While it contains religious content, Televisa claims that the show is not meant to change the religious beliefs of its viewers, but to promote faith and to inspire those in the midst of difficult situations (Trinidad, 2014). Episodes focus on topics such as drugs, divorce, sex, bullying, and teen pregnancy, very much in the Sabido fashion. Since its beginning stages, the show quickly captured the attention of adults as well as teens, who can easily relate to the stories of adolescence in its episodes (Trinidad, 2015).

Noelia Hernandez (27), her daughter Elaine (12), and son Eddie (9) live in a two-bedroom apartment in a largely Italian, Chinese, and Russian neighborhood in Brooklyn. Noelia, who works several hours per day in a restaurant nearby, makes extra income by renting the second bedroom of her apartment to a woman and her young son. Noelia moved to Brooklyn from Mexico City over 20 years ago with her parents and her sister, but due to complications with documents, she and her children rarely visit family back home. She misses her life and family in Mexico, and remembers fondly the smell of the food outside of her church and at the festivals in her borough of Iztacalco. Noelia often wonders if the better life for her is back home, but she knows that the life that she wants for her children is in the United States.

Even so, it is important to Noelia that Elaine and Eddie maintain and improve their fluency in Spanish as well as their appreciation of their cultural heritage. In addition to encouraging her children to communicate with family back home via Facebook, Noelia sends her children to a community center where they learn traditional Mexican regional dances, meet young people from similar backgrounds, and practice their Spanish speaking skills. For Elaine in particular, Noelia views *La Rosa de Guadalupe* as an avenue for language development and cultural maintenance. Elaine, who has been watching since age 10, absolutely loves the stories about adolescent woes, and often binge watches on her tablet or iPhone. She browses through the hundreds of episodes available on Hulu on her iPad, and the more involved she gets in the characters' stories, the more Spanish she picks up along the way.

Noelia fears the ways in which media may affect her children's interpersonal relationships and physical health. She is also apprehensive about Elaine's use of social media for fear of sexual predators and other online dangers. However, none of these fears apply when it comes to *La Rosa de Guadalupe*. Elaine is very into looks, makeup, modeling, and has a strained relationship with eating. Some of Elaine's friends have pressured her to cut class, while others have started to dress more "scandalously." Given these and other factors that concern Noelia about her daughter's transition to adulthood, Noelia has used relevant episodes of *La Rosa de Guadalupe* to talk about how issues in the show might apply to Elaine's life at school, and to reflect on the consequences of the characters' actions. According to Noelia:

> I tell her, "Let's see, you used to watch this type of show, you had to see the signs and think, 'I saw it in the TV show, and also my mom told me [that] I better not do it,' or something like that. 'You have to work hard to prevent things from hurting [or] damaging you . . .'"

Finally, Noelia sees the telenovela as an opportunity to bond with Elaine and to have important conversations with her, which she feels many busy and working parents fail to do. She suggests some of her own favorite episodes of *La Rosa de Guadalupe*—Noelia is a fan, too—so that they can enjoy those stories together. She also uses show material to discuss moral and religious lessons that Noelia feels most mainstream US programming does not provide.

Cross-Case Analysis

We have just presented two very different examples of ethnic media-based boundary objects that supported intergenerational conversations and learning in our Modern Families study. In the first, a father extolled the virtues of *Dora the Explorer* based on co-viewing sessions he's had over the years, initially with his son Junior (age 9) and now with little Katie (age 5). Unlike Kenny, who happened to be in the room when his children would tune into Nickelodeon, Noelia was a regular viewer of *La Rosa de Guadalupe*, and encouraged 12-year-old Elaine to view the show, too. By presenting these contrasting cases, we thought we could most effectively illustrate the diversity of intergenerational interactions around ethnic media observed among our families. The cross-case analysis that follows, therefore, is not meant to draw universal conclusions about the phenomenon; rather, it aspires to be a starting point for others to add to and further refine the notion of the ethnic media-based intergenerational boundary object.

The first list below describes a set of characteristics that the two *media properties* shared in common, and the second describes a set of characteristics that the two *co-viewing experiences* shared in common. Taken together, the two lists illustrate how the content interacted with the specific needs, desires, and situations of the family members we studied to shape learning around these boundary objects.

Characteristics of the Boundary Objects

Plastic and Robust

By definition, boundary objects are "plastic enough to adapt to local needs and constraints of the several parties employing them, yet robust enough to maintain a common identity across sites" (Star & Griesemer, 1989, p. 393). Unlike *Sesame Street* and *Black-ish*, which were engineered to entertain multiage audiences, *Dora the Explorer* and *La Rosa de Guadalupe* were intentionally created for child and adult audiences, respectively. And yet both held the attention and interest of the nonintended party of each parent–child pair without losing their identities as a children's cartoon and an adult-oriented drama among family members.

Serial

La Rosa de Guadalupe and *Dora the Explorer* are television series, which means viewers can tune in on a weekly basis to view new episodes, watch reruns and, over longer stretches of time, establish regular routines around these programs. *La Rosa de Guadalupe* has no recurring characters, as each episode is a stand-alone narrative unto itself. However, the formulaic nature of the show keeps viewers coming back for more each week, as though an alternative to attending Sunday mass. *Dora the Explorer*, on the other hand, employed its protagonist's spunky charm to foster allegiances from its young viewers. Preschoolers grow up with and then outgrow *Dora*, but families maintain relationships with the show as younger siblings inherit their older siblings' loyalties.

Universally Known

Since its 2009 US debut, *La Rosa de Guadalupe* has earned solid ratings on Univision (Crain Communications, 2014; Vasquez, 2016). Consequently, most viewers of Spanish-language television in the United States are familiar with the show as either devoted fans or critics of the melodrama. *Dora the Explorer* consistently topped the children's TV show charts during its 14-year run (2000–2014), which is why she's a household name in Spanish- and non-Spanish speaking families alike (Calvert, Strong, Jacobs, & Conger, 2007; Frey 2004). Because these programs are widely recognized across the US Latino population, they are less likely to be foreign to family members not in their target audience, and therefore of potential interest to them.

Culturally Latino

Ethnic media are produced *by* and *for* immigrants and racial, ethnic, and linguistic minorities (Matsaganis et al., 2010), and this designation is the basic criterion upon which we selected boundary objects to analyze. However, the definition does not require that the program itself possess culturally specific themes or identifiers. Hence, it is noteworthy that the producers of both shows meant to communicate important cultural themes. *La Rosa de Guadalupe* revolves around the modern-day miracles performed by Mexico's patron saint, the Virgin of Guadalupe, and is steeped in Mexican Catholic morals and folklore. *Dora the Explorer* was created to embody the pan-Latino world, and its producers made Spanish language learning an important focus of the program's curriculum.

Problem-Based

Each episode of both the telenovela and the children's cartoon presents at least one dilemma for its protagonist(s) to negotiate. Dora, with the help of her viewing friends, often use Spanish to save her from tricky situations, but sometimes these dilemmas require decision-making or physical skills to resolve. Whatever strategy is called for, it's intended to be an interactive experience for young viewers. *La Rosa de Guadalupe*, on the other hand, is less participatory but presents the viewer with alternatives to consider, which typically involves taking the moral high road. While the scenarios presented by *Dora* and *La Rosa* could not be more different, a goal of both shows is for viewers to transfer lessons learned on screen to their own lives.

Characteristics of the Co-Viewing Experiences

Identification with Characters

Like Dora Marquez, Junior and Katie could understand English and Spanish, but spoke mostly English. While this connection was probably lost on the children, Kenny appreciated the resemblance, along with the fact that "she's Spanish," like his Ecuadorean and Puerto Rican-blended family. The pan-Latino world depicted in *Dora the Explorer* felt as inclusive to Kenny as the show's producers intended it to be. Noelia, on the other hand, identified with the characters in *La Rosa de Guadalupe* as fellow believers in the miracles of a saint she has worshiped as a Catholic Mexican. In contrast to Kenny, the specificity of the show to her native country mattered.

Cultural Maintenance

By encouraging Elaine to watch *La Rosa de Guadalupe*, Noelia hoped to foster a sense of religious identity and devotion in her US-born daughter, especially since American schools do not cover lessons in morality and faith. That Elaine had no choice but to view episodes in Spanish was, at least to Noelia, a secondary benefit of this routine. As a New York City-born Puerto Rican, Kenny grew up speaking mostly English himself and was therefore concerned about Junior and Katie's chances of maintaining their native tongue at all. He felt that any exposure to Spanish beyond what his children heard spoken by family members—including a cartoon character's lessons—could only help.

Separate and Shared Motivations

Kenny and Noelia held high hopes for their children to get further in their formal educations than they ever did. But raising them with a strong sense of family identity and values was an equally important goal and, given how much their children liked *La Rosa de Guadalupe* and *Dora the Explorer*, they recognized the role these shows could play in fulfilling both aims. Junior and Elaine were aware of their parents' motives and indulged them by being willing learners. But they might not have given in on just *any* show. Elaine relished the racy plotlines of the telenovela and Dora and her sidekicks made Junior and Katie laugh. What all parties enjoyed in common, however, were the occasions to spend intentional time together, as media time in both families was typically spent apart.

Conversations

La Rosa de Guadalupe and *Dora the Explorer* grounded family conversations on topics that may not have otherwise come up in their everyday interactions. The telenovela, for instance, presented examples of the impending challenges of adolescence and adulthood. By discussing these fictional scenarios, Noelia helped Elaine see them as lessons to apply to her own life, as opposed to just an evening's entertainment. The problem-based nature of both shows provided sufficient hooks for inquiry and reflection, which meant that Noelia and Kenny could, for the most part, allow the narratives to do the teaching while they simply reinforced their lessons. Kenny and his children typically discussed *Dora* while viewing it together, but since Noelia and Elaine sometimes watched together and sometimes apart, their conversations frequently took place away from the TV set.

Enduring Engagement

Both case parents described an ongoing relationship with their children around the featured programs. Kenny cited the quizzes as something that he and Junior enjoyed whenever the Bridge Troll made a guest appearance on *Dora*, which were sporadic and unanticipated events, suggesting that father and son watched often enough to recount it as familiar practice. Furthermore, Kenny was able to continue his relationship with Dora across the preschool years of both Junior and Katie, who were 4 years apart in age. Elaine, aged 12, had been watching *La Rosa de Guadalupe* since age 10, which means that she and her mother had a long list of past episodes to revisit and reflect upon whenever a related dilemma presented itself in real life.

How the Boundary Objects Supported Learning

As the above comparisons illustrate, *La Rosa de Guadalupe* and *Dora the Explorer*—despite their surface differences—hold quite a bit in common, as did the parent–child interactions they supported. As boundary objects, the two shows provided a point of connection between adult and child worlds. And as a specific variety of boundary object, these ethnic media properties opened up unusual opportunities for intergenerational conversation and learning within the Latino families we studied. By watching *Dora the Explorer* and *La Rosa de Guadalupe* together, adults and children alike ended up crossing into new territory in terms of learning something about themselves and each other. The shows encouraged the parents, for example, to view the world through their children's eyes: Kevin became acquainted with Dora, a beloved heroine to his children, and her pan-Latino world, which Junior and Katie have, to some extent, come to associate with "being Latino." Noelia had to view each episode of *La Rosa de Guadalupe* through the eyes of her 10-, 11-, and now 12-year-old daughter to be able to help her interpret their moral lessons. As a result of their conversations about the moral dilemmas presented in the telenovela, Elaine granted her mother access to details of her social life that she may not have otherwise shared.

Watching these particular shows with their parents also required some boundary crossing on the children's behalf. Elaine had to adopt a more mature perspective in order to make sense of the adult-targeted telenovela. And in watching *Dora* with Kevin, Junior came to see how important it was to his father for him to learn Spanish and, in doing so, developed a stronger sense of his father's commitment to maintaining their heritage. In fact, in both families—and we would argue in other families in which ethnic media-based boundary objects ground intergenerational interactions—the parents and children mutually shaped and solidified their family identity, as proud members of the lands left behind and the one they now call home. The television shows provided both the gathering grounds and the material needed for the adults and children to discuss what it means to be Latino.

Discussion

We have just described how *La Rosa de Guadalupe* and *Dora the Explorer* served as the focal point for intergenerational engagement even this was not the explicit intention of either show's producers. Indeed, there are producers who aspire to bring multiage audiences together to both enjoy and meaningfully discuss show content, with *Black-ish* and *Fresh Off the Boat* being two contemporary examples of programs that are catalyzing family conversations around race and ethnicity (Genzlinger, 2014; Haithman, 2015). But if there are mainstream media producers committed to these causes, what value lies in our dissecting the ethnic media-based intergenerational boundary object? Here are our parting thoughts on the value of this research and implications for further work.

Parents Know Best

To date, opportunities for children to learn in home settings have gone largely untapped, as out-of-school learning has only recently received the research attention it deserves in relation to its school-based analog. While scholars have managed to identify the many ways in which parents can foster their children's academic learning (Epstein, 1995; Hill & Taylor, 2004; Mapp, 2003), less attention has been paid to how parents are already supporting their moral, cultural, socioemotional, and other forms of development. Understanding the factors that support naturally occurring forms of family learning may provide useful insights into how to support school-based learning at home as well. This chapter documents some of these practices in the context of a leisure-time activity that both adults and children benefit from and enjoy.

Following in the footsteps of Moll, Amanti, Neff, and Gonzalez's (1992) work on family "funds of knowledge," this research contributes to the still largely uncharted realm of parental pedagogical knowledge. Teachers may have a sense for students' needs and capabilities, but parents still know their children best. As their earliest and most intimate caregivers, parents know their children's likes and dislikes, strengths and weaknesses, moods and levels of maturity. In the cases featured in this chapter, both parents recognized qualities in the two programs that could enrich their children's cultural and character development in ways that the school curricula weren't currently providing. Noelia, for instance, would not have had Elaine watch *La Rosa de Guadalupe* if she did not think young Elaine could handle its adult themes, much less find the program entertaining. This is one of the most basic and original forms of "personalized learning" (U.S. Department of Education, 2016), an ideal that schools have been challenged to provide students in classroom settings (Kiderman, 2016). By involving parents more integrally in crafting their own child's school-based curricula—by querying them on their child's home-based interests as well as their moral, cultural, and socioemotional needs—educators can create connections between students' home-based interests and school and, consequently, effectively engage students in what they are learning at school.

Redefining "Educational Media"

Our analyses have raised the question of what it means for media to be "educational." By mainstream standards, telenovelas would hardly be considered edifying. Yet, Noelia appropriated *La Rosa de Guadalupe* to help communicate important life lessons to her daughter, as she found this to be the most pragmatic way to do so in the absence of a morality/ethics curriculum at school. It was effective in that both she and Elaine enjoyed the episodes enough to consistently watch them and look forward to the discussions that followed. A less dramatic or more didactic alternative would not have enlisted such committed participation on both of their behalves. Yet, by many people's standards, encouraging a 10-year-old to watch racy telenovelas would be considered poor judgment in parenting. *Dora the Explorer*, on the other hand, was produced to meet specific curricular objectives, but the lessons that Junior and his father took away from their co-viewing sessions involved more than new Spanish phrases and problem solving strategies. In both families, the adults and children recognized the value of these shows in enriching their understandings of one another, their family, and the larger world they live in, regardless of the producers' original intentions for the show.

There are normative notions of what counts as educational media (Rideout, 2014), and yet historically, some of the most enriching media-based experiences documented to date have not involved properties with explicit educational objectives. The video game *Minecraft* is an example of a commercial property not originally designed for the education market that has captivated millions of children around the world on the sheer basis of it "being fun." And yet, in playing the game, children are developing critical thinking, design, and/or collaboration skills (Burnett & Bailey, 2014; Duncan, 2011; Tromba, 2013). Media scholars have written extensively on how other mainstream properties such as Star Wars, Harry Potter, and Pokémon motivate children to participate in the fan-based narratives that extend far beyond the original property in both format and content (e.g., Ito et al., 2009; Jenkins, 2009). Meanwhile, the educational technology marketplace is saturated with game, app, and software titles touting explicit learning objectives, most of which have been unable to deliver empirical evidence of their educational efficacy (Hirsh-Pasek et al., 2015; Vaala, Ly, & Levine, 2015). The value placed on "educational media" over other forms of media—commercial, entertainment, ethnic, and otherwise—has had the effect of narrowing the universe of potentially educative material to the stuff that children are not very interested in. We need to expand our notions of educational media such that the term possesses far more utility for those seeking its benefits.

Intergenerational Media for Latino Families

While *Dora the Explorer* and *La Rosa de Guadalupe* grounded family learning experiences in two of the families we studied, we are certainly not prescribing these programs to others. The telenovela and the cartoon worked for the Hernandezes and the Ortiz-Galarzas because they accommodated the preferences and routines specific to each family. That said, certain qualities of the two shows—their emphasis on culturally specific content and promotion of problem solving, for instance—fulfilled needs that many Latino families also possess, such as the desire to maintain a cultural identity or raise well educated, morally driven children. Furthermore, the serial format of the shows made it more likely that the co-viewing routines they supported endured over time. We believe that these features contributed to the programs' durability and flexibility as intergenerational boundary objects and are more universal in this regard. While this chapter argues that there is potential in adult- and child-target television shows to bring families together, we are also advocating for the creation of more programs that simultaneously appeal to Latino adults and children, as *Black-ish* has done for the African-American community and *Fresh off the Boat* has done for Asian-Americans. Currently and historically, there has been a dearth of intergenerational programs for Latino-American families, despite the fact that Latinos are the largest minority group in the United States.

Final Thoughts

Even in this era of rapidly proliferating content streams and ever-shrinking gadgets, family members are still congregating around television content at a rate these newer media have yet to catch up to. This chapter highlights two very different shows—a telenovela and a cartoon—that managed to ground meaningful conversations between parents and children about family identity and values. The boundary object, as an analytic device, has provided an unusual view into the living rooms of families with young children, making more visible some of the unexpected yet effective ways in which parents and children are learning together. In closing, we encourage other researchers and media designers—as well as educators and parents—to continue to identify the magic ingredients of intergenerational engagement around other objects of ethnic identity, including sports, cooking, photography, and other arts and crafts. There is still much to be learned from these everyday pastimes and routines.

Note

1. Kenny refers to Dora as "Spanish" the same way New York Latinos refer to other Spanish-speaking individuals, whether they hail from Puerto Rico, Ecuador, Mexico, the Dominican Republic, or the Bronx (Rivera, 2003); the term is synonymous with "Latino" or "Latin."

References

Acosta-Alzuru, C. (2003). Tackling the issues: Meaning making in a telenovela. *Popular Communication, 1*(4), 193–215.

Adair, J., & Tobin, J. (2008). Listening to the voices of immigrant parents. In C. Genishi, & L. Goodwin (Eds.), *Diversities in Early Childhood Education: Rethinking and Doing* (pp. 137–150). New York: Routledge.

Adoni, H., Caspi, D., & Cohen, A. A. (2006). *Media, minorities, and hybrid identities: The Arab and Russian communities in Israel.* New York: Hampton Press.

Akkerman, S. F., & Bakker, A. (2011). Boundary crossing and boundary objects. *Review of Educational Research, 81*(2), 132–169.

Altamirano, S. L. (2012). La Representación Social del Guadalupanismo en el programa de televisión La Rosa de Guadalupe. *Comunicación: Revista Internacional de Comunicación Audiovisual, Publicidad y Estudios Culturales, 10*(1), 991–1005.

Bendixen & Associates. (2005). *The ethnic media in America: The hidden giant in plain sight.* Coral Gables, FL: New California Media in partnership with Center for American Progress Leadership Conference on Civil Rights Education Fund. Retrieved from www.npr.org/documents/2005/jul/ncmfreport.pdf

Bureau of Labor Statistics. (2016). *American time use survey—2015 results.* Washington, DC: US Department of Labor. Retrieved from www.bls.gov/news.release/pdf/atus.pdf

Burnett, C., & Bailey, C. (2014). Conceptualising collaboration in hybrid sites. In C. Burnett, J. Davies, G. Merchant, & J. Rowsell (Eds.). *New literacies around the globe: Policy and pedagogy* (pp. 50–71). Abingdon, UK: Routledge.

Calvert, S. L., Strong, B. L., Jacobs, E. L., & Conger, E. E. (2007). Interaction and participation for young Hispanic and Caucasian girls' and boys' learning of media content. *Media Psychology, 9*(2), 431–445.

Chozick, A. (2010, November 5). The turf war for tots. *Wall Street Journal.* Retrieved from www.wsj.com/articles/SB10001424052748704462704575590231467452448

Colby, S. L., & Ortman, J. M. (2015). Projections of the size and composition of the US population: 2014 to 2060. *US Census Bureau, Ed,* 25–1143.

Crain Communications. (2014). *11th annual Hispanic fact pack.* Retrieved from http://gaia.adage.com/images/bin/pdf/Hispanic_Fact_Pack_2014_web_rev0730.pdf

Díaz-Wionczek, M., Lovelace, V., & Cortés, C. E. (2009). Review and commentary: *Dora the Explorer*—Behind the scenes of a social phenomenon. *Journal of Children and Media, 3*(2), 204–209.

Duncan, S. C. (2011). Minecraft, beyond construction and survival. *Well Played: A Journal on Video Games, Value and Meaning, 1*(1), 1–22.

Durham, G. M. (2004). Constructing the "new ethnicities": Media, sexuality, and diaspora identity in the lives of South Asian immigrant girls. *Critical Studies in Media Communication, 21*(2), 140–161.

Epstein, J. L. (1995). School/Family/Community partnerships. *Phi Delta Kappan, 76*(9), 701.

Fisch, S. M., & Truglio, R. T. (2010). *G Is for Growing: Thirty years of research on children and* Sesame Street. New York: Routledge.

Frey, J. (2004, March 5). Hello, "Dora," Hola. *Washington Post.* Washington, DC. Retrieved from https://www.washingtonpost.com/archive/lifestyle/2004/03/05/hello-dora-hola/f785c6d3-99cd-4c69-bc75-73fa6ca70b3a/

Gardner, H. (1993). *Multiple intelligences: The theory in practice.* New York: Basic Books.

Genzlinger, N. (2014, September 23). "Black-ish," a New ABC comedy, taps racial issues. *New York Times.* Retrieved from www.nytimes.com/2014/09/24/arts/television/black-ish-a-new-abc-comedy-taps-racial-issues.html

Gomez Parga, A. C. (2014). *Que no te eduque la Rosa de Guadalupe! A textual analysis of gender and stereotypes in Mexican telenovelas* (M.A.). El Paso, TX: The University of Texas at El Paso.

Haithman, D. (2015, June 11). *"Black-ish" & "Fresh Off The Boat" among networks' new family comedies for all.* Retrieved from http://deadline.com/2015/06/black-ish-fresh-off-the-boat-networks-family-comedies-1201440975/

Hamilton, M. (2013, July 12). *Adorable Dora.* Retrieved from www.nickjrparents.com.au/2013/07/12/adorable-dora

Hill, N. E., & Taylor, L. C. (2004). Parental school involvement and children's academic achievement. Pragmatics and issues. *Current Directions in Psychological Science, 13*(4), 161–164.

Hirsh-Pasek, K., Zosh, J. M., Golinkoff, R. M., Gray, J. H., Robb, M. B., & Kaufman, J. (2015). Putting education in "educational" apps lessons from the science of learning. *Psychological Science in the Public Interest, 16*(1), 3–34.

Horst, H. A. (2010). Families. In M. Ito, M. Bittani, d. boyd, R. Cody, B. Herr-Stephenson, H. A. Horst, et al. (Eds.), *Hanging out, messing around, geeking out: Kids living and learning with new media* (pp. 149–194). Cambridge, MA: MIT Press.

Itō, M. et al. (2010). *Hanging out, messing around, and geeking out: Kids living and learning with new media*. Cambridge, MA: MIT Press.

Jenkins, H. (2009). *Confronting the challenges of participatory culture: Media education for the 21st century*. Cambridge: MIT Press.

Kiderman, J. (2016, March 17). *The elusive "f word" in personalized learning*. Retrieved from https://www.edsurge.com/news/2016–03–17-the-elusive-f-word-in-personalized-learning

Kondo-Brown, K. (2006). *Heritage language development: Focus on East Asian immigrants* (Studies in bilingualism, vol. 32). Amsterdam: John Benjamins.

Leigh Star, S. (2010). This is not a boundary object: Reflections on the origin of a concept. *Science, Technology & Human Values, 35*(5), 601–617.

Mapp, K. L. (2003). Having their say: Parents describe why and how they are engaged in their children's learning. *School Community Journal, 13*(1), 35.

Mastro, D. E., & Behm-Morawitz, E. (2005). Latino representation on primetime television. *Journalism & Mass Communication Quarterly, 82*(1), 110–130.

Matsaganis, M. D., Katz, V. S., & Ball-Rokeach, S. J. (2010). *Understanding ethnic media: Producers, consumers, and societies*. Thousand Oaks, CA: Sage.

McCabe, J. J. E., & Akass, K. (2013). *TV's Betty goes global: From telenovela to international brand*. London and New York: I.B. Tauris.

Miller, J. L. (2010). Ugly Betty goes global: Global networks of localized content in the telenovela industry. *Global Media and Communication, 6*(2), 198–217.

Moll, L. C., Amanti, C., Neff, D., & Gonzalez, N. (1992). Funds of knowledge for teaching: Using a qualitative approach to connect homes and classrooms. *Theory into Practice, 31*(2), 132–141.

Pardo, C., & Dreas, C. (2011). *Three things you thought you knew about U.S. Hispanic's engagement with media . . . and why you may have been wrong*. New York: Nielsen. Retrieved from www.nielsen.com/content/dam/corporate/us/en/newswire/uploads/2011/04/Nielsen-Hispanic-Media-US.pdf

Park, E. (2006). Grandparents, grandchildren, and heritage language use in Korean. In K. Kondo-Brown (Ed.), *Heritage language development: focus on East Asian immigrants* (pp. 57–86). Amterdam: John Benjamins.

Pearson, R. C. (2005). Fact or fiction? Narrative and reality in the Mexican telenovela. *Television & New Media, 6*(4), 400–406.

de la Pérez, M. L. C. (2005). Cultural identity: Between reality and fiction: A transformation of genre and roles in Mexican telenovelas. *Television & New Media, 6*(4), 407–414.

de Sá Pires, F. (2014). *The coviewing experience in the age of transmedia storytelling*. Barcelona, Spain: Universitat Pompeu Fabra.

Portes, A., & Rumbaut, R. G. (2006). *Immigrant America: A portrait*. Berkeley, CA: University of California Press.

Rideout, V. (2014). Learning at home: Families, educational media use in America. A report of the Families and Media Project. New York: The Joan Ganz Cooney Center at Sesame Workshop. Retrieved from www.joanganzcooneycenter.org/publication/learning-at-home/

Rivera, R. Z. (2003). *New York Ricans from the hip hop zone*. New York: Palgrave Macmillan US.

Roca, A., & Colombi, M. (Eds.). (2003). *Mi lengua: Spanish as a Heritage Language in the United States, Research and Practice*. Washington, DC: Georgetown University Press.

Rumbaut, R. G., Massey, D. S., & Bean, F. D. (2006). Linguistic life expectancies: Immigrant language retention in Southern California. *Population and Development Review, 32*(3), 447–460.

Rumbaut, R. G., & Portes, A. (2001). *Ethnicities: Children of immigrants in America*. Berkeley, CA: University of California Press.

Sáenz, R., & Morales, M. C. (2015). *Latinos in the United States: Diversity and change*. New York: John Wiley & Sons.

Singhal, A., & Rogers, E. M. (1999). *Entertainment-education: A communication strategy for social change*. Mahwah, NJ: Lawrence Erlbaum Associates.

Star, S. L., & Griesemer, J. R. (1989). Institutional ecology, "translations," and boundary objects: Amateurs and professionals in Berkeley's Museum of Vertebrate Zoology, 1907–39. *Social Studies of Science, 19*(3), 387–420.

Takeuchi, L., & Ellerbe, B. (in preparation). Joint media engagement around ethnic media.

Takeuchi, L. M. (2011). *Families matter: Designing media for a digital age*. New York: The Joan Ganz Cooney Center at Sesame Workshop.

Trinidad, M. (2014). Acerca de La Rosa de Guadalupe. Retrieved from http://television.televisa.com/programas-tv/la-rosa-de-guadalupe/noticias/2014-02-25/mas-alla-milagro-rosa-guadalupe/

Trinidad, M. (2015). La Rosa de Guadalupe, 8 años de éxito. Retrieved from http://television.televisa.com/programas-tv/la-rosa-de-guadalupe/noticias/2015-02-04/la-rosa-de-guadalupe-8-anos-de-exito/

Tromba, P. (2013). Build engagement and knowledge one block at a time with Minecraft. *Learning & Leading with Technology, 40*(8), 20–23.

U.S. Department of Education. (2016). *2016 National Educational Technology Plan*. Washington, DC: Office of Educational Technology. Retrieved from http://tech.ed.gov/files/2015/12/NETP16.pdf

Vaala, S., Ly, A., & Levine, M. H. (2015). *Getting a read on the app stores: A market scan and analysis of children's literacy apps*. New York: Joan Ganz Cooney Center at Sesame Workshop.

Vasquez, D. (2016, June 29). Hispanic TV: "El señor de los cielos." Retrieved from www.medialifemagazine.com/el-senor-de-los-cielos-flies-high/

Wallace Weeks, M. (2014, September 30). *Minority groups are energizing the U.S. consumer market as never before, according to annual Multicultural Economy report*. Athens, GA: Terry College of Business. Retrieved from www.terry.uga.edu/news/releases/minority-groups-are-energizing-the-u.s.-consumer-market-as-never-before-acc

Wikia. (n.d.). Grumpy old troll. Retrieved from http://dora.wikia.com/wiki/Grumpy_Old_Troll

Wolf, E. R. (1958). The virgin of Guadalupe: A Mexican national symbol. *Journal of American Folklore*, 7(279), 34–39.

10

LATINO IMMIGRANT FAMILIES BRIDGING HOME AND SCHOOL LEARNING WITH TECHNOLOGY

Amber Maria Levinson

How might technology help to connect home and school learning? Education research has defined a need for stronger connections between the ways children learn at school, and their home settings and practices. This chapter shares results from an ethnographic study of Latino immigrant families, focusing on three resourceful strategies some families used to "bridge" home and school. First, parents, all primarily Spanish speakers, employed free translator apps (such as Google Translate or iTranslate) to *bridge understanding*: deciphering children's homework assignments in English and as an English learning tool. Second, families used other digital resources such as mobile applications and an online library to *bridge skills*: bolstering children's academic learning and language. A third way in which parents connected home and school was by *bridging interest*: using online video (e.g., YouTube) to further explore topics that children had discovered at school, thus extending school learning into the home space. Several strategies identified in this chapter are "workarounds," or ways of creatively solving problems, that could be made easier and more effective if more tools were tailored for the express purpose of connecting home and school, and if educators and community leaders helped to support parents in taking advantage of online resources to link learning across settings.

Engaging families as partners in children's education has been increasingly recognized as a way to strengthen children's learning and the health of communities (Henderson & Mapp, 2002; Mapp & Kuttner, 2014). Educators and researchers alike stress that engaging families as well as aligning home and school learning are key to children's academic success. For low-income and/or immigrant parents however, there are often challenging disconnects between school and family approaches and expectations (Lareau, 2003; Rodela, 2014; Valdés, 1996). Meanwhile, as devices such as computers, smartphones, and tablets have become more accessible, questions of equity still persist. How do families use Internet tools? Who has access to learning opportunities, supports, and content that enable users to fully leverage the power of technology? Meanwhile, schools themselves are acquiring more technology infrastructure, presenting unique opportunities to create continuities between home and school settings (see Penuel et al., 2002, for a review).

Among those adopting new technologies most rapidly are our nation's growing population of Hispanic-Latinos, particularly Spanish-speaking and foreign-born Latinos (López, Barrera, & Patten, 2013). A large proportion of Hispanic-Latino immigrants are low-income, and their children, particularly those who begin school with limited English language experience, often face stark challenges in school (Valdés, Capitelli, & Álvarez, 2011). Research on the television show *Sesame Street* also suggests that many Spanish-speaking parents have watched the program with their children to improve their own English (Wright et al., 2001). Given these insights, and the great array of media available today, the research presented in this chapter set out to understand (a) how Hispanic-Latino immigrant families with young children are using digital media; (b) what kinds of language and literacy experiences these resources are bringing into their family life, and (c) what the opportunities might be for media and technology to support families who may be learning English and navigating the education system in a new country. Among the many findings from the study, this chapter shares how families used Internet technologies to bridge home and school settings.

Research focused on Hispanic-Latino immigrant families points in large part to relationships between home practices and school expectations including "home-school discontinuities" that become problematic early on and can set off a pattern of academic failure and disengagement that persists into their middle and high school years (e.g., Reese & Gallimore, 2000; Valdés, 1996). Disentangling these patterns, studies of language learning among low-income, language minority Latino families (not specific to learning with media) have stressed the importance of considering the particular social and cultural practices of families when designing and implementing interventions. Valdés' (1996) detailed 3-year ethnography of 10 Mexican-origin families in the Southwestern United States sheds light on the ways in which traditional family and child-rearing practices favor children's roles in supporting the joint family enterprise. These practices, Valdés argues, serve their own important purpose in the family's survival as a unit, however, they also often clash with the expectations of mainstream school culture. Valdés reveals via rich examples how efforts that seek to help children and their families succeed often fail due to a lack of understanding of this disconnect.

In-depth research suggests that these home-school discontinuities do not occur because Latino parents place a low value on schooling, or lack understanding of how success works. Goldenberg, Gallimore, and Reese (2005) instead argue that it is not the parents' values or goals that diverge from the mainstream; in fact most Latino families share the same desires for their children to do well in school as do teachers and middle-class families. Rather, it is children's *literacy experiences* at home that may help reveal the underpinnings for some discontinuities. Goldenberg et al. identify a cultural model by which parents' literacy activities with children at home are related to—among other factors—parents' own experiences with schooling and literacy development in their home countries. As they reveal parents' cultural model of literacy development, Reese and Gallimore (2000) also point out that these models are not always etched in stone and may evolve and change across generations or an individual's life:

> . . . parents' literacy practices and beliefs do not simply mirror those of their own parents and their childhood. Despite the existence of a shared model of literacy development, families respond to new challenges or demands in the environments in which they find themselves.
>
> (p. 121)

Applying this concept to the context of changing technology tools and access, the dynamic view of parents' frameworks is particularly important to consider. Most parents of young children today did not grow up in a world with smartphones, tablets or for many, even the Internet.

Today's rapidly changing technology landscape poses new challenges or demands for people to adapt to new technologies, and how they choose to take up these tools becomes the focus of attention here. In addition, following Valdés' (1996) emphasis on understanding social and cultural context, investigating the aspect of media use in family homes has the potential to shed light on home practices that in turn shape outcomes in schools or other settings.

The seven case families participating in the study resided in an urban area of Northern California, and were primarily Spanish-speaking, with parents originating from Mexico, El Salvador, Nicaragua, and Peru. All families had low incomes and there was a broad range of education levels among parents. The parents with the least formal schooling had finished up to third grade, and those with the most had completed college coursework in their countries of origin, with many falling in between. The parents were also frequent users of technologies that were not present during their own upbringing. Each family had at least one child between 5 and 7 years old (siblings ranged from 2 to 9 years old) and all school-aged children attended local public elementary schools, where they were enrolled in dual immersion or biliteracy programs (Spanish-English). The study followed these seven families for a 6-month period, through a series of ethnographic observations and interviews, as well as a survey and quantitative app use data (see Appendix, Study 10). Although part of the study included introducing a new tablet device to families, the practices described in this chapter were all happening prior to this intervention—they were existing strategies that families had developed independently of the research.

Three Family Strategies in which Media Helped Bridge Home and School

Over the course of the study, the seven families used technology in a variety of ways to make sense of their environment, access meaning, further their knowledge, and obtain information. This chapter shares several explicit, strategic, and often sophisticated ways in which families used Internet tools to bridge different settings, particularly home and school. These observations offer examples of some of the possible connections between in- and out-of-school learning that are not currently supported, encouraged or developed in families in any systematic way.

The following examples show ways that *media helped bridge learning across settings* including home and school. These practices included using technology to decipher homework assignments, searching for and exploring new English words online, and using an e-book library both in and out of school. Some of these bridging practices were also used toward parents' own pursuits—learning English or furthering their education or their careers.

Media tools can be particularly powerful in allowing people to connect across settings and boundaries. Among the case families in this study, whose primary home language was Spanish, media facilitated links between the home context and children's schools, where children received both Spanish and English instruction, and English was the language of many peers. As mentioned above, the specific ways that families "bridged" home and school using media were as follows:

1. Bridging understanding: Using translator apps (such as Google Translate or iTranslate) to understand children's homework assignments in English and to explore words heard at school;
2. Bridging skills: Using computer and mobile apps to strengthen children's academic skills including English language and reading;
3. Bridging interest: Using Internet video to expand upon topics a child learned about and became interested in at school.

The sections that follow offer examples of ways that families engaged in these bridging practices.

Strategy 1: Use of Translator Apps to Bridge Understanding

> They give him Spanish and reading homework in Spanish, but for math the instructions come in English, and sometimes I do not understand but I downloaded the translator application [. . .] So sometimes [my son] says to me, 'Mom, I need you to help me with this,' so then we go get the cell phone, we write what is written there and it tells us what it means, and then I tell him: ah, look, this is what it's saying . . .
>
> Érica, mother of Saúl, third grader

Throughout the study, parents from six of the seven families—five of the mothers and three of the fathers—spoke about and demonstrated how they used digital translator apps (chiefly Google Translate and iTranslate) for various purposes in their daily lives. Translator apps were a commonly used technology among families and served several different purposes. The examples below highlight in particular the ways that translator programs on smartphones, computers, and tablets supported families in understanding children's homework instructions in English. In this way, translator apps acted as a bridge that facilitated parents' attempts to access meaning from materials assigned at school in order to engage with the school-based learning activities children were involved in.

Translator apps do not always provide accurate output, and in some instances they added confusion. At the same time, this practice between parents and children allowed children to more successfully understand and complete the assignments, because parents accessed meaning from the texts and thus were able to support the task at hand. As shown in the examples, translator use involved and relied on both parent and child participation, and sometimes resulted in a collaborative meaning making between the two.

Some parents and children utilized the audio input feature (voice recognition via microphone), which allowed them to enter words as they were heard without having to spell them. The audio output feature enabled families to listen to the pronunciation of words in English. As with many of the apps and resources they downloaded, most parents discovered translators through word of mouth. José Rubén Orozco, whose son Brandon participated in speech support sessions at school, reported that the speech specialist recommended using a translator app to explore vocabulary and word pronunciation (further discussed below). The fact that these tools are free to download was a likely factor in their popularity across several families.

Parents, many of whom considered themselves to have a limited command of English, used translator apps to help understand the children's homework assigned in English. The following example describes how 8-year-old Naomi and her mother Lorena used iTranslate on their tablet to help understand homework instructions, specifically a two-part math word problem. It also illustrates the role that the technology played in a parent's effort to support her child's schooling.

Naomi (Age 8) and Lorena

Parents Lorena and Eduardo Aguirre had been the first generation in their rural families to attend university in Mexico. They immigrated to the United States with the dream of saving money with which to start a business back home, but have as yet been unable to save enough. Lorena is a stay-at-home mother caring for their two children, 6-year-old Eduardo Jr. and 8-year-old Naomi, both US-born. Eduardo works full time as a carpenter. Naomi is an avid reader and enjoys creating her own talk shows with her iPod, while Eduardo is passionate about sports.

During one observation, Naomi and Lorena were working with a pair of math word problems on a homework worksheet that Naomi's third grade teacher had assigned for homework. The word problems read:

1. The newspaper cost 50¢. Ron pays with a $5.00 bill. How much change should he get back?
2. The newspaper has three sections. The news section is 16 pages long. The arts section is 22 pages long. The sports section is 20 pages long. How many pages are in the paper?

Naomi read the problems and as she did so, translated them aloud into Spanish for her mother as she went:

Lorena: ¿Qué dice?
Naomi: Dice: El periódico cuesta 50 centavos, Ron pagó con 5 dólares. ¿Cuánto dinero le van a regresar?
Lorena: Es "shou" . . . "should" . . . Mmm . . . ¿Leíste bien la pregunta? "Should . . ." [Lorena types into the translator]. Dice que cuánto cambio debería volver. [. . .] Dice: Cuánto debería . . . Dice: Should he get back? Entonces . . .
Naomi: Debería volver . . .
Lorena: Debería volver. Entonces, ¿cuánto le deberían devolver a él, si el periódico costó 50 centavos?
Naomi: Mmm . . . 5 dólares . . .

Lorena: What does it say?
Naomi: It says, the newspaper costs 50 cents, Ron paid with five dollars. How much money are they going to give back to him?
Lorena: It's "shou" . . . "should" . . . Mmm, Did you read the problem right? "Should . . ." [Lorena types into the translator]. It says how much change should be returned. [. . .] It says: How much should . . . It says . . . "should he get back?" So . . .
Naomi: Should be returned . . .
Lorena: Should be returned. So, how much should they return to him, if the newspaper cost 50 cents?
Naomi: Mmmm . . . 5 dollars . . .

Having fully understood the language in the problem, at this point mother and daughter went on to discuss how to complete the actual math operation and with Lorena's support, Naomi was able to solve it.

Naomi's initial oral reading/translation of the problem served a dual purpose: it helped enable Lorena to understand the problem as well as to test whether Naomi understood it. In order to understand the problems and be sure that she knew what they were asking, Lorena typed the key question at the end of the word problem into iTranslate on her iPad and translated it to Spanish. For the first question, Naomi had translated the meaning of the question correctly when she read it to her mother, but Lorena used the translator to in order to validate Naomi's translation and reassure herself that they both understood it fully before determining the math operation needed.

From this point, Lorena was able to help Naomi reason through the math problem, focusing on the mathematical operation rather than on ambiguities in the language of the problem. In this instance, the translator app acted as a support that helped Lorena feel more confident she understood the homework instructions and helped enable her to guide Naomi with the math task itself.

Lorena used the translator app as a way to bridge a language proficiency gap that may have prevented her from supporting Naomi's school work. While helping Naomi complete another problem, Lorena clearly called out the value of the translator app and explicitly tried to instill in Naomi the strategy of first making sure she understands the problem and using the translator app as a tool if she is not sure. Naomi, not clear on what the question was asking, admitted, "It's that I don't understand," to which Lorena replied, "Ah, well there is this. [Lorena picks up the iPad and types the question in]. How many . . ." In this way, Lorena not only used the translator app as a support for her own comprehension, but she also modeled and explicitly encouraged this practice as something her daughter should do to clarify or confirm her understanding of text in a problem. From a Vygotskian perspective, the word problems were, mathematically and linguistically speaking, within Naomi's *zone of proximal development* (ZPD; Vygotsky, 1986)—within the range of tasks she could accomplish alone or with help. However, while Lorena possessed the mathematical knowledge to support her daughter, she needed support to accomplish the task of deciphering the language. In this case, the translator app was part of the repertoire of tools that Lorena, as the supporting adult in the situation, enlisted—not only to enable herself to guide Naomi, but also to introduce to Naomi as a form of support she could eventually use independently.

Translator apps also came with shortcomings, which parents had become familiar with, namely that they do not always provide a correct or sensible translation. For example, in one case where a sentence was referring to a duck's bill (*pico*), the translator offered *proyecto de ley* (bill of law), as the translation, completely mystifying the parent and child. When translating text that contains words with multiple meanings, the translator apps did not always choose the one that best fit. In fact, sometimes they added confusion by selecting a translation that hit far off the mark.

Families' use of translator apps to make sense of children's homework highlight an important way that media facilitated bridging home and school. Lorena used the app strategically, bringing a critical understanding of how the technology works to make the best possible use of the translations it provided. In this practice, she also explicitly modeled translator use and emphasized for Naomi that this tool was available and should be used, rather than approaching an exercise without understanding it fully. Naomi contributed to the task using her own knowledge of English, which Lorena tested by having her translate items aloud and then supplemented with the translator. Lorena brought her content knowledge as well as savviness with the technology itself. In this way, the translator app elicited a collaborative meaning-making practice between mother and child that not only supported Naomi in completing her homework assignments, but also supported Lorena in developing a deeper understanding of her daughter's current schoolwork. Finally, the translator app helped empower mothers in the study like Lorena to support their children in completing her homework, whereas they may otherwise have needed to seek help from either teachers or the child's father (the men in this study had more opportunities to develop their English at work).

An additional way that families used translator apps to bridge understanding was to further research English words and expressions often heard at school together at home. The voice recognition and "speak" features required the parents and children, regardless of their fluency with text or spelling, to speak English words they had heard (but might not know how to write), as well as hear the translator model the pronunciation. In this way, some parents and children took up the translator app, which offers the opportunity to explore vocabulary in a multimodal manner (text, audio, speech, etc.) in lieu of a dictionary or other print word reference resource. Unlike large print dictionaries, the app was also portable and could be taken along and used in any setting for—to use the popular phrase—"anytime, anywhere learning."

Although they expanded the realm of possibilities for families that used them, translator apps also had serious limitations in these learning contexts. The apps are not necessarily subjected to the same kinds of editorial or academic review as published print dictionaries, and it is unclear how complete or accurate their output might be. In addition, the audio feature, while useful, does not necessarily represent different regional variants of English or Spanish. For example, in an interview one child modeled how he input words into Google translate, using the Spanish word *piyama* (pajamas). However, Google translate did not recognize the Latin American variant and suggested the correction of *pijama*, invalidating Brandon's legitimate use of language and leading his father José Rubén to comment that he had not said the word correctly. This last anecdote raises the question of how translator apps might reflect the various regional forms of Spanish (or other languages) and if they are to be used as reference tools, how they might more inclusively reflect the particularities in vocabulary and pronunciation across the very diverse Spanish-speaking world.

Strategy 2: Bridging Skills: Using Technology as a Source of Academic Support

In some cases, families used other specific Internet resources in targeted ways to bolster their children's learning and progress in academic domains. Sometimes these tools were recommended and/or subscribed to by the child's school. In other cases, parents took the initiative themselves to find resources that would support their children in a given area. Emergent examples of both (school-recommended tools and parent choices) are presented here, and the examples shared represent all of the instances observed or reported of using apps or other technology resources to support children's learning in specific academic skills such as math or reading.

Jessica (Age 7) and Rebeca

Rebeca Rivera is a separated mother in her late twenties, with two daughters—Jessica, age 7 (in second grade), and Yoli, age 3. With some help from the girls' father, who does not live with them but does co-parent them, Rebeca juggles working nights and weekends. She also strives to further her own education, taking GED classes when she can. Jessica likes science as well as hula-hooping and the cartoon series *Monster High*.

For the Rivera family, YouTube helped bridge home and school by acting as a source of homework help. Rebeca used YouTube to review math concepts herself, in order to help Jessica with her math homework.

Rebeca: También si buscas en YouTube, por ejemplo tutorías para algo de matemáticas o . . .

Interviewer: ¿Usted busca en YouTube? Podría explicarme un poco más que busca?

Rebeca: Sí, como tutoría para ayudarme con las tareas, por ejemplo las matemáticas ahorita que no está en la escuela si no le entendía le busca en YouTube y ya le dan tutoría [. . .] Tutoría de matemáticas, tutoría de padres de matemáticas de primer grado.

Interviewer: Oh para los padres ¿entonces para apoyar a Jessica?

Rebeca: Si, para apoyar a Jessica.

[buscando el video en YouTube]

Interviewer: ¿Entonces ustedes han mirado esto juntos?

Rebeca: Bueno la miro yo para ayudarle en la tarea.

Rebeca: Also if you search on YouTube, for example tutorials for something about math, or . . .

Interviewer: You search on YouTube? Can you explain a bit more what you search for?

Rebeca: Yes, like tutorials to help me with homework assignments, for example math since right now [Jessica] is not in school. If I didn't understand I search on YouTube it gives a tutorial [. . .] Math tutorials, tutorials for parents for first grade math.

Interviewer: Oh for the parents, so it's to support Jessica?

Rebeca: Yes, to support Jessica.
Interviewer: So you have watched this together?
Rebeca: Well I watch it in order to help her with her homework.

In addition to seeking out online videos that explained math concepts with the purpose of supporting Jessica in her homework efforts, Rebeca used the iPad the family received as part of participating in this study to download math practice applications for Jessica to use. The Aguirre family (described above) had also downloaded the math application *Monkey Math* to their smartphone the year prior to the study, to help Naomi (then in second grade) practice basic math operations and increase her speed for timed quizzes her teacher gave in school.

E-books, particularly ones that offer the combination of illustrations, text, and audio narration, have shown some promise in research studies particularly where second language learners are concerned. Books that present the story in several modalities at once, in ways that support story comprehension meaningfully, can help readers' comprehension and vocabulary learning (Bus, Verhallen, & deJong, 2009). Although research comparing the use of print books to ebooks has returned mixed results with children reading in their first language (Warschauer & Miller, 2014), some research with second language learners has suggested a difference in how electronic books support these learners, and that they may benefit from the multimedia aspects of e-books in ways that native speakers do not (Bus et al., 2009). The case example below shares how one family in the study engaged with a literacy tool that the child's school subscribed to, and the challenges they encountered.

Saúl (Age 8) and Érica

Saúl Martínez, aged 8, had recently arrived from Mexico and was attending third grade. His teacher recommended that over summer break he continue to use MyOn, an online library of ebooks subscribed to by the school, to continue developing his English skills. The family of four lived in a single room, and they did not have a working computer with reliable internet at home, so Saúl's mother Érica frequently took Saúl and his younger brother to the local library, both to use the computers and to enjoy a leisure space outside their cramped quarters.

Online libraries such as MyOn, which can be logged on to from any device, offer potential to extend school activities into out-of-school spaces (e.g., by allowing a child to explore the same book used in the classroom from home) as well as easy access to a wide variety of books. At the same time, Saúl's particular experience with this kind of tool illustrates ways that e-reading materials could do better to reach diverse learners.

When Saúl logged on to MyOn at the library, he began navigating the site, searching for books that were grouped based on interest areas. Saúl became excited when he encountered a collection of books entitled "Favorite Characters," marked by a comic-book illustration icon that caught his eye, and found a Batmanthemed book—*Dark Knight: Cat Commander.* "Batman!," exclaimed Saúl, enthralled. However, when Saúl began to read and listen to the narration, the complexity of the vocabulary and lack of illustrations made it difficult for him to access meaning form the text. The first page began, "On the roof of Gotham Museum, Batman stood motionless in the moonlit shadow of an air conditioning unit. . . ." There were no illustrations to support what was happening in the story.

Saúl's mother Érica was also concerned that Saúl could not make sense of the language in the book. She pressed him to read out loud along with the narrator. "It's hard," Saúl commented softly in Spanish, after a few minutes with the book. "Let's find something easier," his mother suggested.

Saúl returned to the main menu and pointed at the "Picturebooks" collection and the "Readers" collection. "This is where my teacher told me to read, I don't remember if it was this one, or that one," he mused. Saúl chose "Picturebooks," which presented a selection of books for preschoolers such as *Duck goes Potty*, *Bunny Eats Lunch*, and *Busy Truck*. Saúl settled on *Crabby Pants*, a picture book about a young child learning to deal with disappointment. Saúl could understand more of the *Crabby Pants* story—which displayed one or two sentences per page and full-page illustrations—than he could of the *Batman* plot. Clearly however, the topic and plot were not appropriate for his age or interests. Saúl's reading became an academic exercise, rather than an exploration of interesting books.

As suggested above, Saúl had some difficulty finding a good match between his *interests* (particularly in the Favorite Characters/superhero genre as illustrated by his enthusiasm for the *Batman: Dark Knight* text) and his zone of proximal development (Vygotsky, 1986) in terms of English reading and comprehension. In this mismatch that occurred between Saúl's interests and the level of the text, the MyOn books aimed at his age group assumed a level of both English and reading skills that were far from Saúl's zone of proximal development as a beginning English learner. For this reason, Saúl may have had a difficult time accessing meaning from the *Dark Knight* text he chose and become discouraged with the book. The vocabulary in the text is fairly complex, and although Saúl demonstrated an interest in the theme of the story and was attracted by the cover illustration, the language used in the book and lack of illustrations to contextualize them likely made it very challenging for him to grasp at the content of the story. On the other extreme, books with simpler text and a plentiful visual support were targeted at preschoolers and the kinds of topics that children of that age might prefer. Although Saúl perhaps had a better chance of understanding the story, the aspects that had grabbed his interest in the first two titles were missing in these books.

Strategy 3: Bridging Interest—Deepening Inquiry across Settings

As shown in prior research, families may use media—and specifically online videos—to further explore topics of children's interest (Barron, Levinson, Matthews, & Vea, in preparation; Rideout & Katz, 2016). During the present study, a case example from 6-year-old Brandon Orozco and his father José Rubén illustrated the way that media facilitated parent-child exploration of a theme the child became interested in at school—in this case history and historical figures.

Internet resources provided the means for families to access the types of information included in school curricula, but also allowed families to explore *beyond*, expanding upon interests that were ignited in school or elsewhere. In the following case, free online video provided the means for a father and son to further explore an interest that was sparked at school. It is worth noting that for families in the study, YouTube was also used as a reference tool for other types of information, including recipes, repair instructions, hairstyles, and more—much of which could be found in Spanish-language videos.

Brandon (Age 7) and José Rubén

Brandon, aged 6, whose parents are from El Salvador, is an active boy who loves to play outside as well as play video and board games, especially ones related to sports and superheroes. He attends first grade and speaks predominantly Spanish although his parents report based on observing him at school that he understands and speaks some English as well. Brandon also had begun to demonstrate a keen interest in history, and often asked his parents detailed questions about historical figures that he was learning about at school such as Martin Luther King, Jr. and César Chávez.

A curious and inquisitive child, Brandon often asked questions about famous people that had come up in the school curriculum, either because of a particular holiday such as Martin Luther King Jr. Day or other thematic units his first grade class was studying at the time. Brandon's father José Rubén turned to YouTube as a way of learning more. The two began searching for videos on YouTube about Martin Luther King, Jr., George Washington, and other famous leaders Brandon wanted to know about in the moment. As José Rubén explained:

> Entonces, ya, para que él vaya . . . porque él nos pregunta mucho también de César Chávez, de Martin Luther King, de Washington, de todos . . . porque me imagino que en la escuela se los mencionan y él viene con la idea de eso o quiere ver cómo son más o menos, a veces hay videos donde hay fotos, a veces hay videos donde está Martin Luther King hablando, y está ya con una idea de quién es, ya se percata de quién es la persona, quiénes son . . .
>
> So, well, for him to . . . because he also asks us a lot about César Chavez, about Martin Luther King, Washington, about all of them . . . because I imagine that at school they mention them and he comes home with that idea or wants to see what they are like, sometimes there are videos with photos, sometimes there are videos where Martin Luther King is talking,

> and that way gets an idea of who he is, and he starts realizing who the person is, who they are.

Although numerous text resources are available online about any of these important names in history, in José Rubén's view the videos provided a way of representing information that was easier for Brandon to connect to at his age:

> Porque es más fácil para él, para que él lo visualice y le entienda más bien, y todo, y así como uno de adulto, pues lo pongo a leer y todo y a veces entendemos más bien. Pero a veces si nos ponen a leer, a veces tal vez no lo entiende uno bien. Y así se lo representan o . . . como que él entiende un poquito más así la representación de los personajes . . .
>
> Because it's easier for him, for him to visualize it and understand it better, and everything, and as adults sometimes we read and understand things better. But sometimes if we're given something to read, sometimes we don't understand it well. And this way [on the videos] they represent it or . . . like he understands the way the representation of the figures better that way.

Though José Rubén and Brandon began exploring online videos in order to learn about history-related topics, they expanded this to explore other interests as well. Brandon was also interested in animals, so father and son researched videos on animals and dinosaur species. José Rubén also described one case in which Brandon's questions were actually sparked by watching one of the Disney *Ice Age* movies:

> Dice 'Papi, ¿en esa época cómo era, que no había buses, no había . . .?' entonces vemos documentales donde aparecen y todo.
>
> He said 'Dad, at that time what was it like, there weren't any buses, there weren't . . .?,' so we watched documentaries where it's shown and everything.

In this way, media and particularly Internet video became a go to resource for Brandon and José Rubén to learn about topics Brandon was interested in, taking advantage of both the information available as well as the visual nature of the material and in the case of historical figures, even seeing and hearing people from the past.

Discussion

The three strategies presented above categorize several language and literacy experiences in which media helped bridge home and school settings. Families showed ingenuity "in tight circumstances" (McDermott & Raley, 2011) or *inventos* (Schwartz & Gutiérrez, 2013, 2015) by leveraging technology in innovative ways in situations of limited resources. Families showed these kinds of inventive strategies that have been traditionally present in non-dominant communities (Schwartz & Gutiérrez, 2015).

In the *bridging understanding* practices, Internet translating tools mediated families' understanding of assignments, allowing families to collaboratively access meaning in ways they may not have been able to do otherwise, while also bringing some limitations and challenges. In Saúl and Érica's session with MyOn, we see a media program's unique potential to span in-school and out-of-school settings, as well as how both content and parent participation powerfully mediate the experience in positive and challenging ways. Online video provided oral and visual explanations available online were a tool to support parents' *content* knowledge, as in Rebeca's example of using YouTube videos to better understand how to help her daughter with math homework. It also provided a means for Brandon and his father to explore a history interest sparked in school.

With regard to the *bridging skills* category, Saúl's example shows a unique way that technology can span in-school and out-of-school settings, and illustrates two directions for further research and design to support second language learners via e-books, in particular from the out-of-school perspective less frequently represented in the literature. The first is to investigate the opportunities to leverage technology to create customized e-reading tools that can take into account both children's age/potential interests *and* language skills, rather than automatically linking these two aspects in design. For example, one could imagine a *Dark Knight* book that used simpler vocabulary and employed illustrations to help readers contextualize the story. Such a book would have the potential to capture the interest of a child Saúl's age, but also fall within his individual zone of proximal development in the given scenario. Although MyOn offers a wide variety of books integrated with assessments and a multitude of ways to customize the selection made available, the books themselves do not offer multiple options for difficulty. In other words, books targeted at a given age range are written at a particular level. More nuanced and varied combinations of text difficulty and interest area could be possible given technology tools available today, and for English learners these multiple permutations may more closely tailor content for meaningful literacy experiences.

Saúl's online reading example also draws specific attention to the role of guided participation in the child's activities (Rogoff, 1990) in this case, and the ways in which Saúl's mother Érica's own framing of the literacy activity impacted the young learner's experience. As Goldenberg, Reese, and Gallimore (1992) point out, "Just as a teacher might design and send materials and activities to children's homes, so too does the child's home receive and interpret them" (p. 499). Érica placed a very high value on her son's education and was motivated to support him, much as are other Hispanic-Latino parents documented in prior research

(Goldenberg, 1987; Reese & Gallimore, 2000; Valdés, 1996). Érica's motivation to further Saúl's education and specifically his English skills is strong and led her to intentionally seek out an out-of-school literacy tool prescribed by Saúl's teacher. As in the case of Brandon and his father exploring words on Google Translate, this case also shows the important role teachers and other trusted individuals can play in supporting families as they try to understand how to best leverage technology. It also shows some shortcomings that literacy tools not necessarily designed with English learners or struggling readers in mind can have.

The *bridging interest* practices point to some potential ways that digital technologies might allow for children to further explore topics of inquiry across settings and engage in interest-driven learning (Barron, 2006). The ability to search online and encounter multimedia representations of nearly any topic offers distinct advantages, as compared to using encyclopedias or consulting a library book collection, for example. First is the ease of accessing such material from the home for "anytime, anywhere learning." Second is the auditory and visual nature of the resources, which may be more accessible for pre-readers or emerging readers. However there are also disadvantages, namely that online searching can return results that provide inaccurate information or even inappropriate content, and thus young children need the presence of an informed adult to navigate.

There are three points to highlight across all three strategies shared. First, the rich examples show how deeply motivated parents in these case families are to support their children's schooling and learning, echoing prior work with Hispanic-Latino immigrant families (Goldenberg, 1987; Rodela, 2014; Valdés, 1996). Parents in this study actively supported their children's efforts, modeled ways of leveraging media tools for their own knowledge, and sought out ways to understand and expand upon what children were learning in school. Parents reached out for technology tools to connect home and school because they were motivated to do so, and because they offered unique forms of support that were not provided by another mechanism.

Second, families' strategies here represent innovative workarounds or creative approaches to solve problems where no ideal tool is available. For example, YouTube serves as a means of locating further information for families to explore based on topics introduced at school. However, YouTube presents content of varying quality and appropriateness. A tool designed to help families further explore school topics could be created, where families may find video, images, or other materials to elaborate on areas of interest related to the school curriculum or assigned projects.

Finally, the examples shared here present considerations for educators and designers serving families of language learners. Digital media offer the opportunity to explore topics in visual and other modalities besides text that can support these emerging bilinguals' grasp of new concepts and language. Freely available content online can be harnessed to help support students and their families. The example of Saúl engaging with e-books also reveals a potential affordance of e-reading, which could be to offer varying levels of text complexity for any one book title (e.g., superhero books that can be read either at third grade level, or at earlier reading levels). In this way, electronic texts can offer reading material for children based on their interests, at any reading level. This will require producers of electronic books to think of their titles not as onscreen versions of print books, but as a different tool with the capability to transform uniquely to serve students' needs.

Conclusion

The cases shared here have shown the important roles that that Internet-based apps (translators, online video, online libraries, etc.) played in bridging understanding, skills, and interests across the divides between home and school settings. Moreover, although the technologies themselves provided the means, the bridging was realized through the ways in which these immigrant families *used* digital tools and harnessed them to advance toward particular goals. Parents varied in their savvy with technology and the degree to which they leveraged the tools available to them. However, families' use of these technologies included sophisticated strategies for learning as well as inventiveness and ingenuity in approaching challenges, often with limited resources. These examples also revealed ways in which media tools may be leveraged for purposes that designers and producers had not necessarily intended or conceived of, such as using translator apps for support in completing homework. In turn, families' strategies illuminate new possibilities and opportunities for design. These implications, discussed in more depth in Levinson (2014), might include e-reading tools that can adapt text difficulty for English learners or other diverse readers, translation tools that are tailored for use in language study or for understanding homework items, and curation tools that allow teachers to set up video collections that draw expand upon what has been learned in school—to suggest a few.

Finally, family media practices among this case study sample support evidence presented in prior research of the high value Hispanic-Latino immigrant families place on education (e.g., Valdés, 1996), which can be more effectively tapped into by educators and schools. This value was applied both to their children's education, which was a priority, and parents' own continued learning as adults. Case parents in this study actively pursued knowledge and leveraged media in intentional and strategic ways to support their children's schooling and/or to advance their own studies or careers for the benefit of their families. While parents' knowledge and overall comfort with technology varied (even between parents in the same family), the data indicate many opportunities where existing technologies can support families, and where technology design can do better to tailor resources for Hispanic-Latino immigrant families and their communities. Finally, variability in parents' comfort and experience with technology could contribute to already existing inequities, as parents who are more tech savvy leverage these tools to support children's learning, while others may not. Schools, libraries, and other community organizations can play an important role in helping provide opportunities for all parents to gain experience with digital technologies and learn strategies for supporting their children's schooling.[1]

Note

1. As an example of a community program for parents technology fluency, see the Latina Tech Mentors program at Mission Graduates in San Francisco.

References

Barron, B. (2006). Interest and self-sustained learning as catalysts of development: A learning ecology perspective. *Human Development, 49*, 193–224.

Barron, B., Levinson, A., Matthews, J., & Vea, T. (in preparation). Digital media as a catalyst for learning: Contributions of parent & child learning biographies, expertise and interests.

Bus, A. G., Verhallen, M. J. A. J., & deJong, M. T. (2009). How onscreen storybooks contribute to early literacy. In A. G. Bus & S. B. Neuman (Eds.), *Multimedia and literacy development: Improving achievement for young learners* (pp. 153–167). New York: Routledge.

Goldenberg, C. (1987). Low-income Hispanic parents' contributions to their first-grade children's word-recognition skills. *Anthropology and Education Quarterly, 18*, 149–79.

Goldenberg, C., Reese, L., & Gallimore, R. (1992). Context effects on the use of early literacy materials in Spanish-speaking children's homes. *American Journal of Education, 100*(4), 497–536.

Goldenberg, C., Gallimore, R., & Reese, L. (2005). Using mixed methods to explore Latino children's literacy development. In T. Weisner (Ed.). *Discovering successful pathways in children's development: Mixed methods in the study of childhood and family life* (pp. 21–46). Chicago, IL: University of Chicago Press.

Henderson, A.T., & Mapp, K. (2002). *A new wave of evidence: The impact of school, family, and community connections on student achievement.* Austin, TX: Southwest Educational Development Laboratory.

Lareau, A. (2003). *Unequal childhoods: Class, race, and family life.* Berkeley, CA: University of California Press.

Levinson, A. M. (2014). *Tapping in: Understanding how Hispanic-Latino immigrant families engage and learn with broadcast and digital media.* Doctoral dissertation, Stanford University (3781 2014 L).

Lopez, M. H., Gonzalez-Barrera, A., & Patten, E. (2013). *Closing the digital divide: Latinos and technology adoption.* Washington, DC: Pew Hispanic Center.

Mapp, K. L., & Kuttner, P. J. (2014). *Partners in education: A dual capacity-building framework for family–school partnerships.* Austin, TX: Southwest Educational Development Laboratory.

McDermott, R., & Raley, J. (2011) Looking closely: Toward a natural history of human ingenuity. In E. Margolis & Luc Pawels (Eds.), *The Sage handbook of visual research methods* (pp. 372–391). Los Angeles, CA: Sage.

Penuel, W. R., Kim, D., Michalchik, V., Lewis, S., Means, B., Murphy, R., et al. (2002). *Using technology to enhance connections between home and school: A research synthesis.* Prepared for the Planning and Evaluation Services, U.S. Department of Education. Menlo Park, CA: SRI International.

Reese, L., & Gallimore, R. (2000). Immigrant Latinos' cultural model of literacy development: An evolving perspective on home-school discontinuities. *American Journal of Education, 108*(2), 103–134.

Rideout, V. J., & Katz, V. S. (2016). *Opportunity for all? Technology and learning in lower-income families*. A report of the Families and Media Project. New York: The Joan Ganz Cooney Center at Sesame Workshop.

Rodela, K. C. (2014). Ni el problema, ni el remedio (neither the problem, nor the solution): Latina immigrant mothers negotiating deficit perspectives in U.S. early childhood education. Doctoral dissertation, Stanford University. Retrieved from https://purl.stanford.edu/gn022nj4118

Rogoff, B. (1990). *Apprenticeship in thinking: Cognitive development in social context*. New York, NY: Oxford University Press.

Schwartz, L., & Gutiérrez K. (2013). Turn-taking and *Inventos*: Examining the everyday lives of latino families and designing learning ecologies with youth and under-graduates. Paper presented at the Digital Media and Learning Conference, Chicago, IL.

Schwartz, L., & Gutierrez, K. (2015). Literacy studies and situated methods: Exploring the social organization of household activity and family media use. In J. Rowsell & K. Pahl (Eds.), *The Routledge handbook of literacy studies* (pp. 575–592). London: Routledge.

Valdés, G. (1996). *Con Respeto: Bridging the distances between culturally diverse families and schools: An ethnographic portrait*. New York: Teachers College Press.

Valdés, G., Capitelli, S., & Álvarez, L. (2011). *Latino children learning English: Steps in the journey*. New York: Teachers College Press.

Vygotsky, L. (1986). *Thought and language*. Cambridge, MA: The MIT Press.

Warschauer, M., & Miller, E. B. (2014). Young children and e-reading: Research to date and questions for the future. *Learning, Media and Technology, 39*(3), 283–205

Wright, J., Huston, L., Murphy, K. C., St. Peters, M., Piñon, M., Scantlin, R., et al. (2001). The relations of early television viewing to school readiness and vocabulary of children from low-income families: The early window project. *Child Development, 72*(5), 1347–1366.

AFTERWORD

Heather Weiss

Stepping back to reflect, I am struck by how much this book advances the conversation about digital media and learning in at least four pivotal ways. First, it moves us beyond Turkle's usefully provocative portrait of families alone together to paint a different and powerful alternative picture in the mind's eye. This alternative picture is more complex and optimistic, one in which many families have and use their agency to shape media in support of increasingly essential lifelong learning and recognize that they learn anywhere and anytime, not just in class or school. The research shows we have a lot to learn from and about families, and their voice and views need to play a bigger role as we move forward to reap the benefits of media for lifelong learning.

Second, the book is a leading example of how to employ Bronfenbrenner's multilayered ecological framework and its related process, person, context, and time (PPCT) research model to understand complex family processes in order to address a consequential challenge: how to shape media to support learning for all families, not just the economically and otherwise advantaged. It showcases the value of funding multidisciplinary and mixed methods teams to get both a broad overview and a deep examination of proximal processes in families in multiple and under researched ecological niches, thereby bringing the experiences and array of possibilities for shaping media use from a broader range of families to the table. It is my hope that this book will inspire more funders and researchers to pursue this fruitful research model, thereby continuing to expand understanding and action around how diverse families do and can use media to support learning.

Third, as the book's introduction notes, more widespread access to smart phones and tablets is closing the digital access divide, opening up a whole range of out-of-school learning opportunities for young people, and challenging libraries, after school providers and other community-based organizations to embrace and support families' and not just children's use of digital media. With its nuanced, more inclusive and optimistic picture, the book will inform the work of a range of organizations as they support and scaffold families use of digital media for learning.

Last, and overall, the book pushes us to pivot from a stance in which researchers inform practice to a broader one in which researchers share their work and encourage and build the inclusion of families, community-based organizations and others in a process of designing practices, apps, programs, and other supports to better meet their needs. Human-centered design, aka design thinking, a process bringing together diverse perspectives and experiences to develop and test solutions to complex challenges, is well suited for this. The four pivots together create a bridge to new ways of thinking and doing that hold substantial promise. Echoing the preface, I hope many people read the book and take it to heart.

APPENDIX

Study Methods

STUDY 1

Learning at Home—National Survey of Educational Media Use

Principal Investigator: Vicky Rideout, VJR Consulting

This study is based on a nationally representative survey of 1,577 parents of children ages 2–10 years old, including an oversample of Black (290) and Hispanic-Latino (682) parents. It is the first study to quantify, on a national level, how much of children's media time is devoted to educational content—platform by platform, age by age. The study also provides a measure of parents' experiences with and beliefs about the educational media their children use, and assesses the degree to which children and parents use media together, which researchers call "joint media engagement" (JME). It is also the first study to employ a nationally representative sample to document both the proportion of children's reading that occurs online or on electronic reading devices and the amount of time that parents spend reading along with their children.

Purpose and Research Questions

Today there are more platforms for educational media content than ever before. There are scores of cable channels, hundreds of computer games, thousands of apps, and millions of websites. There are e-readers, tablets, smartphones, gaming consoles—the list goes on and on. With young children spending hours a day with these screen media, one question has never been answered: How much of this content is educational? The survey aimed to answer this as well as the following research questions:

- How are children using educational media, with whom, and for how long?
- Which subjects do parents feel their children are learning the most about from media? Which platforms do they perceive as being most effective in teaching their children these subjects?

- What do parents believe it means for media to be "educational," and how do media fit in children's broader learning ecologies?
- What are the reasons some children do not use educational media?
- How are the above questions mediated by age, gender, race/ethnicity, and socioeconomic status?

Researchers defined "educational media" for parents who took this survey as content that "is good for your child's learning or growth, or that teaches some type of lesson, such as an academic or social skill." The survey did not independently evaluate or certify the educational value or quality of the media children are consuming, nor did it attempt to assess its impact or effectiveness.

Methods

Vicky Rideout of VJR Consulting designed the instrument with help from FAM researchers from the Joan Ganz Cooney Center, Sesame Workshop, and Stanford University. Research firm GfK administered the online survey.

The 20-minute online survey asked parents of 2- to 10-year-olds questions about their children's use of media. Respondents were given the choice to take the survey in either English or Spanish to increase participation of Spanish-speaking parents. By asking parents to focus on a specific "focal" child and a specific day in their child's life (the day prior to taking the survey), the survey aimed to elicit more precise estimates of children's media use than by asking about a "typical day." Fielding of the survey was spread out across the 7 days of the week during the field period of June 28–July 24, 2013. Because most students were out of school during this time, it is possible that the results do not reflect media use patterns during the school year among the school-aged portion of the sample. Parents may relax rules for media use in the summer; children may use more media because they are not in school, or, conversely, they may spend less time with media because they are occupied with other activities. The margin of error for the full sample was 2.1 percentage points. The completion rate for the survey was 40 percent.

Participants

GfK employs an online research panel that is representative of the entire US population, the KnowledgePanel. KnowledgePanel members are randomly recruited through probability-based sampling, and households are provided with access to the Internet and hardware if needed. The use of a probability sample means that the results are substantially more generalizable to the population of the United States than are results based on convenience panels. The 1,577 parents of the 2- to 10-year-olds who took the survey included 290 Black and 682 Hispanic-Latino parents. Fifty-two percent of respondents were male and

52 percent of the "focal" children were male. Surveyed households earning less than $25,000/year comprised 26.6 percent of the sample, those earning $25,000–$49,999 comprised 25.4 percent, those earning $50,000–$74,999 comprised 18.2 percent, those earning $75,000–$99,999 comprised 13.5 percent, and households earning more than $100,000 comprised 16.3 percent of the sample. In 61 percent of surveyed households, English was the only language spoken, and in 5 percent only a non-English language was spoken. Twenty percent of surveyed households spoke mainly English and some other language, and 15 percent spoke mainly another language and some English.

STUDY 2

Joint Media Engagement—Case Studies of Children and Parents Learning Together Using Media

Principal Investigators: Brigid Barron and Amber Levinson, Stanford University

This study examined how parents conceptualize the presence of screen media (television, video, electronic games, apps, etc.) in their children's lives, how specific child-oriented media come to be used in ways that support learning, and the role of both child and parent interests as contributors to the media practices that emerge. Given the complexity of a rapidly changing media ecology and vastly different family configurations and patterns of use, this mixed methods study sought to understand these dynamics for a small number of families.

Purpose and Research Questions

This study sought to uncover rich examples of how families are taking up media resources and how these might be used for learning. National surveys of children's media use paint a portrait of preschool and elementary school children increasingly immersed in technologically mediated activities (Common Sense Media, 2013; Rideout, 2014). Recent nationally representative surveys indicate that children 2–10 years old use over 2 hours of screen media per day (Rideout, 2014), and that mobile media use time for young children tripled between 2011 and 2013 from an average of 5 minutes a day to an average of 15 minutes a day (Common Sense Media, 2013), with 75 percent of families owning some kind of networked device. Mobile devices are used to play games, use apps, watch videos, access TV or movies, and read books. These rapidly changing use patterns have raised many questions about the benefits and drawbacks of media time. Of particular importance is gaining a better understanding of how the quality and quantity of young children's engagement with digital media might influence children's well-being more generally. At this stage, large survey work is useful but other methods are needed to identify how media might catalyze productive learning opportunities.

Methods

Each of the eight participating families completed one audio recorded ethnographic interview, and one video recorded "play session" in which a parent and child dyad (in one case, a child with both parents) played with preselected apps provided by the research team on a tablet, as well as with an app or technology that the family owned and selected to share. Interviews were semi-structured, following a set of questions as well as the use of follow-up questions and probing based on participant responses. The interview questions included items that asked parents to elaborate on their responses to an online survey that participants had filled out as part of their recruitment. Interview questions explored topics such as how parents selected media for their children, what a typical scene might look like when children engaged with media at home (setting, other people present, and so forth), and the relationship between media content and other areas of children's lives such as school subjects and extracurricular interests.

Participants

Our case study participants were eight families from the San Francisco Bay Area with children ages 4–6, evenly divided with four boys and four girls. All participating parents and seven of the children were Caucasian, and one child was of mixed Asian and Caucasian heritage. Seven of the case families were two-parent households with annual incomes ranging from $76,000 to more than $150,000 a year, while one family was headed by a single mother, with an annual income between $30,000 and $76,000. In seven of eight cases, mothers took the survey and volunteered to be interviewed—one of these mothers was also joined by her partner (the child's father) in the interview. The remaining parent was a stay-at-home father who completed the survey and participated in the interview. Each household had at least one parent with an advanced degree and four parents indicated they had a science hobby or interest. Career industries included publishing, real estate, health care, education, and the film industry. Participants were recruited via a survey (Barron, Levinson, Matthews, & Vea, in preparation), distributed to local parent e-mail lists, which allowed respondents to indicate if they were interested in participating in a follow up interview and play session.

Data Analysis

We used a grounded theory approach to generate categories of learning rich practices (Charmaz, 2006). Multiple rounds of coding led to a more restricted set of codes. Reliability was calculated using percentage agreement and Cohen's kappa for each pair of coders. PRAM (Program for Reliability Assessment with Multiple Coders) reliability software was used for calculations. From among three possible coder pairs, we selected the most reliable pair. Across variables, percentage agreement for this pair ranged from 90.9 percent to 99 percent, with a mean agreement of 95.5 percent. Cohen's kappa ranged from 0.74 to 0.83, with an overall pair mean of 0.779. Following the recommendations of Banerjee, Capozzoli, McSweeney, and Sinha (1999) for the interpretation of Cohen's kappa, reliability was determined to be good to excellent for all four codes. Play session videos were transcribed and some analyses were performed on select cases.

STUDY 3

Joint Media Engagement, Play, Literacy, and Learning among Mexican-American Families

Principal Investigators: Elisabeth Gee, Arizona State University and Sinem Siyahhan, California State University, San Marcos

Digital media, ranging from video games to YouTube, can be important resources for informal teaching and learning in the home and among families. The value of such media depends not only on their content, but on how they are perceived by adults and children, and how they are incorporated into household routines and family interactions. The aim of this study was to investigate how Mexican-American families with young children engage with digital media in the context of home and family life. The study had two particular emphases: (a) the role of siblings in the family media ecology, and (b) video gaming and intergenerational play as potentially distinctive opportunities for family engagement and learning.

Purpose and Research Questions

Similar to other studies in this volume, we focused on Mexican American families due to the growing numbers of Latino school age children, now the largest demographic group (45 percent) in Arizona schools, and the challenges they face in achieving academic success. Despite the significance of siblings in children's development, few studies have explored the influence of siblings on the home media ecology. We posited that siblings might be particularly important in these families, with greater English proficiency or familiarity with US culture than parents. While video gaming is a popular practice in all families, including Hispanics, little attention has been given to how video gaming is situated in the context of family life, or how gaming might be a focal point for teaching and learning in the home. Our key research questions were as follows:

- How do Mexican-American families engage with digital media in the physical context of their homes and in the social and cultural context of family practices and routines?
- What role does video gaming play in the home media ecology and practices of these families?
- How does a "game literacy" intervention support joint engagement, language use, and learning around digital games?

Methods

Data were collected during three home visits over approximately 6 months with each participating family. Our data collection protocols varied across each home visit. During the first visit, one or both parents, the focal child, and siblings were interviewed separately. These interviews included completion of the Families and Media Survey (see Study 1), for the purpose of comparison with the national survey sample. As a group, the family was interviewed to inventory the digital technology in their homes and asked to play a digital game together. Between home visits, parents were asked to take photos of everyday family media use, with a disposable camera provided by the researchers. Subsequent home visits included semi-structured interviews about technology practices identified in the first home visit and in the photos taken by the parent. Families also were asked to participate in game play and game design activities together in each visit. We used several additional data collection methods to further develop our understanding of families' digital media practices and beliefs. For example, in the second home visit, parents and children were interviewed separately to elicit their beliefs about educational media. We also introduced cards with discussion prompts that parents could use to elicit family conversations about video games. In the third home visit, participants completed a timeline to illustrate when and why the family acquired digital technologies, juxtaposed with key life events.

Three researchers participated in each home visit. Two members of the research team were bilingual; most parent and family interviews were conducted in Spanish. All home visits were videotaped; interviews were transcribed and translated into English when necessary.

Participants

We recruited 16 families of Mexican origin through contacts with Hispanic-serving organizations, flyers, and word-of-mouth. All families had at least one focal child between the ages of 4 and 6, and at least one child age 7 years and above, and owned at least one platform for gaming (e.g., console, computer, cell phone, tablet). All except two families were first generation immigrants with both parents, and in some cases the older sibling, born in Mexico. All young children were born in the United States. In 14 households, Spanish was the primary home language. All families were nuclear families, with between two and four children. Family income was generally low, with only two families reporting household incomes of $60,000 or more. Parents' highest level of formal schooling ranged from elementary school to undergraduate degrees. These demographics were comparable to the general Phoenix metropolitan area where we conducted our field study: 32.8 percent of Latinos live below poverty line and 81 percent of the Latino population speaks a language other than English at home (United States Census Bureau, 2013).

STUDY 4

Collecting and Connecting: Intergenerational Learning with Digital Media

Principal Investigator: Katie Headrick Taylor, University of Washington

Technology is transforming how and what young people and their families learn together. While families are demographically diverse and idiosyncratic, using technology together (and apart) is a quality of household life that unites us. Together, parents and children continue to push the possibilities of intergenerational learning with technology. This study examines this complexity of learning with digital media in the home to highlight young people's adeptness at negotiating with, trouble-shooting, and making technology work when it resists their efforts. We compare cases of digitally mediated, collaborative activities that were organized by, or produced, teaching and learning opportunities in the home. We found that young people's digital media use was often active and followed a pattern of "collecting and connecting." This finding highlights the often difficult and intensive effort children and their parents expend on the opportunity to engage with digital media well before the desired activity even takes place. We argue this research provides a counter-narrative to the popularized view that children are passive consumers of digital media and that technology prohibits children and parents from learning and engaging together.

Purpose and Research Questions

This investigation to better understand the complexity of intergenerational learning with digital media and technology is based on observations of children ages 9 through 13. Considering the impact technology has had on families' daily routines and activities related to learning, we ask: How do technologies and digital media reorganize family activities, and create new ones, in and around the household? By answering this question, we aimed to highlight young people's adeptness at negotiating with, trouble-shooting, and making technology work when it resists their efforts. Learning with digital media was often a family endeavor that brought parents, caregivers, and siblings together in unexpected ways.

Methods

We video recorded at least three home-based observations per participating family over the course of 6 weeks. We also asked focal children to wear GoPro cameras either on their heads or on their chests. This angle on the activity provided us with a closeup perspective on the mobile device screens children were often using. Wearable cameras were especially useful on car trips where mobile device use by focal children was common.

We took photos in homes when something particularly pertinent to our research interests might not be captured within the video frame. For example, a pile of devices and chords on a kitchen countertop, an old computer, and a stack of games were photographed within families' homes with an eye toward understanding how tools and media saturated scenes. The use of various visual methods of documenting observations and home organization afforded unique insights into the often unseen, difficult to access, activities in homes and families.

We also conducted interviews and over-the-phone surveys with focal children to get a more complete picture of the range of media and technology young people engaged with while in the study as well as where and with whom such engagement took place. We interviewed one parent per family at the beginning of the study and at the end of the study.

Participants

We recruited families after parents responded to flyers that we placed in local community centers. A total of nine families from the urban and suburban Midwest participated. Twelve focal children between the ages of 9 and 13 years old participated. Ten nonfocal children were included in the observations. Nine parents, all mothers, were the focal adults. Two grandmothers were also part of two different families' observations. Three families were Black families and nine families were White families. Of the 12 focal children, there were three sibling pairs. Family pets—dogs, cats, chickens, and a snake—were also important actors within our family-based observations.

STUDY 5

Parents' Social Networks

Principal Investigators: Alexis Lauricella and Ellen Wartella, Northwestern University

This study examines how low- and middle-income Hispanic parents of young children (under age 6) find parenting advice and information. We conducted an online survey with 185 Hispanic parents and asked about their online and offline social networks and support systems. The results from this study demonstrate that the vast majority of respondents speak in person, on the phone, or through text messaging to communicate with their support network. E-mail, video chat, and social networking sites are used much less frequently but are an additional support system for many parents.

Purpose and Research Questions

The purpose of this study was to examine low- and middle-income Hispanic parents' use of online and offline social networks for parenting support and advice. Our primary research questions were as follows:

1. How do low- and middle-income Hispanic parents engage with their parenting support networks?
2. What types of social support do low- and middle-income Hispanic parents receive online?
3. How are low- and middle-income Hispanic parents using online social networking sites for parenting social support?

Methods

An online survey instrument was designed to assess parents' online and offline social support and use of social networking sites for parenting-related information. The instrument included the following measures:

- *Parenting network.* Using a modified network analysis procedure (e.g., Campbell & Lee, 1991; Marin & Hampton, 2007), participants were asked to list up to five family members or friends with whom they most often discuss general parenting issues. For each person provided, the participant answered questions regarding how they knew this person, if the person was a parent, if the person was a parent of a child aged 6 or below, how long they had known this person, where this person lived or worked in relation to the respondent, how often and the ways in which they communicated with this person. We coded information for Person 1 and Person 2 as "primary network" to distinguish individuals listed first from those later in the list of support individuals.
- *Technology access.* Participants were asked to report which types of digital media they had in their household including: laptop or desktop computers with Internet access, smartphones, and tablet devices.
- *Social networking site use.* Participants were asked to rate how often they used Facebook, Twitter, Instagram, Tumblr, or other self-identified sites on an 8-point Likert scale from never to several times a day.
- *Parenting support and communication on social networking sites.* Using items adapted from social support survey measures developed by Sherbourne and Stewart (1991), participants were asked about their experience of three types of parenting support: (1) informational support (offering of advice and guidance around parenting issues, for example, how to teach child how to tie their shoes); (2) tangible support (provision of new information that helps you as parent, for example, healthy nutrition, school-related skills); and (3) emotional support (expression of positive affect, empathetic understanding) on each social networking site. Each item was measured on a 5-point Likert scale from never to always. Participants were also asked to report if their social networking support came from (1) friends, (2) people you sort of know or follow, or (3) companies or websites.
- *Income.* Income was broken down into two groups for the purpose of this study: "lower income" families refers to those earning less than $30,000 a year and "middle income" refers to those earning $30,000 to $75,000 per year.

Participants

To increase our lower income Hispanic sample, we worked with the National Center for Families Learning (NCFL) to recruit parents of children 6 years of age or younger at NCFL support centers and offered parents a $10 Amazon.com gift card for completing the survey. The final sample included 185 participants who were of Hispanic, Latino, or Spanish origin with a household income of less than $70,000. The majority of participants were Mexican (78 percent), followed by Dominican (5 percent), Salvadorian (5 percent), Puerto Rican (2 percent), and

Columbian (1 percent), with the remaining 7 percent from other backgrounds. The vast majority of the sample was low-income, with 72 percent of respondents reporting a household income of less than $30,000 and another 28 percent of parents reported a household income between $30,000 and $70,000. Most respondents (82 percent) were female. Respondents ranged in age from 20 to 50 years old: 25 percent of the respondents were 27 years old or younger, 50 percent were between 28 and 36 years old, and 25 percent were 37years old or older. Educational attainment was relatively low, with 34 percent of respondents not having a high school diploma, 34 percent having a high school diploma or GED, and 32 percent having at least some college experience.

STUDY 6

Responding to Classroom Change—How Low-Income Latino Parents View Technology's Impact on Student Learning

Principal Investigator: Vikki Katz, Rutgers University

In schools across the United States, technology is being integrated into classroom learning at rapid rates. While classroom technology use shows promise for closing opportunity gaps between lower and higher income students, in-school initiatives seldom account for how parents' perceptions of such programs might constrain or enable students' learning experiences. The aim of this study was to explore how low income Latino parents feel about technology being introduced into their children's classroom learning and how they interpret the consequences of local technology initiatives on their children's educational trajectories. We focused specifically on Mexican-heritage families because they experience greater social disparities than other US families and therefore stand to gain more from programs that enable access to learning opportunities. Findings from the study also informed actionable recommendations for increasing parental engagement with technology initiatives to support their children's learning experiences.

Purpose and Research Questions

This study investigated how Latino parents are responding to technological innovations occurring in their children's schools (e.g., digital curricula, computerized testing, one-to-one laptop programs), and consequently, in their learning practices. We recruited families in three districts serving high-poverty, predominantly Mexican-heritage students in three states (Arizona, California, and Colorado) to examine how specific initiatives to increase educational opportunity for underserved students were being received by their families. We asked:

1. How do low-income Latino parents respond to the introduction of technology into their children's classroom learning?

2. How do parents interpret the consequences of specific district and state-level technology initiatives for their children's educational trajectories?
3. What are the implications of parents' perspectives on technology and learning for educators and for the successful deployment of future technology initiatives?

Methods

Study Design. In each district, we worked with administrators to identify two K-8 schools with student populations that were predominantly Mexican-heritage and financially qualified to receive subsidized school meals. Staff members from each school recruited families for interviews; to meet study criteria, they had to identify as Latino or Hispanic, have a focal child between ages 6 and 13 who received subsidized lunch, and have any kind of Internet service at home. Data collection took placed between July 2013 and September 2014.

Interviews were conducted with parents and children separately and simultaneously in their preferred language (i.e., Spanish or English) and location (i.e., at school or at home) for between 45 and 60 minutes each. Parents were compensated with $25 in cash and children received a $10 iTunes gift card. Parents were asked fixed-answer demographic questions, and both parents and children answered open-ended questions about motivations and decisions for adopting technology, their perspectives on how connectivity affects family relationships, routines, and learning activities, and the extent to which families engage technology to connect with local resources and institutions (including schools). The final section of parents' interviews asked questions about specific technology initiatives (e.g., one-to-one computing, digital standardized testing) in their local school and district. While we interviewed both parents and children, we focus on the parent interviews only in this chapter.

Participants

We interviewed 170 Mexican-heritage parents in three US cities: Chula Vista, California (N = 52); Tucson, Arizona (N = 58); and Denver, Colorado (N = 60). Over 90 percent of interviewed parents were mothers, and most parents in the California (75 percent) and Arizona (60 percent) sites opted to be interviewed in Spanish. In Colorado, about half (52 percent) were interviewed in English, reflecting a greater proportion of US-born respondents. In California, 75 percent of parents chose to be interviewed at school when they picked up their children; in Colorado, that proportion was even higher (89 percent). Arizona parents were mostly chose to be interviewed at home (60 percent).

With a median household size of five and a majority reporting annual household incomes under $25,000, many interviewed families were living under the federal poverty line. Parents in Arizona were more likely to have graduated high school (68 percent) than parents in California (50 percent) or Colorado (49 percent). Most parents were foreign-born in all three sites, with at least one immigrant parent in each family from Mexico. Immigrant parents' median US tenure ranged from 13 to 20 years across sites, suggesting that respondents were not "new" immigrants. In fact, 39 percent and 28 percent of foreign-born parents in Arizona and Colorado, respectively, had attended their last year of school in the United States rather than in Mexico.

Data Analysis

Interviews were audio-recorded and transcribed verbatim. These transcripts and field notes that researchers compiled directly after each interview constituted our data corpus for analysis. These documents were entered into Dedoose, an online platform commonly used for collaborative qualitative data analysis. We engaged a grounded theory approach to analysis, beginning with open, followed by axial, and then selective, coding.

STUDY 7

Online Information Brokering

Principal Investigator: Jason Yip, University of Washington, Seattle

In the United States, there is a large proportion of families where one or both parents are English language learners (ELL). Children in these families often serve important roles as *brokers*, by engaging their linguistic capabilities, cultural familiarity, and technological skills to bridge their families' access to information resources. Despite the central role that child brokers play, scholars know little about how they search for, interpret, and translate online information. Using data from an exploratory study with 10 Latino youth (ages 11–14) that involved interviews, online search tasks, and group discussions, we investigate the learning processes, challenges, and strategies that youth employ as they broker online information for their ELL parents. We believe the findings of this exploratory study highlight the need to examine brokering and family responsibilities in the context of digital literacy and connected learning. Our findings suggest that as more information (both urgent and nonurgent) is digitized and accessible online, youth brokers will face a flood of complex information decisions (e.g., query formation, information reliability) that will require deeper learning and connections to different domains.

Purpose and Research Questions

We conducted this study to understand the intersection of family responsibilities, culture and language, and digital technologies. By becoming more familiar with the challenges that youth brokers face during online searching for families, and what strategies they develop to support their families' information needs, we are seeking to develop more informed strategies to promote connected learning as part of supporting family learning and wellbeing. Our investigation expands work in the fields of information and communication by examining youth online brokers' processes and experiences as they navigate complex online information. Our focus on brokering moves away from a deficit perspective, which presumes families lack knowledge resources, and instead highlights the strategies that online brokers employ to broaden their information access. Therefore, our research questions are as follows:

1. What learning roles do online information brokers play with their parents?
2. What strategies and challenges shape learning roles in online information brokers?
3. What are the affordances and limitations of digital technologies in brokering and learning?

Methods

We conducted 10 one-on-one interviews and search tasks with youth brokers in four sessions in an afterschool setting. We asked questions about family demographics, ICT usage, and general search behavior. Next, for 40 minutes, we asked youth to engage in a series of search using school laptops:

1. If your parent needed information on the public schools in this area, what information would you look up for them?
2. Can you show me how you find information for something your parents have asked you to search before?
3. Can you show me how you find information for a problem you think your parents might have today?
4. If one of your parents was not feeling well or had been sick for a few days and wanted to know why, what information would you look up for them?

During these search tasks, we had the respondent narrate how they were conducting the search and their opinions on the task. We video recorded screen interactions as the children explained their search tasks. During this time, we asked children to search as if their parents were present. After the search tasks, we had the youth engage in a 20-minute group discussion about how they search for information for their ELL parents.

Participants

This study occurred in a major metropolitan area in the Northeast United States. In the middle school where we recruited participants, 72 percent of children were receiving free- or reduced-cost meals and 59 percent were Latin American. We conducted this study with 10 youth participants who met the following criteria: (1) self-identified as the child of a Latin American immigrant; (2) has at least one parent with limited facility in verbal or written English; (3) between ages 11 and 14; and (4) reported helping his/her parent(s) understand and navigate online content and ICTs.

Data Analysis

The data for analysis consisted of verbatim individual and group interview transcripts, transcripts of the video-recordings, and detailed field notes. We adhered to the inductive analytical approach developed by Corbin and Strauss (2007) to develop themes and categories to capture children's search and learning experiences for their ELL parents. Two researchers open-coded the data independently for themes, such as parental interaction, affect, search challenges and frustrations, and strategies for brokering. We categorized, sorted, and compared the themes to further develop categories for analysis. We then systematically compared and contrasted the themes between the researchers. Following the open-coding analysis, we used axial coding to make connections between a category and its subcategories more explicit. We used selective coding to see if additional categories were needed. This sorting, comparing, and contrasting was performed until we reached theoretical saturation and no new codes or categories were generated.

STUDY 8

Learning with Media in Modern Families

Principal Investigator: Lori M. Takeuchi, Joan Ganz Cooney Center at Sesame Workshop

Due to recent trends in immigration and parental living arrangements, as well as trends in parental work schedules, military deployment, and the consumer technology landscape, media and technology are playing more central roles in family routines and functioning than ever before. The aim of this study, therefore, was to understand how technology and media are being used for learning in *modern families*—a catchall to describe families in which children spend significant stretches of time physically apart from at least one parent as a result of these modern-day phenomena. In particular, the study aimed to understand modern Hispanic-Latino families, and how assimilation needs, custody and child care arrangements, and cultural values and norms shaped media use and decisions in these families, and how the affordances of the devices may further shape family learning with media.

Purpose and Research Questions

This investigation aimed to identify and better understand the factors that ground meaningful interactions around play, learning, and connection in families with children ages 6 through 9. Considering the issues facing the growing number of Hispanic-Latino families in the United States today, we posed the following research questions to drive our investigation:

1. How do *family characteristics*—including nativity status, parent marital status, parent and child age, English language proficiency, and cultural values and norms—shape media use and decisions in these families (e.g., time and resource allocations, content selections)?

2. How do *environmental characteristics*—including size and layout of the home, access/availability of community resources, and neighborhood safety—shape media use and decisions in these families?
3. How do the *affordances of the devices* that family members use (e.g., mobility, connectivity) shape how they spend time alone and with friends and relatives in both public and private spheres and, consequently, the learning that occurs with and around media?

By answering these questions, we aimed to determine how the precious little time family members spend using media might also be leveraged for learning, if not in colocated situations, then virtually, asynchronously, or during transitions between settings. The findings, we hoped, would inform the design of media to better serve Latino children's learning needs and fit into time- and budget-stretched family routines.

Methods

To gain a greater understanding of the natural flow of play, learning, and connection around media and technology in modern Hispanic-Latino families, we observed and interviewed 15 families with children between the ages of 6 and 9 in their ordinary settings, namely home and in the community. We visited each family at least five times—usually more—over the course of 6–8 weeks, and, when possible, tracked a focal child's (age 6–9) media use as they moved across settings. We employed a variety of data collection protocols, including the Learning at Home: National Survey of Educational Media Use (see Study 1), and adapted the some of the same procedures from the Collecting and Connecting: Intergenerational Learning with Digital Media Study (see Study 4) to accommodate the younger ages of our child participants.

In addition to these common methods, at both the start and end of the study we separately interviewed the parents and children about their personal and family routines around media and technology use in the home. We also conducted at least three observations, each lasting between 2 and 3 hours, over both weekdays and weekends. Given our interest in how children are using media and technology across settings, we scheduled at least one observation outside of the home, or in transit between primary settings. We videotaped these visits and occasionally asked the focal children to wear GoPro cameras on their chests to capture a first-person perspective of the screens while we watched from afar.

Participants

We recruited 15 Hispanic-Latino "modern families" with at least one child ages 6–9 living in the urban Northeast, most from New York City (Manhattan, Brooklyn, Bronx, Queens), and a few from New Jersey and Philadelphia. Families were offered $200 cash for participating, and the focal child of the study (age 6–9) was given a $50 gift card upon completing the study. Most families were Mexican, Ecuadorean, Puerto Rican, Dominican, or some combination of these ethnicities; three families comprised White European and Latino mixes. The number of children per household ranged from 1 to 6 (mean = 3, median = 2, mode = 2). Total family income ranged from low to middle, and seven of the 15 qualified as low. In only one family were the parents married; the rest were single parent (4) or domestic partnership households (9). English was the primary language spoken in seven of the homes, Spanish was in one, and the remaining seven were equal Spanish-English language households.

STUDY 9

Understanding How Hispanic-Latino Immigrant Families Engage and Learn with Broadcast and Digital Media

Principal Investigator: Amber Levinson, Stanford University

This study explores what kinds of language and literacy experiences Hispanic-Latino immigrant families engage in via broadcast and digital media. Seven case families, each of whom had at least one child between the ages of 5 and 7, participated in interviews and home observations over the course of 6 months, receiving visits every 2 weeks. The study included documentation of families' existing media infrastructure and practices, as well as an "intervention" in which families each received a tablet device loaded with language and literacy apps (available to them for the second half of the data collection period). In this way the study sought to understand how families were taking up resources they already had available to them, as well as what they might do with new tools. In addition to ethnographic data collected via interviews and observations, the study also included a survey and quantitative app use data generated on the tablets provided.

Purpose and Research Questions

A large and growing proportion of US public school children are of Hispanic-Latino origin, and many face daunting challenges in school. Many of these children, particularly those who are immigrants themselves or children of immigrants (first generation) are learning a new language while their families learn to navigate a school system that is unfamiliar to them. Meanwhile, Hispanic-Latinos are taking up digital technologies at rapid rates. Although research has shown a positive relationship between computer access and scores on early cognitive development scores, and a negative relationship between watching television and these scores (Espinosa, Laffey, & Whittaker, 2006), existing large-scale research has not been able to pinpoint what impact media use patterns may have on children's schooling and learning. This dissertation seeks to contribute toward informing researchers, educators and media producers about how low-income Latino immigrant families—whose primary language is not English—engage with media, and what entry points for English learning media might provide. This study seeks to answer the following research questions:

1. What language and literacy experiences does media provide or facilitate for children who are developing as dual language learners and for parents who are also learning English?
2. What language- and literacy-related media practices and activities do families engage in, either solo or together, as part of their daily routines?
3. What family dynamics and practices develop around a newly introduced tablet device loaded with a small set of high-quality literacy and language resources?

Methods

The study methodology consisted of the following major components:

1. *Ethnographic case studies* of families based on 6 months of qualitative data collection, including parent interviews, child "artifact-based" interviews where children showed and explained their media use, and 2 monthly home observations per family.
2. *A tablet intervention* that provided families with their own iPad tablet computer, starting halfway through the 6-month data collection period, which subsequently became part of the ethnographic observations and interviews. Each iPad was equipped with a selection of applications related to language and literacy learning, and included an app that collected quantitative app use data (which apps were used, for how long, and how many each app was opened);
3. *Quantitative survey responses* from each family on the Learning at Home Survey (see Appendix, Study 1) were compared to the national dataset.

Participants

Case families were low-income families of Hispanic-Latino origin who resided in an urban area of Northern California. Parents were all born and raised in Latin America (countries of origin included Mexico, El Salvador, Nicaragua, and Peru). Each family included at least one "focal" child between the ages of 5 and 7; some of these children had older or younger siblings. Eleven children total participated in the study (four boys and seven girls). The formal schooling completed by parents ranged widely, from third grade to bachelor's degree. All families spoke Spanish as their primary home language. In one family, parents were separated and lived apart, and in the remaining six families children resided with their mother and father.

Data Analysis

Interview transcripts and field notes were coded with Dedoose software, using a grounded theory approach to uncover emergent themes from the data (Charmaz, 2000). The study yielded rich case studies that were reported in Levinson's (2014) doctoral dissertation. Chapters 2 and 10 share a subset of examples from the overall findings.

References

Banerjee, M., Capozzoli, M., McSweeney, L., & Sinha, D. (1999). Beyond kappa: A review of interrater agreement measures. *Canadian Journal of Statistics*, *27*(1), 3–23.

Barron, B., Levinson, A., Matthews, J., & Vea, T. (in preparation). Digital media as a catalyst for learning: Contributions of parent & child learning biographies, expertise and interests.

Campbell, K. E., & Lee, B. A. (1991). Name generators in surveys of personal networks. *Social Networks*, *13*(3), 203–221.

Charmaz, K. (2000). *Constructing grounded theory*. London: Sage.

Charmaz, K. (2006). The power of names. *Journal of Contemporary Ethnography*, *35*(4), 396–399.

Common Sense Media (2013). *Zero to eight: Children's media use in American*. Retrieved from https://www.commonsensemedia.org/research/zero-to-eight-childrens-media-use-in-america-2013

Corbin, J., & Strauss, A. (2008). *Basics of qualitative research: Techniques and procedures for developing grounded theory*, 3rd ed. Thousand Oaks, CA: Sage.

Espinosa, L., Laffey, J., & Whittaker, T. (2006). *Language minority children analysis: Focus on technology use*. Final report published by CREST/NCES. Washington, DC: National Center for Education.

Levinson, A.M. (2014). Tapping in: Understanding how Hispanic-Latino immigrant families engage and learn with broadcast and digital media. Doctoral dissertation. Retrieved from Stanford Digital Repository: https://purl.stanford.edu/bb550sh8053

Marin, A., & Hampton, K. N. (2007). Simplifying the personal network name generator: Alternatives to traditional multiple and single name generators. *Field Methods*, *19*(2), 163–193.

Rideout, V. (2014). *Learning at home: Families, educational media use in America*. A report of the Families and Media Project. New York: The Joan Ganz Cooney Center at Sesame Workshop. Retrieved from www.joanganzcooneycenter.org/publication/learning-at-home/

Sherbourne, C. D., & Stewart, A. L. (1991). The MOS social support survey. *Social Science & Medicine*, *32*(6), 705–714.

United States Census Bureau. (2013). *Phoenix city, Arizona QuickLinks from the US Census Bureau*. Retrieved from http://quickfacts.census.gov/qfd/states/04/0455000lk.html

INDEX

Page numbers in *italics* show illustrations; those in **bold** show tables; n indicates an endnote